MANAGING FOR RESILIENCE

In an era of longer hours and shorter contracts, of tighter margins and frequent organizational change, stress can undermine both the mental health and performance of employees. A culture of resilience in the workplace, however, offers the potential to support psychological wellbeing and improve the performance of both people and organizations.

This is the first book to provide managers with a guide to fostering psychological resilience within their teams. It synthesises not only the latest cutting-edge research in the area, but also translates this into practical advice for a range of organizational settings.

Chapters cover the following important issues:

- Key personality factors related to resilience
- How job design and routines can improve employee resilience
- How to build a resilient team
- Communicating change and improving teamwork
- Modelling resilient thinking and behaviour as a leader
- Selecting the right resilience training for your organization

This is the ideal book for anyone interested in fostering a high-performance and emotionally resilient workforce, whether they are a manager, HR professional or occupational psychologist. Its cutting edge approach will also make it important reading for students and researchers of organizational and occupational psychology.

Dr. Monique F. Crane, PhD, is a lecturer and researcher in Organisational Psychology at Macquarie University, Sydney, Australia. She is also a director in a private consulting firm which provides evidence-based resilience training to private and public organizations.

MANAGING FOR RESILIENCE

A Practical Guide for
Employee Wellbeing and
Organizational Performance

Edited by
Monique F. Crane

Routledge
Taylor & Francis Group

LONDON AND NEW YORK

First published 2017
by Routledge
2 Park Square, Milton Park, Abingdon, Oxon OX14 4RN

and by Routledge
711 Third Avenue, New York, NY 10017

Routledge is an imprint of the Taylor & Francis Group, an informa business

© 2017 selection and editorial matter, Monique F. Crane; individual chapters, the contributors

The right of Monique F. Crane to be identified as the author of the editorial material, and of the authors for their individual chapters, has been asserted in accordance with sections 77 and 78 of the Copyright, Designs and Patents Act 1988.

British Library Cataloguing in Publication Data
A catalogue record for this book is available from the British Library

Library of Congress Cataloging in Publication Data
A catalog record for this book has been requested.

ISBN: 978-1-138-12463-9 (hbk)
ISBN: 978-1-138-12464-6 (pbk)
ISBN: 978-1-315-64803-3 (ebk)

Typeset in Bembo and Stone Sans
by Florence Production Ltd., Stoodleigh, Devon, UK

Printed and bound by CPI Group (UK) Ltd, Croydon, CR0 4YY

To Eyal and our son Noam.

CONTENTS

ILLUSTRATIONS

Figures

Tables

Boxes

CONTRIBUTORS

Monique F. Crane, PhD. Dr. Monique Crane is a lecturer at Macquarie University teaching on the Organisational Psychology Masters Programme. Dr. Crane consults to the Australian Commonwealth Department of Defence regarding resilience in military personnel. Her research, higher degree research student supervision, and teaching focus on occupational resilience and mental health in the workplace. Dr. Crane is also the founder of Resilience Research and Training Systems, which provides evidence-based resilience training to private and public organisations.

Professor Robert R. Sinclair, PhD. Professor within the Department of Psychology Clemson University, South Carolina. Dr. Sinclair is a founding member of the Society for Occupational Health Psychology and a Fellow of the American Psychological Association and the Society for Industrial-Organisational Psychology. His current research programme focuses on health-related aspects of organisational climate, economic stress and the employment relationship.

Janelle H. Cheung, PhD. Dr. Janelle Cheung is a post-doctoral researcher at Oregon Health and Science University. Her research focuses on occupational health psychology, with a specific emphasis on economic stress and employee wellbeing, and the promotion of employee safety, health and wellbeing in the workplace.

Phoebe E. Stoddart, D.Org Psych. Dr. Phoebe Stoddart holds a professional Doctorate in Organisational Psychology from Macquarie University, Australia. Specialising in the impostor phenomenon and how to manage impostor cognitions in the workplace.

Professor Pauline Rose Clance, PhD, ABPP. Clinical Psychologist and Emerita Professor at Georgia State University, Atlanta, GA, US. Professor Clance specialises in the ethology and treatment of the impostor phenomenon.

Professor Carolyn M. Youssef-Morgan, PhD. Redding Chair of Business, College of Business, Bellevue University, Nebraska, US. She is co-author of *Psychological Capital and Beyond* (Oxford University Press, 2015), and a leading researcher, author, speaker and consultant on positivity in the workplace.

Jason L. Stratman. Dean of Instruction and Workforce Development for Western Nebraska Community College. Stratman holds a Masters in Business Administration and is nearing completion of his PhD in Human Capital Management from Bellevue University and specialises in workforce skill development and career-technical education.

Professor Thomas W. Britt, PhD. Trevillian Distinguished Professor, College of Behavioral, Social and Health Sciences, Department of Psychology, Clemson University, South Carolina, US. His current research investigates how stigma and other barriers to care influence employees in high-risk occupations seeking needed mental health treatment, and the identification of factors that promote resilience among employees.

Kristen S. Jennings. Kristen Jennings is a doctoral candidate in Industrial-Organisational Psychology at Clemson University. Kristen's research interests broadly include work stress and worker health, with an emphasis on supporting employees in high-stress occupations.

Ben J. Searle, PhD. Organisational psychologist in the Department of Psychology, Macquarie University, Sydney, Australia. Dr. Searle is a senior lecturer on the Organisational Psychology Masters Program at Macquarie University and specialises in employee wellbeing, engagement, stress appraisal, proactive behaviour and work attitudes. Podcasts and videos by Dr. Searle on these topics are available at mindonthejob.com.

Frances McMurtrie, MOrg. Frances McMurtie holds a Masters in Organisational Psychology from Macquarie University, Sydney, Australia. Specialising in the role of professional identification in occupational resilience.

Professor Jill Flint-Taylor, PhD. Founding director of business psychologists Rusando and an adjunct faculty member and research fellow at Ashridge Hunt International Business School.

Professor Sir Cary L. Cooper, CBE. Sir Cary Cooper is the 50th Anniversary Professor for Organisational Psychology and Health at the Alliance Manchester Business School, University of Manchester, UK.

Niklas K. Steffens, PhD. Dr. Niklaas Steffens is a Lecturer in Psychology in the School of Psychology at The University of Queensland, Australia. His research focuses on self and identity, leadership and followership, motivation and creativity, and health and wellbeing.

Professor S. Alexander Haslam, PhD. Professor Alex Haslan is an Australian Research Counsel Laureate Fellow, School of Psychology, The University of Queensland, Australia. Professor Haslam's research focuses on the study of group and identity processes in organisational, social and clinical contexts.

Amy B. Adler, PhD. Dr. Amy Adler is a leading US clinical psychologist in military resilience at the Walter Reed Army Institute of Research, Silver Spring. Dr. Adler co-chairs the US Army's psychological health and resilience research programme.

CPT Kristin N. Saboe, PhD. Dr. Kristin Saboe is an Industrial-Organisational Psychologist currently serving as an officer in the U.S. Army at Army Headquarters in the Army Resiliency Directorate where she manages science and research integration for the army's strategy to promote personal readiness and resilience among service members.

CPT Danny Boga. CPT Danny Boga is a military psychologist with the Australian Army and PhD candidate at Macquarie University, Sydney, Australia. His research focuses on the role of autonomous motivation in the tolerance of distress and the capacity for resilience.

Bernd Carette, PhD. Dr. Bernd Carette obtained his PhD in Industrial/ Organisational Psychology at Ghent University (Belgium). His area of expertise is in development and change at the individual, team, organisational level.

Mustafa Sarkar, PhD. Dr. Mustafa Sarakar is lecturer in Sport and Exercise Psychology at the College of Arts and Science, School of Science and Technology, Nottingham Trent University, UK. Dr. Sarkar specialises in the psychology of sporting excellence and its application to other high performance domains (e.g., business).

David Fletcher, PhD. Dr. David Fletcher is a senior lecturer in Sports and Performance Psychology in School of Sport, Exercise and Health Sciences, Loughborough University, UK. Dr. Fletcher is an expert in thriving and resilience in the context of sports performance.

1

A MANAGER'S INTRODUCTORY GUIDE TO RESILIENCE

Dr. Monique F. Crane

If you manage people or are in a leadership position and you are concerned about workplace stress among your employees, you are not alone. Stress in the workplace is a growing concern for both employees and their employers. Such concern is reflected by the increasing prevalence of dialogue among managers about how to address the effects of employee stress within their organisations. This hot topic is also recognised by major business news outlets, such as Forbes, and leading management consulting institutes (e.g., *Gallup*). A report by the Safe Work Australia (2015) indicated that work-related mental stress cost the Australian economy over 3 billion between 2012–13. Moreover, 'while mental stress cases comprise 2 per cent of the total number of cases, they contribute 5 per cent of the total economic cost' (p. 33). Similar trends are evident across the globe. The American Institute of Stress reports that *"Job stress carries a price tag for U.S. industry estimated at over $300 billion annually"* (www.stress.org/workplace-stress/).

Increasing stress in the workplace is considered to correspond to several trends such as the decline of manufacturing in several countries, downsizing and resulting lay-offs, the advance of the IT and service sector, more short-term contracts, outsourcing, mergers, automisation, globalisation and greater international competition (Randall, Griffiths & Cox, 2005). Moreover, the increased use of mobile phones, laptop computers and PDAs means that essentially employees may never leave their work. This increases stress by limiting downtime available for employees to recover from work stress (Luthans, Vogelgesang & Lester, 2006).

In an interview with Jennifer Robison from the *Gallup* business journal (27 March 2014) Damian Byers, PhD executive director of People, Learning, and Culture at the Benevolent Society, reported that management practices and processes had a significant role to play in the stress experienced by employees in the workplace. Byers suggests that the solution to these issues is, at least in part, in the hands of organisational management. Given this, and similar observations, the question on the minds of many managers is: '*As a manager, how can I reduce work stress in my employees and increase their resilience?*' Fortunately, research within the field of organisational psychology suggests that organisations can invest in the resilience of their employees (Luthans, *et al.*, 2006), not only via resilience training, but as a consequence of the way managers can shape the work environment (Piccolo & Colquitt, 2006). The aim of this book is to provide evidence-based recommendations about how managers and leadership can reduce workplace stress and improve employee resilience.

The complex world of resilience

Resilience primarily describes the emergence of good outcomes despite significant risk factors (Masten, Best & Garmezy, 1990). Historical work in the area of resilience by Anne Masten and colleagues, observed that many children developed well despite significant risks, such as poverty or chronic abuse. These observations led psychologists to try to understand why some people resisted these highly risky, or at least undernourishing situations, while others did not. If you are a manager you may have similarly observed distinctive outcomes in your employees. Two employees might be exposed to similar workload or work stressors, and yet experience quite different emotional and behavioural outcomes. One employee may be visibly stressed and you might observe a change in their demeanour and the way he/she interacts with their colleagues. In contrast, the other employee might appear much more collected with no obvious outward signs of distress. Such observations have led scientists and managers alike to ask *why* do some people seem to be more resilient to stressors than others?

Although managers are able to impact on some dimensions of an employee's resilience, there may also be other factors that are beyond a manager's positive influence. Having said this, managers and the organisational setting most certainly play a role in how robust employees will be to the stressors imposed by the modern workplace. The influence of good leadership on resilience and mental health outcomes should not be underestimated; for example, greater levels of perceived leadership, morale and team cohesion have been found to be associated with lower levels of self-reported PTSD symptoms from UK personnel deployed to Afghanistan (Jones *et al.*, 2012). This means that managers, broader leadership and the organisational culture are likely to impact employee resilience at work.

Defining resilience

Resilience is one of those terms that has attracted numerous definitions. At times, it seems that there are as many definitions of resilience as there are research studies. Although the definitions may vary there is some general consensus about what resilience is and therefore what it looks like if we were to observe it in the work-place that provides a useful benchmark for our discussion. First, a theme captured by several prominent definitions is that resilience is characterised by good outcomes despite adversity or risk factors (Fergus & Zimmerman, 2005). Thus, in order to observe resilience, risks or adversity need to be present testing the individual's capacity for adaptive coping. Without adversity it is very difficult to observe a person's level of resilience. This makes the workplace an excellent context for the observation of adult resilience because the nature of the current work-place is constantly challenging the ability of employees to cope with various demands.

Second, resilience is considered to be the ability to 'bounce back' in the face of this adversity. This does not mean personal growth after adversity, which is considered conceptually distinct to resilience, but is where an individual may experience a mild disruption (e.g., disturbed sleep) in functioning that quickly returns to normal (Bonnano, 2005). It is also widely accepted that resilience is also not *recovery*. The expectation is that the disruption in functioning is mild, too mild to require recovery, which would be preceded by a more severe downturn in functioning (Bonnano, 2005).

The generally accepted definition of resilience reflects both aspects described above, which can be summed up in the following definition: *Resilience describes the capacity to adapt effectively to life adversity with a short-lived downturn in functioning* (Bonnano, 2005; Masten *et al.*, 1991).

Let's start by addressing some common myths about resilience

Myth 1: Seeking support from a professional means that the individual lacks resilience. The idea that seeking support means that an individual lacks resilience is a common myth and one that probably needs to be addressed early on. When this belief is held among managers, employees and the broader community it can be responsible for significant stigma and barriers to coping resources that could enhance resilience. Going to see a psychologist or mental health practitioner does not necessarily mean one's resilience has failed or that the person lacks resilience. Often this means that the most appropriate support networks are engaged serving to buffer the impact of stressors (Cohen & Wills, 1985). Moreover, going to a psychologist or another professional support person does not necessarily mean that someone is suffering considerable distress. Actually, it can mean quite the opposite. It may indicate that the person has quickly responded to present stressors by engaging a strategy appropriate for them. Talking about stressors with a professional support person may be helpful to the individual. Therefore, part of that person's resilience is about engaging the correct strategies to continue to remain resilient.

Depending on the nature of the stressor, the best person for that supportive role might be a professional, particularly in the case of potentially traumatic events or seismic life-adversity. In such instances, a professional support person is trained to identify risk factors and minimise their impact before they detrimentally affect wellbeing. Those who proactively engage such support early on are therefore less likely to suffer significant and debilitating distress and maintain resilience.

The issue of seeking professional support will be addressed in further detail later in this book when we reflect on the role of social support because it is useful for organisations to allow as many options for accessing support as possible. This might include practical structures that facilitate access to support such as time off work to attend appointments (Chapter 6) or cultural structures that reduce feelings of stigma associated with support seeking (Chapter 5).

Myth 2: Coping strategies that are resilient in one area of one's life are useful for all areas in all situations. The idea that certain behaviours or thinking styles that promote resilience do so in all areas of one's life has been challenged in a few lines of research. What serves to promote resilience in one area of a person's life may actually create difficulty or be maladaptive in another (Bonnano, 2005). Research by Bonnano and colleagues demonstrated that individuals with trait self-enhancement had greater resilience coping in the face of trauma and loss (Bonanno, et al., 2002). Self-enhancers are those people who tend to overestimate their positive qualities and do not mind expressing the existence of these qualities to others. Although self-enhancement might be useful for coping with trauma and loss, when it came to social relationships there was a considerable social cost. These self-enhancers were considered to be lower on social adjustment as rated by friends and relatives and their social relationships tended to suffer. It also appeared that high self-enhancers were unaware of the strain they placed on their relationships, continuing to rate their relationships as healthy and positive. Thus, adaptive strategies for coping with the stressors of life may not necessarily be desirable in other life domains, such as maintaining good interpersonal relationships.

Other research has demonstrated that strategies effective for maintaining resilience to one stressor may not be effective for *all* stressors. For example, several studies have demonstrated that problem solving is a generally adaptive coping strategy for dealing with a range of stressors (Billings & Moos, 1984; Folkman & Moskowitz, 2004). However, recently Britt, Crane, Hodson and Adler (2016) have shown that for stressors that are uncontrollable, such as many present in military training (e.g., being away from home), problem-solving was not as effective as acceptance coping. Acceptance coping in this study was the ability to accept the stressors as just part of being a good soldier. In the typical workplace, both uncontrollable and controllable stressors are also likely to exist. The implication of this research is that for a work setting containing uncontrollable stressors acceptance of the situation seemed to be much more adaptive in reducing longer term distress symptoms.

Of course, it is not just the military setting that contains uncontrollable stressors. For example, in the case of organisational change there are frequently both controllable and uncontrollable aspects. Change may be inevitable, but some elements of that change may be open to influence. Uncontrollable aspects might include the potential for an employee to experience changes in their responsibilities. However, the employee might be able to control some other aspects related to that change, such as the types of changes to responsibilities or how well prepared they are for the new role. The latter issues can be addressed by problem-solving (e.g., negotiating with managers and discussing the scope of new responsibilities, preferences for duties, professional development and training). However, the fact that change will occur is inevitable and this is the aspect that needs to be *accepted*, rather than solved. Continuing to problem-solve or resist uncontrollable aspects of a stressor can lead to on-going frustration and unhappiness. More critically, it blinds them to any potential opportunities that may emerge as a consequence of change.

Employees, like anyone else, can have difficulty breaking situations down into controllable and uncontrollable component parts and this may mean that the strategies do not fit the realities of the situation. Managers can play a role in helping employees to distinguish between parts of a stressor that they have control over, versus those they do not by having honest conversations about these aspects with their employees. In practice, I have seen managers attempt to 'ease the pain' of organisational change by giving employees a false sense of control over aspects that are ultimately immovable. This is a problematic strategy because employees will often respond, and rightfully so, with attempts to engage in problem-solving and influence strategies when what is actually needed is acceptance. There will be some aspects of change that can be influenced and managers are in a position to direct employees to understand what these aspects are and also the limits of employee influence.

More resilient and adaptive employees seem to apply coping strategies flexibly depending on the nature of the stressor. Research in resilience emphasises the importance of flexibility in coping (Cheng, 2001). Rather than providing a proscribed strategy about how to cope, it is important that individuals engage in a process of making coping attempts that are later reflected upon for their level of success. Thus, returning to my previous point, coping strategies that work for one stressor will not necessarily work effectively for *all* situations. The nature of the stressor event and its level of controllability appear to be important to determining the effectiveness of the coping strategy applied.

Myth 3: Some people are just resilient whereas others are not. In some workplaces resilience has been thought of as something employees either have or do not. However, there is now increasing evidence that resilience can actually be developed. It is now commonly thought that resilience is associated with certain individual differences, such as personality traits, and is therefore somewhat consistent over time. The personality dimensions related to resilient functioning will be addressed in greater detail in Chapter 2. However, there is also emerging evidence to suggest that it is also open to development (e.g., Coutu, 2002; Reivich & Shatte, 2002). Researchers now understand that resilience, at least in part, changes over the course of someone's life and experiences. Windle, Bennett, and Noyes (2011) argued "the defining point which distinguishes hardiness from resilience is that it [hardiness] is a stable personality trait whereas resilience is viewed as something that will change across the lifespan" (p. 163). Our research recently demonstrated that even workplace events could serve to enhance or decrease perceived psychological resilience over a period as short as three months (Crane & Searle, 2016). Other researchers have shown that successfully dealing with one's problems can enhance factors related to resilient functioning, in particular confidence in one's ability to cope with difficulties (Thoits, 1994). Thus, there seems to be some scope for individuals to change their level of resilience given the tools to do so, which is where the role of both managers, but also where resilience trainers come in (Chapter 14). Studies demonstrate several mechanisms for building resilience including: encouraging support seeking, providing employees with challenges, achieving good daily respite from work and developing employee self-efficacy (Carette, Anseel & Lievens, 2013; Craig & Cooper, 1992; Crane & Searle, 2016; Lagerveld et al., 2012). These mechanisms can all be promoted in the workplace by managers and are discussed in detail in the chapters of this book.

Myth 4: Resilience is rare. Previously, resilience was thought of and studied by researchers as an uncommon response to adversity. However, this view has been challenged and the currently prevailing view is that resilience is surprisingly commonplace. Several studies have demonstrated that despite the loss of spouses or exposure to extremely traumatic events, such as the September 11 terrorist attacks, the majority of people demonstrate remarkable resilience (Bonanno, Galea, Bucciarelli & Vlahov, 2007; Bonanno, Moskowitz, Papa & Folkman, 2005). Although an estimated 50–60 per cent of the adult population has been exposed to some form of potentially traumatic stressor, only around 7–8 per cent ever met the criteria for Post-Traumatic Stress Disorder (Kessler et al., 2005). The ordinariness of resilience is not only observed in adults, but also in children. In her research, Masten (2001), describes that a majority of children growing up in threatening or disadvantaged environments experience resilient outcomes.

So, what does this mean for managers of employees? This appears to indicate that a majority of employees are quite resilient in the face of difficulties. People somehow naturally know what they need to get through difficulties and have developed adaptive strategies over the course of their lives. This seems to hold true for both acute traumatic events or more chronic stressors such as caring for a spouse with a life threatening illness (Bonanno et al., 2005). Thus, managing for employee resilience is in part about allowing employees the opportunity to convey what they need, responding openly to those needs, not creating barriers for employees to access the support or resources they require to cope effectively and trying to minimise additional unnecessary drains on resilience.

How to use this book: what managers can do to maintain resilience in their employees

This book is a call to managers and all levels of organisational leadership to give greater consideration to their role in maintaining the psychological resilience of their employees, but also to give managers some essential tools to meet this challenge. Many managers have turned to resilience trainers to help workers cope with greater workplace demands. However, there are also on-the-job opportunities for management to play a critical role in the maintenance of employee resilience. For example, Barbara Fredrickson and her colleagues suggest that it is critical to remind employees to maintain positive thinking and find meaning even when undesirable events occur within an organisational context. Managers are able to model resilient behaviours by continuing to maintain a positive outlook despite hardship and manage the meaning of difficulties in a way that promotes hope and the value of stressors in relation to the organisation's mission (Fredrickson, 2001; Piccolo & Colquitt, 2006).

This book provides a readable synthesis of cutting-edge psychological resilience research for the purpose of giving managers practical strategies for supporting the resilience of their employees. The five sections of this book will address: (1) individual characteristics that promote resilience and common personality styles that erode resilience, (2) how managers can facilitate employee resilience in the workplace by promoting effective support structures, (3) how to manage common organisational-level factors that erode resilience including job design and facilitating adequate daily rest, (4) using the team to engender resilience and build team resilience and (5) how managers can promote resilient behaviour and thinking styles. To get the greatest benefit from these chapters we suggest that the reader consider two questions while reading each chapter. The first, is the way I currently manage my team supporting their resilience? The second, how would I change my management style in the future? In the final chapter, you will get an opportunity to reflect on your own management style and consider in more detail what changes you would make.

The role for managers in maintaining the resilience of employees

The role for managers in maintaining the resilience of employees can be summarised in the below illustration. Via these roles managers can help to support employee resilience. As illustrated in Figure 1.1, these four roles for managers include: (1) reducing unnecessary drains on staff resilience, (2) promoting adaptive workplace behaviours and thinking in the face of difficulties, (3) supporting the development of both personal and social resources and (4) allowing employees the opportunity to access needed resources. Each of the following chapters addresses at least one of these roles.

(1) Reducing unnecessary drains on resilience. This might include attempts to alleviate unnecessary stressors, particularly *hindrance* stressors. Hindrance stressors are defined as stressors that tend to be perceived as impeding goal achievement or personal development (Podsakoff, LePine & LePine, 2007). A good example of a hindrance stressor is bureaucracy or considerable administration that is a barrier to actual work

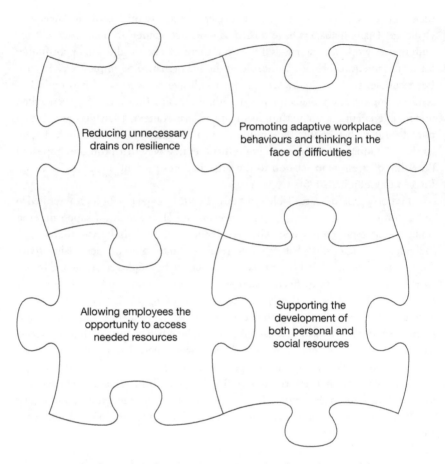

FIGURE 1.1 The four roles of managers in maintaining the resilience of their employees

outcomes. These types of stressors have been shown to reduce employee resilience (Crane & Searle, 2016). There are two critical points to be made in relation to this. The first is that managers can play an important role in buffering their employees from hindrance stressors, and second, there is a real human cost to hindrance stressors not always considered when making workplace changes that increase the amount of hindrances (e.g., increased red-tape). In Chapter 7, we discuss how managers can spot these hindrance stressors and make attempts to minimise or mitigate their impact on employee resilience.

(2) Promoting adaptive workplace behaviours and thinking in the face of difficulties. This piece of the puzzle largely reflects the manager's role in modelling resilient behaviour and thinking and inspiring it in others. These behaviours and thinking styles might encompass: identification of controllable and uncontrollable parts of

a problem, promoting optimism and agency regarding the achievement of organisational goals, celebrating successes and promoting learning from, but not dwelling, on failures. Managers have the ability to engender some critical resources in their employees such as self-belief, realistic optimism, hope and agency, particularly when an employee's personal resources might be undergoing assault. For example, the first few years of academic life is often filled with self-doubt and frustration. Initial attempts at securing grants and research publications in good journals are often marked by setbacks and rejection letters. Our university was one of those to adopt annual professional development reviews whereby an initial plan was set at the commencement of the year and reviewed with a supervisor at the end of the same year. In my initial year, with some apprehension I had to admit to my supervisor that I had not met my publication goals that year. To my surprise and relief he simply stated: "*That's okay, you will. I know you will*". I do not know whether he believed this at the time or not, but his confidence and optimism in my ability was enough to challenge my personal feelings of self-doubt. He could have responded very differently, perhaps dissecting where I had gone wrong or given me some 'tips of the trade' relevant to achieving my goals. In fact, I think that even the best managers would have reacted in just that way. In doing none of this he gave me exactly what I needed: *self-belief*. In the following year, I exceeded my publication goals. Thus, managers can embrace a thinking and behavioural style that allows them to support the personal resources of their employees.

(3) Supporting the development of both personal and social resources. The third tool is somewhat related to the previous one. Managers can use their position to support both the personal and social resources of employees. In particular, emerging research is demonstrating the importance of social identification for wellbeing and resilience and this will be addressed in Chapter 10. For many years, researchers in the area of organisational psychology have been demonstrating the benefits of organisational identification during times of organisational change (Iverson, 1996). Moreover, work in the area of family resilience also reflects this idea. Families that promote family cohesion, celebrate key family events, develop their own culture, support and advocate for one another and display good communication tend to be more resilient (McCubbin & McCubbin, 1996; McCubbin & McCubbin, 1988). Behaviours of managers can both promote and erode the team cohesion necessary to promote employee resilience. For example, managers that vent or complain about employees within the workplace are likely to quickly poke holes in the cohesive fabric that knits a team or organisation together. Conversely, a manager who is willing to celebrate team success can serve to unite employees in their common goals. Managers are also in a position to promote behaviours and thinking styles that are related to resiliency. A manager's response to workplace stressors and setbacks can either be a model for building resilience or eroding it. For example, in the face of difficulties managers play a role in shaping the perception of stressors as opportunities for growth and this style of response is likely to promote resilience in those who model this approach. In contrast, if a manager

responds to stressors as though they are nuisances or exhibit catastrophising, those that follow such an example may find their resilience eroded. Further, after workplace setbacks managers can either highlight the merit or growth opportunities promoting self-efficacy and learning. In contrast, managers can also focus negatively on setbacks and take a punitive approach to employee failure having quite a different effect.

(4) Allowing employees the opportunity to access needed resources. Finally, managers can make concerted efforts to allow employees access to the resources they need to cope with the demands of their job. Access to coping resources can be many and varied and may be as simple as allowing employees control over the timing of break periods to allow recovery when needed. A burnt-out social worker once expressed to me that one of the things that would have helped her is if she could have just taken breaks when she needed them, rather than having her daily schedule controlled by someone else. For this social worker, control over her recovery opportunities was something that she believed would have helped her to cope with the stressors of an occupation with a high risk of burnout. While this is not the solution for everyone, the point is that managers need to be willing to listen and respond where possible to the strategies that employees believe will help them to cope. Again, this point comes back to the earlier observation that most people are resilient and have some intuitive understanding of how to adapt resiliently to the stressors they face.

Each chapter in this book reflects one or more of the above themes and includes recommendations regarding how managers can achieve these broad objectives in their role. However, because every workplace is different we also encourage the reader to think flexibly about how these recommendations and strategies might be adapted to their workplace to achieve the same underlying goal.

References

Billings, A. G. & Moos, R. H. (1984). Coping, stress, and social resources among adults with unipolar depression. *Journal of Personality and Social Psychology, 46*, 877–891.

Bonnano, G. (2005). Resilience in the face of potential trauma. *Current Directions in Psychological Science, 135*, 14, 135–138.

Bonanno, G. A., Field, N. P., Kovacevic, A. & Kaltman, S. (2002). Self-enhancement as a buffer against extreme adversity: Civil war in Bosnia and traumatic loss in the United States. *Personality and Social Psychology Bulletin, 28*, 184–196.

Bonanno, G. A., Galea, S., Bucciarelli, A. & Vlahov, D. (2007). What predicts psychological resilience after disaster? The role of demographics, resources, and life stress. *Journal of Consulting and Clinical Psychology, 75*, 671–682.

Bonanno, G. A., Moskowitz, J. T., Papa, A. & Folkman, S. (2005). Resilience to loss in bereaved spouses, bereaved parents, and bereaved gay men. *Journal of Personality and Social Psychology, 88*, 827–843.

Britt, T. W., Crane, M., Hodson, S. E. & Adler, A. B. (2016). Effective and ineffective coping strategies in a low-autonomy work environment. *Journal of Occupational Health Psychology, 21*, 154–168.

Carette, B., Anseel, F. & Lievens, F. (2013). Does career timing of challenging job assignments influence the relationship with in-role job performance? *Journal of Vocational Behavior*, *83*, 61–67.

Crane, M. F. & Searle, B. J. (2016). Building resilience through exposure to stressors: The effects of challenges versus hindrances. *Journal of Occupational Health Psychology*. Retrieved from http://dx.doi.org/10.1037/a0040064

Cheng, C. (2001). Assessing coping flexibility in real-life and laboratory settings: A multimethod approach. *Journal of Personality and Social Psychology*, *80*, 814–833.

Cohen, S. & Wills, T. (1985). Stress, social support, and the buffering hypothesis. *Psychological Bulletin*, *98*, 310–357.

Coutu, D. L. (2002). How resilience works. *Harvard Business Review*, *80*, 46–55.

Craig, A. & Cooper, R. E. (1992). Symptoms of acute and chronic fatigue. In A. P. Smith & D. M. Jones (eds), *Handbook of human performance* (Vol. 3, pp. 289–339). London: Academic Press.

Fergus, S. & Zimmerman, M. A. (2005). Adolescent resilience: A framework for understanding healthy development in the face of risk. *Annual Review of Public Health*, *26*, 399–419.

Folkman, S. & Moskowitz, J. T. (2004). Coping: Pitfalls and promise. *Annual Review of Psychology*, *55*, 745–774.

Fredrickson, B. L. (2001). The role of positive emotions in positive psychology: The broaden-and-build theory of positive emotions. *American Psychologist*, *56*, 218–226. Peterson, S. J. & Luthans, F. (2003). The positive impact and development of hopeful leaders. *Leadership & Organization Development Journal*, *24*, 26–31.

Froh, J. J., Yurkewicz, C. & Kashdan, T. B. (2009). Gratitude and subjective well-being in early adolescence: Examining gender differences. *Journal of Adolescence*, *32*, 633–650.

Iverson, R. D. (1996). Employee acceptance of organizational change: the role of organizational commitment. *The International Journal of Human Resource Management*, *7*, 122–149.

Jones, N., Seddon, R., Fear, N. T., McAllister, P., Wessely, S. & Greenberg, N. (2012). Leadership, cohesion, morale, and the mental health of UK Armed Forces in Afghanistan. *Psychiatry*, *75*, 49–59.

Kessler, R. C., Berglund, P., Demler, O., Jin, R., Merikangas, K. R. & Walters, E. E. (2005). Lifetime prevalence and age-of-onset distributions of DSM-IV disorders in the National Comorbidity Survey Replication. *Archives of General Psychiatry*, *62*, 593–602.

Lagerveld, S. E., Blonk, R. B., Brenninkmeijer, V., Wijngaards-de Meij, L. & Schaufeli, W. B. (2012). Work-focused treatment of common mental disorders and return to work: A comparative outcome study. *Journal of Occupational Health Psychology*, *17*, 220–234.

Luthans, F., Vogelgesang, G. R. & Lester, P. B. (2006). Developing the psychological capital of resiliency. *Human Resource Development Review*, *5*, 25–44.

Masten, A. S. (2001). Ordinary magic: Resilience process in development. *American Psychologist*, *56*, 227–238.

Masten, A. S., Best, K. M. & Garmezy, N. (1990). Resilience and development: Contributions from the study of children who overcome adversity. *Development and Psychopathology*, *2*, 425–444.

McCubbin, M.A. & McCubbin, H. I. (1996). Resiliency in families: A conceptual model of family adjustment and adaptation in response to stress and crises. In H. I. McCubbin, A. I. Thompson & M.A. McCubbin, *Family assessment: Resiliency, coping and adaptation – Inventories for research and practice* (pp. 1–64). Madison, WI: University of Wisconsin System.

McCubbin, H. I. & McCubbin, M. A. (1988). Typologies of resilient families: Emerging roles of social class and ethnicity. *Family Relations*, *37*, 247–254.

Medibank Private (August, 2008). *The cost of workplace stress in Australia*. Retrieved from www.medibank.com.au/client/documents/pdfs/the-cost-of-workplace-stress.pdf.

Piccolo, R. F. & Colquitt, J. A. (2006). Transformational leadership and behaviors: The mediating role of core job characteristics. *Academy of Management Journal, 49*, 327–340.

Podsakoff, N. P., LePine, J. & LePine, M. (2007). Differential challenge stressor-hindrance stressor relationships with job attitudes, turnover intentions, turnover, and withdrawal behavior: A meta-analysis. *The Journal of Applied Psychology, 92*, 438–454.

Randall, R., Griffiths, A. & Cox, T. (2005). Evaluating organizational stress-management interventions using adapted study designs. *European Journal of Work and Organizational Psychology, 14*, 23–41.

Robison, J. (27 March 27 2014). *Easing the global (and costly) problem of workplace stress*. Retrieved from www.gallup.com/businessjournal/167921/easing-global-costly-problem-workplace-stress.aspx

Reivich, K. & Schatte, A. (2002). *The resilience factor*. New York: Broadway Books.

Safe Work Australia (2015) *The cost of work-related injury and illness for Australian employers, workers and the community: 2012–13*. Canberra, ACT. Retrieved from www.safework australia.gov.au/sites/swa/about/publications/pages/cost-injury-illness-2012-13.

Thoits, P. A. (1994). Stressors and problem-solving: The individual as psychological activist. *Journal of Health and Social Behavior, 35*, 143–159.

Tugade M. M. & Fredrickson, B. (2004). Resilient individuals use positive emotions to bounce back from negative emotional experiences. *Journal of Personality and Social Psychology, 86*, 320–333.

Windle, G., Bennett, K. M. & Noyes, J. (2011). A methodological review of resilience measurement scales. *Health and Quality of Life Outcomes, 9*, 8–26.

PART 1

Personality, psychological resources and employee resilience

2

THE RIGHT STUFF

Employee characteristics that promote resilience

Professor Robert R. Sinclair and
Dr. Janelle H. Cheung

Tom Wolfe's famous book *The Right Stuff* explored the qualities and character of United States Air Force pilots flying experimental aircraft and ultimately working to become astronauts. By nearly any measure, these were exceptional individuals, selected from larger pools of personnel who were themselves among the best of the best. *The Right Stuff*, for Wolfe, was an elusive mix of skills, abilities and traits that enabled pilots to thrive in the most demanding situations. Although pilots are an extreme example, Wolfe's classic illustrates a challenge that all organisations face: how to find and develop employees who can rise to the challenge of adverse circumstances and who are capable of persevering with relatively few health or performance-related problems.

Most occupations require at least some level of resilience. For example, military personnel experience long separations from their families and experience combat-related death and destruction. Health care workers face life and death situations with patients on a daily basis, as well as risks to their own health and wellbeing. Call centre representatives deal with frustrated and sometimes abusive customers. Workers in other occupations also experience stressors such as abusive supervisors or colleagues, the threat of job loss, interpersonal conflict at work or work role demands that exceed employees' capacity to respond. So, a critical challenge for organisations is how to develop and maintain employee resilience in the face of the demands of the contemporary work environment.

One perplexing challenge in developing employee resilience is that people differ considerably in how they respond to stressors – even among workers with similar levels of training and experience. Some people experience no problems or only report minor symptoms such as a short-term decline in job satisfaction. Others may experience some significant short-term consequences such as lower performance, physical and mental health problems and thoughts of quitting their job, but ultimately recover relatively quickly and get back to business as usual. Still others develop longer-term negative physical outcomes such as cardiovascular disease or mental health outcomes such as depression and burnout. Some may even come to believe dealing with the stressor was ultimately beneficial and helped them grow as individuals. For example, many military service members report personal and work related benefits as a consequence of being deployed on combat or peace-keeping missions (Wood *et al.*, 2012).

Clearly, there are individual differences in how people respond to demanding circumstances; managers need to understand these differences in order to develop and maintain a resilient workforce. Thus, the central goal of this chapter is to discuss the nature of individual differences related to resilience, with a particular focus on personality traits. Specifically, we will define the broad concept of personality, describe some core themes that emerge from personality literature regarding personality traits related to resilience, and discuss possible steps managers can take to enhance employees' personal capacities for resilience.

Defining personal capacities for resilience

Personality can be defined as "an individual's characteristic patterns of thought, emotion, and behaviour, together with the psychological mechanisms behind those patterns" (Funder, 2001, p. 2). Personality research encompasses many ideas and approaches, including evolved patterns of behaviour common to the human species, behavioural tendencies that reflect biologically-based dispositions, learned ways people typically respond to specific situations, and even each individual's unique personal life story (McAdams & Pals, 2006). Although some people assume that personality traits are relatively stable throughout adulthood, evidence suggests that people continue to experience at least some personality changes throughout their lives (cf. Roberts & Del Vecchio, 2000). Such changes are in part due to their experiences in key life roles such as work. This is a critical point for organisations interested in resilience as it implies that personal capacities for resilience may be developed (or undermined) through organisational policies and practices.

The scientific literature on personality and health is vast and specific interest in resilience appears to be on the rise. For example, in a recent search we found over 20,000 peer-reviewed references using the keywords *personality* and *stress* and over 5,000 references using the keywords *personality* and *health*.[1] A similar search revealed over 6,000 citations to *resilience* and over 200 of those specifically mentioning *resilience* and *employee*. One problem in this literature is that scholars have developed many different definitions of the term resilience (Meredith *et al.*, 2011), adding to confusion in understanding the scientific literature. Perhaps the most important problem is that scholars sometimes ignore the distinction between the *demonstration* of resilience (i.e., showing little or no adverse outcomes following exposure to demanding events) and the *capacity* for resilience, which involves knowledge, skills, motives, etc. that promote resilient functioning, but are not resilience per se (Bonanno, 2004, Britt, Sinclair & McFadden, 2013, Fikretoglu & McCreary, 2012).

Drawing on this distinction, personality traits may be viewed as individual differences that reflect the capacity for resilience in stressful circumstances.

A Personal POWER model of personality-based resilience

There is no universally accepted list of resilience-related personality traits. Therefore, we will review several relevant models and describe central themes in the literature. As the reader will see, each model contributes different but overlapping content, sometimes using different terms for very similar concepts. We propose that these models can be integrated into what we call a Personal POWER model of personality-based resilience. Our Personal POWER model represents an effort to highlight both the common and unique features across models in order to provide general understanding of the aspects of personality most likely to be related to resilience.

Table 2.1 lists several commonly studied personality constructs in the occupational health literature. All of the models listed have been discussed extensively in prior reviews (e.g., Bowling & Jex, 2013; Perrewé & Spector, 2002; Sinclair & Tucker, 2006; Sinclair et al., 2013) and we encourage readers to consult these sources for in-depth discussion. For this chapter, we note the following general characteristics of these traits. First, each of the traits can be viewed as a personal resource, defined as "aspects of the self that are generally linked to resiliency and refer to individuals' sense of ability to control and impact upon their environment successfully" (Xanthopoulou et al., 2007, pp. 123–124). In other words, each trait reflects a personal resource that promotes individual functioning in adverse circumstances. Second, at least some research in each model assumes that the traits are subject to change through intervention and experience and therefore potentially able to be influenced by organisational policies and practices. Thus, they are relevant to the workplace as potential targets for personnel selection systems or training programmes, and may possibly change in response to changes in job design/working conditions.

Third, the traits are interrelated; people with higher scores on some of the traits are quite likely to have higher scores on others. This idea is formally stated in the case of hardiness, core self-evaluations and psychological capital, where a few personality traits are considered to be part of a broader theme. For example, we will see in Chapter 3 that traits such as hopefulness, optimism, resilience and self-efficacy share some common elements that allow them to be collectively considered to reflect one's level of psychological capital (Luthans et al., 2007a; Luthans, Youssef & Avolio, 2007b). Similarly, the Five-Factor Model (FFM) is a prominent model of personality that proposes the existence of five core personality traits: openness, conscientiousness, extraversion, agreeableness and neuroticism (Costa & McCrae, 1992). Students in undergraduate psychology are commonly trained to remember these five important personality dimensions by using the acronym 'OCEAN'. Researchers have demonstrated that these five personality dimensions are not completely distinct, but rather can be organised into one or

TABLE 2.1 Frequently studied personality constructs related to resilience

Model (Citation)	Construct	Definition
Five-Factor Model (Costa & McCrae, 1992)	Conscientiousness	The extent to which one is responsible, hardworking and detail-oriented.
	Extroversion	The extent to which one is sociable and friendly, and experiences positive emotions.
	Neuroticism	The extent to which one experiences feelings of anxiety and vulnerability, and displays self-consciousness.
Core Self Evaluations (Judge, Locke, & Durham, 1997)	Locus of Control	Internals: individuals believe that they can control a variety of factors in their lives. Externals: individuals believe that events in their lives are out of their control.
	Emotional Stability	One's tendency to be confident, secure, and steady.
	Self-Esteem	The overall value one places on him or herself.
	Generalised Self-Efficacy	One's estimate of their fundamental ability to cope and perform successfully.
Psychological Capital (Luthans et al., 2007b)	Resilience	Bouncing back from adversity and sustaining momentum in attaining goals.
	Hope	Continuously expecting successful goal attainment and being read to redirect paths to goals as needed.
	Optimism	Making positive, stable and internal attributions about one's success.
	Self-Efficacy	Having confidence about one's ability to successfully execute a task.
Hardiness (Kobasa, 1982; Maddi & Kobasa, 1984)	Commitment	The predisposition to be engaged in things, people, and contexts; it gives the person a sense of purpose and meaning.
	Control	The extent to which a person believes that he or she has control over one's life and life events.
	Challenge	The extent to which a person seeks growth and leaning from life experiences and makes challenge appraisals (as opposed to threat appraisals) in the face of difficult situations.
Affective Dispositions (Watson, Clark, & Tellegen, 1988)	Positive Affect	The extent to which a person generally experiences positive emotions, such as excitement and enthusiasm.
	Negative Affect	The extent to which a person generally experiences negative emotions, such as depression and frustration.
Regulatory Focus (Wallace & Chen, 2006)	Promotion Focus	An eagerness focus in seeking positive outcomes, such as accomplishing greater quantity of work more quickly and emphasising on productivity.

continued . . .

TABLE 2.1 Continued

Model (Citation)	Construct	Definition
	Prevention Focus	A vigilance focus in avoiding negative outcomes, such as adhering to rules, responsibilities and regulations.
Proactive Personality (Bateman & Crant, 1993)	Proactive Personality	The extent to which a person generally takes initiative to manage and control their environment to their advantage.
Type A Behaviour Pattern (Friedman & Rosenman, 1959)	Type A Personality	The extent to which a person tends to be competitive and self-critical, experiences a constant sense to time urgency, and is easily aroused to anger or hostility.
Self-control (Baumeister et al., 2007)	Self-control (Ego Control)	The extent to which people can adjust their responses according to a standard such as "ideals, values, morals, and social expectations, and to support the pursuit of long-term goals" (p. 351).

two broader themes (van der Linden, te Nijenhuis & Bakker, 2010; Rushton & Irwing, 2008).

Lastly, the models share similarities in the kinds of traits expected to serve as personal resources, although each model also contributes some unique content. For example, self-efficacy and control appear in several models, suggesting their central role in resilience. On the other hand, only hardiness includes the concept of a dispositional ability to find purpose in one's life. As shown in Table 2.2, we identified five core themes that summarise the content in these models: *Purpose, Optimism, Will-power, Emotional Stability, and Resourcefulness* (POWER). We do not view these as five completely distinct concepts; rather, we conceptualise them as overlapping concepts that share the common feature of being personal resources thought to be associated with the capacity for resilience. We discuss each of these below.

(1) Purpose. The sense that life activities are filled with purpose and meaning plays a critical role in psychological health and wellbeing (Glazer *et al.*, 2014). Some personality theorists view the ability to find meaning and purpose in major life activities as at least partly a dispositional tendency. The concept of commitment from the hardiness literature best illustrates this idea (Kobasa, 1982; Maddi & Kobasa, 1984). Hardiness is a cognitive personality trait reflecting the way people tend to think about events in their lives. Commitment, a dimension of hardiness, is defined as a dispositional tendency to find meaning and purpose in life events. The ability to find meaning in life events may be particularly critical for those exposed to adverse circumstances such as soldiers on extended combat deployments (Bartone, 2005). Of course, the sense that life events are meaningful also can be

TABLE 2.2 Personal POWER: Core themes across resilience constructs

	Personal POWER Themes				
	Purpose	*Optimism*	*Willpower*	*Emotional Stability*	*Resourcefulness*
Five-Factor Model	Conscientiousness	Extroversion Neuroticism			
Core Self Evaluations				Emotional Stability	Self-Esteem Generalised Self-Efficacy Locus of Control
Hardiness	Commitment Challenge			Control	
Affective Dispositions		Positive Affectivity		Negative Affectivity	
Psychological Capital		Optimism			Self-Efficacy Hope
Regulatory Focus		Promotion Focus		Prevention Focus	
Proactive Personality					Proactivity
Type A Behaviour Pattern				Type A Behaviour Pattern	
Self-Control			Self-Control		

influenced by environmental forces such as the influence of transformational leaders on perceptions of meaningful work (cf. Arnold *et al.*, 2007). But, literature on hardiness highlights the idea that there is a dispositional basis to these perceptions. We would expect that people with a greater capacity to see events in their lives as meaningful to be more likely to demonstrate resilience under adversity.

(2) Optimism. Several models listed in Table 2.2 describe dispositional aspects of a positive mental outlook on life events, which we refer to as optimism. For example, the hardiness literature describes the idea of challenge as a dispositional tendency to view demanding events as challenges to be overcome, rather than as stressors that threaten the individual. Similarly, people who are higher in extroversion and positive affect are described, in part, as more likely to experience positive emotional states. The psychological capital literature describes optimists as tending to see negative events as influenced by the situation, rather than by stable and enduring aspects of the self, meaning that they can potentially be changed in the future. Similarly, those with a promotion focus are more likely to attend to positive features of events and situations such as opportunities for rewards and personal growth rather than focusing on the negative consequences associated with failure.

(3) Willpower. Willpower concerns a person's general sense of self-discipline and self-control and corresponds to facets of the FFM dimension of conscientiousness such as *hard-working* and *prudent* as well as Baumeister's strength model of self-control (Baumeister, Vohs & Tice, 2007). People with high willpower are driven to success, resist giving up easily, avoid making careless mistakes and display strong impulse control. Conscientiousness is a particularly important attribute to capture in relation to resilience given its links to research on both job performance (e.g., Barrick & Mount, 1991; Judge, Higgins, Thorsen & Barrick, 1999; Sinclair & Tucker, 2006) and health-related outcomes such as mortality (Friedman *et al.*, 1993), marital stability (Roberts & Bogg, 2004), and health maintenance behaviour (Bogg & Roberts, 2004).

(4) Emotional stability. Emotionally stable individuals are poised under pressure; they remain calm, cool and collected in demanding situations. In relation to stress, emotionally stable individuals are less likely to view events as stressful, less likely to have negative emotional or interpersonal reactions to stressors, and more likely to successfully cope with demanding situations. The FFM dimension of neuroticism is the core feature of emotional stability and has been shown to be important to health in a wide variety of contexts (Lahey, 2009). Other traits in this category resemble neuroticism/emotional stability in that they concern either dispositional tendencies to experience negative emotions (negative affectivity), intense arousal in response to stressful situations (e.g., Type A), or a focus on attending to and avoiding negative stimuli (prevention orientation).

(5) Resourcefulness. Many resilience-related traits reflect some sense of individuals' perceived ability to affect their own lives – the sense that they are capable of responding to situations, that they can control whether they receive positive outcomes and that they expect good things to result from their actions. We refer to this as resourcefulness. The idea of resourcefulness underlies traits such as locus of control, hope, proactive personality, challenge, self-esteem and self-efficacy. Although there are subtle differences between these traits, they all emphasise the idea that people who are self-confident and believe in their ability to positively respond to life events should demonstrate higher levels of resilience. Thus, resourceful individuals adopt a head on approach to confronting problems. This enables them to avoid some problems, to respond effectively to others before they become serious, and to remain productively engaged in their work, rather than being debilitated by stressors.

How does the capacity for resilience influence the demonstration of resilience?

We now turn our attention to the question of *how* the capacity for resilience is related to the demonstration of resilience. This is an important issue because personality traits may have multiple kinds of relationships to stress and health outcomes that are not always consistent with a "common sense" perspective on why there are individual differences in reactions to adverse circumstances. Figure 2.1 depicts four pathways that are important to understanding individual differences in the capacity for resilience.

Path (a) reflects the relationship between personality traits and the experience of stressors. Bowling and Jex (2013) discuss three types of processes related to this path: *selection, stressor creation and perceptual effects.* Selection refers to how peoples'

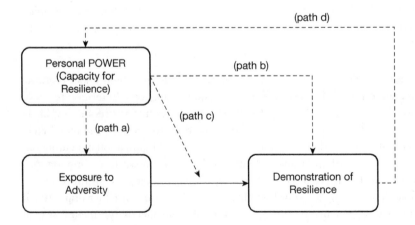

FIGURE 2.1 Pathways through which personal power influences the demonstration of resilience

personalities influence their choices of work environments. Bowling and Jex give the example of a high Type A person who might be predisposed to prefer a fast paced and high pressure work environment, such as being a day trader on the New York Stock Exchange. Regarding resilience, people with higher capacities for resilience might be more willing to work in dangerous environments (e.g., military deployments, commercial fishing) or environments that are intellectually challenging (e.g., medicine, science).

Stressor creation effects involve how peoples' behaviour influences the work environment. Regarding negative effects, people with lower capacities for resilience might engage in behaviours that increase the stress in their work environment. For example, people with lower emotional stability may have greater difficulty getting along with colleagues and therefore create more interpersonal stressors for themselves. Conversely, teams with more emotionally stable and conscientious members who share a strong sense of purpose and a desire for challenging work might be less prone to errors at work, project delays or team conflict, each of which would enhance team functioning. Although research on vocational interests supports the idea that work-related aspects of personality influence peoples' choices of (and satisfaction with) particular jobs (Holland, 1997), little research has directly tested either selection or stressor creation effects with regard to resilience and work stress. One exception is Smith and Zautra's (2002) discussion of exposure effects for neuroticism such that less emotionally stable individuals tend to be more difficult to work with and as a result tend to have less co-worker support.

Bowling and Jex (2013) describe perceptual effects as the tendency of personality to "colour" employees' perceptions of their work environments. In other words, while selection effects refer to the influence of personality on the objective (actual) work environment, perceptual effects refer to the influence of personality on the way people view their work environments. Applied to resilience, perceptual effects refer to the idea that individuals with higher capacity for resilience would be expected to perceive their work environments more favourably and experience less stress as a result. For example, consider two employees experiencing the same high workload and time pressure. Let's say that employee A tends to be more resilient than employee B. Employee A should view the high workload and time pressure as a personal challenge and opportunity for growth (e.g., developing the ability to work effectively under pressure). In contrast, employee B may view the time pressure as a threat to their job performance (e.g., the threat of failing to meet the deadline).

Perceptual effects have been supported by more research than selection effects as studies have found that people who report higher levels of many of the POWER traits listed above also describe their work environments more favourably. Neuroticism and Negative Affectivity have perhaps the strongest support (Bowling & Jex, 2013), but research has also supported these effects for many of the other traits listed (Eschleman, Bowling & Alarcon, 2010; Morris, Messal & Meriac, 2013).

Path (b) depicts the direct relationship between the capacity for resilience and the demonstration of resilience, such that, all other things being equal, people with higher resilience capacities are more likely to demonstrate resilience. This is the relationship most commonly studied in the scientific literature on personality and health and research generally supports the conclusion that people with higher scores on measures of the personal POWER themes tend to have better health outcomes. For example, Eschleman *et al.* (2010) found that higher levels of hardiness were associated with a wide array of measures of psychological strain (e.g., depression, burnout, PTSD, maladjustment), wellbeing (e.g., life satisfaction, happiness, personal growth) and physical strain (e.g., physical health symptoms, fatigue, fitness). Similarly, many studies of the FFM traits have clearly established their ability to predict outcomes such as health behaviour (Bogg & Roberts, 2004), subjective wellbeing (DeNeve & Cooper, 1998), symptoms of clinical disorders (Malouff, Thorsteinsson & Schutte, 2005) and physical activity (Wilson & Dishman, 2015).

It is important to note that each model offers a different theoretical analysis of why traits in the model are linked to health outcomes. We will not provide a detailed review of theoretical issues here, but we encourage interested readers to review this literature. Strictly speaking, the direct relationship can be argued not to reflect resilience per se because it does not require exposure to adverse circumstances, as described above. In other words, even among individuals who have not been exposed to adverse circumstances, people with higher personal capacities for resilience tend to have better health outcomes. However, for organisational staff members tasked with developing and maintaining worker health and wellbeing, this path is an important focus because it has strong levels of scientific support. To the extent that traits can either be selected for or developed, this might be the most feasible path to address in a contemporary workforce. On the other hand, a concern with much of this literature is that it shows stronger effects for personality traits in relation to other self-reported measures as compared with their relationship with objective health status measures. Such findings imply the need for caution and further study before concluding that resilience-related health effects are personality-driven.

Path (c) shows that individual differences in Personal POWER might influence the relationship between exposure to stressors and the demonstration of resilience. This is often called a moderating or buffering effect and can be argued to reflect the classic depiction of resilience as trait-related differences in how people respond to adversity. In statistical terms, a moderated relationship is one in which the strength of the relationship between two variables changes depending on levels of some third variable, which is said to moderate the relationship. For example, the negative health outcomes resulting from exposure to organisational change (e.g., downsizing) may depend on an individual's standing on the Personal POWER traits. From this perspective, high levels of most POWER traits are considered to reduce an individual's negative responses to stressors, thereby enhancing their demonstration of resilience. Other personality traits can increase a person's sensitivity to stressors and in turn lower resilience. Many personality variables have been tested as moderators of the relationship between various stressors and outcomes. However, our impression of this research is that the findings are not consistent from study to study and the size of the observed effects is typically smaller than the effects obtained in studies of direct effects (i.e., path b).

Path (d) is perhaps the least commonly studied relationship between the demonstration of resilience and the capacity for resilience. It portrays a feedback loop between the demonstration of resilience and the subsequent development of higher capacities for resilience. In other words, one of the outcomes of successfully adapting to circumstances may be the subsequent development of enhanced capacity for resilience. In Personal POWER terms, after responding to adversity, some people may develop a stronger sense of meaning in daily events (i.e., purpose), a more positive outlook about the future (i.e., optimism), a stronger sense of self-control/self-discipline (i.e., will power), a calmness in the face of subsequent stressors (i.e., higher emotional stability), and an enhanced sense of confidence in one's ability to respond to future demands (i.e., higher resourcefulness). Thoits (1994) found that individuals who successfully resolved their job and romantic relationship problems tended to experience an increase in mastery and self-efficacy, compared to those who did not attempt to solve their problems or who made failed attempts to solve their problems. Thus, the demonstration of resilience is also likely to feed back into one's capacity for resilience.

Given that the demonstration of resilience is likely to play an important role in increasing the capacity for resilience, some level of exposure to adversity is likely to be necessary for the development of resilience. For example, Seery and colleagues proposed an inverted-U relationship between exposure to traumatic events and resilience such that people who have experienced moderate levels of adversity (two to four potentially traumatic events) seem to be more resilient than those who have experienced either extremely high or very low levels of adversity (Seery, Holman & Silver, 2010). This suggests that managers should avoid both pushing employees to the limits of what they can handle and shielding them from all adversity. Instead, managers can promote resilience by providing employees with reasonably challenging jobs and the resources to respond to those challenges.

What can organisations do to promote resilience?

Organisational approaches to building and fostering a resilient workforce fall under three main categories (Spangler *et al.*, 2012). Partnership for Workplace Mental Health (PWMH), a programme of the American Psychiatric Foundation, has also adopted this three-tier model in its guide for employers on addressing workplace stress and building a resilient workforce (PWMH, 2013). The three categories are primary prevention, secondary prevention and tertiary prevention. These three prevention categories reflect a hierarchical framework commonly used by public health professionals in addressing various health issues and organisations are likely to benefit from implementing a combination of these three types of interventions (At Work, 2006). Readers are encouraged to consult PWMH's employer guide for details regarding the different types of strategies organisations can adopt in promoting a resilient workforce (including training and development, employee assistance programmes and leadership involvement). In this chapter, we will focus mainly on the promotion of resilience in relation to individual traits.

Hiring and selection. A resilient workplace may be developed through strategic hiring and selection practices. Resilience-related traits and other related individual characteristics might be assessed during pre-hire stages using professionally developed and well-validated inventories. Organisations can use the POWER model described above as a basis for the selection of resilient employees. Although there is not one personality inventory specifically designed to fit the POWER model, various psychometrically valid scales may be combined to achieve the assessment of POWER. For example, Luthans and his colleagues (2007a) have developed a measurement of positive psychological capital (including hope, resilience, optimism and efficacy) that is predictive of work performance and satisfaction. Other resilience measurement scales, such as the Connor-Davidson Resilience Scale, the Resilience Scale for Adults and the Brief Resilience Scale, that have been found to have strong psychometric properties should be considered as well (Windle, Bennett & Noyes, 2011). Scales such as these can be incorporated in assessment batteries to evaluate applicants' resilience and stress tolerance tendencies and their expected performance on the job. It is important to note, though, the ability of resilience measures to predict long-term work outcomes is still understudied in the literature. Although additional validation evidence is needed, organisations should also be on the lookout for potential subgroup differences (e.g., race and gender) in resilience that may have discriminatory consequences for selection systems.

The right fit. Hiring managers should also pay attention to person–organisation and person–job fit (PWMH, 2013; Spangler *et al.*, 2012). For example, person-organisation fit may be assessed using an organisational culture profile, individual preferences for organisational cultures and individuals' personality traits (cf. O'Reilly, Chatman & Caldwell, 1991). Person-job fit may be assessed using a profile comparison approach in matching the job requirements, individual competencies and their personality tendencies (Caldwell & O'Reilly, 1990). Comprehensive job analyses consulting subject matter experts (e.g., job incumbents and supervisors) would be beneficial in order to truly consider the nature of the job in question and the individual skills, abilities and traits needed to succeed in the job. For example, a candidate who strives under stressful circumstances and appraises high-pressure situations as challenging may have a greater fit with a high-stress work environment than a candidate who prefers working without pressure. Research suggests that overall person-organisation and person-job fits are related to important human resources outcomes, including job performance, job satisfaction, organisational commitment and turnover rates (Arthur *et al.*, 2006; O'Reilly *et al.*, 1991). Less attention has been paid to the relationship between fit and resilience specifically, although poor fit has long been implicated as a factor in work stress (cf. Edwards, Caplan & Harrison, 1998).

Post-hire practices. Post-hire practices may also be implemented to promote resilience in relation to personality traits, especially targeted at at-risk individuals who are in need of assistance before potential problems lead to severe consequences (i.e., secondary prevention). In the context of workplaces, secondary prevention may include programmes for employees who are at-risk of developing mental health and/or other stress-related problems. For example, individuals who are emotionally unstable may be more vulnerable to stressful situations and may not be able to cope effectively with the consequences of stress. Organisations may provide employees with health risk assessments and other screening tools, and based on the screening results, stress-management programmes and behavioural health interventions may be provided and catered to individual needs. For example, health risk assessments regarding employees' reported levels of stress may increase their awareness of their own mental health and thereby increase their willingness to engage in stress-management programmes, such as resilience-building interventions. Resilience training as part of secondary prevention may focus on reframing the way employees perceive stressors and developing realistic previews and anticipated setbacks so that employees can develop resiliency and realistic optimism (Luthans *et al.*, 2006). A more detailed discussion of the various approaches to resilience training is available in Chapter 14.

It should be emphasised in all work contexts that the mere implementation of strategic policies and practices is not adequate unless leadership involvement and management support are also in play. Values, norms and beliefs espoused by the organisation must be aligned with the behaviours enacted by the leaders. For example, efforts to develop resilience in the workforce through selection require commitment and support from hiring managers and the personnel responsible for resilience assessments. Management support is also essential when health risk assessments or other programmes alike are provided to employees, especially when at-risk employees may need their managers' encouragement and assurance that the programmes in place do not incur negative employment-related consequences and are beneficial to the employees' health and wellbeing.

Final thoughts

In this chapter we described Personal POWER as a set of personal capacities people have that enable them to demonstrate resilience in response to adverse circumstances. These qualities are viewed as somewhat stable but changeable personal qualities that organisations may be able to (a) select for, through the careful use of personality assessments in the selection process, (b) develop in employees through training interventions, or (c) influence through leadership practices aimed at facilitating these qualities. Finally, although our work implies the need for attention to how individual qualities influence responses to adversity, we strongly advocate for a continued primary focus on the work environment and on leadership. Supportive leadership and healthy work design are necessary components of any organisational effort to promote employee health.

KEY MESSAGES FROM THIS CHAPTER

- There are five common themes in personality models that tend to be associated with the capacity for resilience: *Purpose, Optimism, Willpower, Emotional Stability and Resourcefulness* (POWER).
- A resilient workplace may be developed through strategic hiring and selection practices. Organisations can use the characteristics described in the POWER model as a basis for the selection of resilient employees.
- Paying attention to employee fit is also important in developing a resilient workforce. The type and nature of the POWER characteristics expected of employees must match the requirements of the job.
- Post-hiring practices that promote the POWER characteristics are critical. This could be in the form of resilience-building interventions, but can also be management practices and policies discussed throughout this book.

Note

1   Search of PsychINFO, MedLine, ERIC, and Business Source Premier – April 14, 2015.

References

Arnold, K. A., Turner, N., Barling, J., Kelloway, E. K. & McKee, M. C. (2007). Transformational leadership and psychological well-being: The mediating role of meaningful work. *Journal of Occupational Health Psychology, 12*, 193–203.

Arthur Jr., W., Bell, S. T., Villado, A. J. & Doverspike, D. (2006). The use of person-organization fit in employment decision making: An assessment of its criterion-related validity. *Journal of Applied Psychology, 91*, 786–801.

At Work. (2006). What researchers mean by primary, secondary and tertiary prevention. Retrieved from www.iwh.on.ca/system/files/at-work/at_work_43.pdf

Barrick, M. R. & Mount, M. K. (1991). The big five personality dimensions and job performance: A meta_analysis. *Personnel Psychology, 44*, 1–26.

Bartone, P. T. (2005). The need for positive meaning in military operations: Reflections on Abu Ghraib. *Military Psychology, 17*, 315–324.

Bateman, T.S. & Crant, J.M. (1993). The proactive component of organizational behaviour: A   measure and correlates. *Journal of Organizational Behaviour, 14*, 103–118.

Baumeister, R. F., Vohs, K. D. & Tice, D. M. (2007). The strength model of self-control. *Current Directions in Psychological Science, 16*, 351–355.

Bogg, T. & Roberts, B. W. (2004). Conscientiousness and health-related behaviours: a meta-analysis of the leading behavioural contributors to mortality. *Psychological Bulletin, 130*, 887–919.

Bonanno, G. A. (2004). Loss, trauma, and human resilience: Have we underestimated the human capacity to thrive after extremely aversive events? *American Psychologist, 59*, 20–28.

Bowling, N. & Jex, S. (2013). The role of personality in occupational stress: A review and future research agenda, In N. Christiansen & R. Tett (eds). *Handbook of personality at work* (pp. 692–717). New York: Routledge.

Britt, T. W., Sinclair, R. R. & McFadden, A. C. (2013). Introduction: The meaning and importance of military resilience. In R. R. Sinclair & T. W. Britt (eds). *Building psychological resilience in military personnel: Theory and practice* (pp. 3–17). Washington, DC: APA Books.

Caldwell, D. F. & O'Reilly, C. A. (1990). Measuring person-job fit with a profile-comparison process. *Journal of Applied Psychology, 75*, 648–657.

Costa, P. T., Jr. & McCrae, R. M. (1992). *Revised NEO Personality Inventory (NEO PI R) and NEO Five Factor Inventory (NEO-FFI) Professional Manual*, Psychological Assessment Resources, Inc., Odessa, FL.

DeNeve, K. M. & Cooper, H. (1998). The happy personality: A meta-analysis of 137 personality traits and subjective well-being. *Psychological Bulletin, 124*, 197–229.

Edwards, J. R., Caplan, R. D. & Harrison, R. V. (1998). Person-environment fit theory: Conceptual foundations, empirical evidence, and directions for future research. In C. L. Cooper (ed.), *Theories of organizational stress* (pp. 28–67). Oxford: Oxford University Press.

Eschleman, K. J., Bowling, N. A. & Alarcon, G. (2010). A meta-analytic examination of hardiness. *International Journal of Stress Management, 17*, 277–307.

Fikretoglu, D. & McCreary, D. R. (2012). *Psychological resilience: A brief review of definitions, and key theoretical, conceptual, and methodological issues.* Technical Report 2012–012, Defense R&D Canada, Toronto.

Friedman, M. & Rosenman, R. H. (1959). Association of specific behaviour pattern with blood and cardiovascular findings. *Journal of the American Medical Association, 169*, 1286–1296.

Friedman, H. S., Tucker, J. S., Tomlinson-Keasey, C., Schwartz, J. E., Wingard, D. L. & Criqui, M. H. (1993). Does childhood personality predict longevity? *Journal of Personality and Social Psychology, 65*, 176–185.

Funder, D. C. (2001). *The Personality Puzzle.* New York: Norton. 2nd edn.

Glazer, S., Kozusznik, M. W., Meyers, J. H. & Ganai, O. (2014). Meaningfulness as a resource to mitigate work stress. In S. Leka & R. R. Sinclair (eds), *Contemporary occupational health psychology: Global perspectives on research and practice*, Volume 3, pp. 114–130. Chichester: Wiley-Blackwell.

Holland, J. L. (1997). *Making vocational choices: A theory of vocational personalities and work environments* (3rd edn) Odessa, FL: Psychological Assessment Resources, Inc.

Judge, T. A., Higgins, C. A., Thoresen, C. J. & Barrick, M. R. (1999). The big five personality traits, general mental ability, and career success across the life span. *Personnel Psychology, 52*, 621–652.

Judge, T. A., Locke, E. A. & Durham, C. C. (1997). The dispositional causes of job satisfaction: A core evaluations approach. *Research in Organizational Behaviour, 19*, 151–188.

Kobasa, S. C. (1982). The hardy personality: Toward a social psychology of stress and health. In G. S. Sanders & J. Suls (eds), *Social psychology of health and illness* (pp. 3–32). Hillsdale, NJ: Lawrence Erlbaum Associates.

Lahey, B. B. (2009). Public health significance of neuroticism. *American Psychologist, 64*, 241–256.

Luthans, F., Avey, J. B., Avolio, B. J., Norman, S. M. & Combs, G. M. (2006). Psychological capital development: Toward a micro-intervention. *Journal of Organizational Behaviour, 27*, 387–393.

Luthans, F., Avolio, B. J., Avey, J. B. & Norman, S. M. (2007a). Positive psychological capital: Measurement and relationship with performance and satisfaction. *Personnel Psychology, 60,* 541–572.

Luthans F., Youssef, C.M. & Avolio, B. J. (2007b). *Psychological capital.* New York, NY: Oxford University Press.

Maddi, S. R. & Kobasa, S. C. (1984). *The hardy executive: Health under stress.* Homewood, IL: Dow Jones-Irwin.

Malouff, J. M., Thorsteinsson, E. B. & Schutte, N. S. (2005). The relationship between the five-factor model of personality and symptoms of clinical disorders: A meta-analysis. *Journal of Psychopathology and Behavioural Assessment, 27,* 101–114.

McAdams, D. P. & Pals, J. L. (2006). A new Big Five: Fundamental principles for an integrative science of personality. *American Psychologist, 61,* 204–217.

Meredith, S., Sherbourne, C., Gaillot, S., J., Hansell, L., Ritschard, H. V., Parker, A. M. & Wrenn, G., (2011). *Promoting psychological resilience in the U.S. military,* RAND Corporation (MG-966-OSD).

Morris, M. L., Messal, C. B. & Meriac, J. P. (2013). Core self-evaluation and goal orientation: Understanding work stress. *Human Resource Development Quarterly, 24,* 35–62.

O'Reilly, C. A., Chatman, J. & Caldwell, D. F. (1991). People and organizational culture: a profile comparison approach to assessing person-organization fit. *The Academy of Management Journal, 34,* 487–516.

Partnership for Workplace Mental Health (2013). *Employer practices for addressing stress and building resilience.* Retrieved from www.workplacementalhealth.org/Publications-Surveys/Study-Examines-Employer-Perceptions-of-Stress-and-Resilience-Intervention.aspx

Perrewé, P. L. & Spector, P. E. (2002). Personality research in the organizational sciences. In G. R. Ferris & J. J. Martocchio. (eds), *Research in personnel and human resources management,* Vol. 21 (pp. 1–63). US: Elsevier Science/JAI Press.

Roberts, B. W. & Bogg, T. (2004). A longitudinal study of the relationships between conscientiousness and the social-environmental factors and substance-use behaviours that influence health. *Journal of Personality, 72,* 325–354.

Roberts, B. W. & Del Vecchio, W. F. (2000). The rank-order consistency of personality traits from childhood to old age: A quantitative review of longitudinal studies. *Psychological Bulletin, 126,* 3–25.

Rushton, J. P. & Irwing, P. (2008). A general factor of personality (GFP) from two meta-analyses of the Big Five: Digman (1997) and Mount, Barrick, Scullen, and Rounds (2005). *Personality and Individual Differences, 45,* 679–683.

Seery, M. D., Holman, A. E. & Silver, R. C. (2010). Whatever does not kill us: Cumulative 'lifetime adversity, vulnerability, and resilience. *Journal of Personality and Social Psychology, 99,* 1025–1041.

Sinclair, R. R. & Tucker, J. S. (2006). Stress-CARE: An integrated model of individual differences in soldier performance under stress. In A. Adler, T. Britt & and C. Castro (eds). *Military life: The psychology of serving in peace and combat* (Vol. 1, pp. 202–231). Greenwood Publishing Group.

Sinclair, R. R., Waitsman, M., Oliver, C. M. & Deese, N. (2013). Personality and psychological resilience in military personnel. In R. R. Sinclair & T. W. Britt (eds). *Building psychological resilience in military personnel: Theory and practice* (pp. 21–46). Washington, DC: APA Books.

Smith, B. W. & Zautra, A. J. (2002). The role of personality in exposure and reactivity to interpersonal stress in relation to arthritis disease activity and negative affect in women. *Health Psychology, 21,* 81–88.

Spangler, N. W., Koesten, J., Fox, M. H., Radel, J. (2012). Employer perceptions of stress and resilience intervention. *Journal of Occupational and Environmental Medicine*, *54*, 1421–1429.

Thoits, P. A. (1994). Stressors and problem-solving: The individual as psychological activist. *Journal of Health and Social Behavior*, *35*, 143–160.

Wallace, C. & Chen, G. (2006). A multilevel integration of personality, climate, self-regulation, and performance. *Personnel Psychology*, *59*, 529–557.

Watson, D., Clark, L. A. & Tellegen, A. (1988). Development and validation of brief measures of positive and negative affect: The PANAS scales. *Journal of Personality and Social Psychology*, *54*, 1063–1070.

Wilson, K. E. & Dishman, R. K. (2015). Personality and physical activity: A systematic review and meta-analysis. *Personality and Individual Differences*, *72*, 230–242.

van der Linden, D., te Nijenhuis, J. & Bakker, A. B. (2010). The general factor of personality: A meta-analysis of Big Five intercorrelations and a criterion-related validity study. *Journal of Research in Personality*, *44*, 315–327.

Windle, G., Bennett, K. M. & Noyes, J. (2011). A methodological review of resilience measurement scales. *Health and Quality of Life Outcomes*, *9*, 8–25.

Wolfe, T. (1979). *The Right Stuff*. New York: Picador.

Wood, M.D. & Britt, T.W. (2010). Military benefit finding: Turning adversity to advantage. In P. T. Bartone, R. H. Pastel & M. A. Vaitkus (eds), *The 71F advantage: Applying Army research psychology for health and performance gains* (pp. 247–261). Washington, DC: National Defense University Press.

Wood, M. D., Britt, T. W., Wright, K. M., Thomas, J. L., & Bliese, P. D. (2012). Benefit finding at war: A matter of time. *Journal of Traumatic Stress*, *25*, 307–314.

Xanthopoulou, D., Bakker, A. B., Demerouti, E. & Schaufeli, W. B. (2007). The role of personal resources in the job demands-resources model. *International Journal of Stress Management*, *14*, 121–141.

3

IDENTIFYING AND MANAGING PERSONALITY STYLES THAT IMPAIR RESILIENCE IN THE WORKPLACE

Dr. Phoebe E. Stoddart and Professor Pauline Rose Clance

Research examining maladaptive personality styles has illuminated some personality dispositions that have particularly detrimental impacts on the performance of employees, not to mention difficulties with the employee's own private experiences. In this chapter, we reflect on two personality styles that are of particular interest in this regard: perfectionism and impostorism. These related, albeit different personality styles, are particularly interesting in the context of the workplace because on one hand they can motivate employees and even enhance performance, but this often occurs at a significant cost to the individual's wellbeing and to productivity, particularly in a high-pressure workplace. The other interesting feature of these personality styles is that they can often manifest in behaviours that managers would typically find unappealing such as procrastination, turning in reports late, and yet, the cause of these behaviours is not laziness or low motivation. In contrast, such behaviours can be the product of significant concern about one's performance, doubts about the quality of one's work and worry about making mistakes or failure. In this chapter, we will first address perfectionism, how to identify it in yourself and others, and manage it in the workplace. Second, we explore impostorism, its related characteristics and how to manage it.

Perfectionism: a blessing or a curse?

Perfectionism is the setting and pursuit of exceptionally high standards of performance (Burns, 1980; Frost *et al.*, 1990; Hamachek, 1978). Perfectionism is considered a personality disposition (Flett & Hewitt, 2002; Frost *et al.*, 1990; Hewitt & Flett, 1991) and may occur in specific aspects or domains of a person's life but particularly in areas where performance is important such as in sport, school or work. Early conceptualisations of perfectionism (e.g. Hollender, 1965; Burns, 1980) focused on the pathological and negative nature of this trait (Lo & Abbott, 2013). However, it is now understood that perfectionism is multidimensional, with both a positive dimension 'adaptive' dimension as well as a negative 'maladaptive' dimension (Frost et al., 1993; Slaney, Ashby & Trippi, 1995; Rice, Ashby & Slaney, 1998).

From a workplace perspective, perfectionism can be a desirable trait in an employee. In fact, businesses tend to see that perfectionism leads to superior performance. Certainly, research has found that perfectionism is related to increased achievement motivation and striving (Cox, Enns & Clara, 2002; Dunkley et al., 2006; Rice, Ashby & Slaney, 2007; Wang, Slaney & Rice, 2007). Perfectionists also tend to be conscientious; they are organised, meticulous, rule following and reliable (e.g., Stoeber, Otto & Dalbert, 2009). These are necessary characteristics in potentially high-risk or detailed oriented roles such as a surgeon, pilot or audit accountant. Finally, perfectionists can be willing to put in extra effort and work longer than others (Spence & Robbins, 1992) and are more engaged in the workplace (Ozbilir, Day & Catano, 2015).

Despite the potential benefits of hiring a perfectionist, individuals with this trait can be problematic in a workplace setting. Employees with perfectionism might procrastinate (Frost et al., 1990), tend to micromanage (Houpt, Gilkey & Ehrighaus, 2015) and are unwilling to delegate tasks to their team members (Burke, 2001; Paluchowski et al., 2013). Perfectionists can also be intolerant of team members' inability to meet their unrealistically high standards (Hewitt & Flett, 1991) and can be more distressed by events in the workplace that violate their moral perspective (Crane, Phillips & Karin, 2015).

Importantly, perfectionism can be damaging to an individual's psychological and physical wellbeing. A longitudinal study conducted by the Human Synergistics International found that individuals with perfectionism reported more physical and mental health problems, as well as more difficulties at work and with personal relationships (Flynn, 1995). Specifically, perfectionism has been associated with greater feelings of inferiority, anxiety, depression and loneliness, more somatic complaints, self-criticism and higher negative affect (Ashby & Kottman, 1996; Flett, Hewitt & De Rosa, 1996; Mor et al., 1995; Stornelli, Flett & Hewitt, 2009; Periasamy & Ashby, 2002; Rice & Slaney, 2002). Taken together, the accumulation of research on perfectionism seems to broadly demonstrate that perfectionists experience high amounts of stress and exhaustion that leads to significant health problems and dissatisfaction with life (Flett & Hewitt, 2015).

Measures of workplace outcomes have revealed that perfectionism can lead to lower work engagement (Childs & Stoeber, 2010) and low job satisfaction (Flett, Hewitt & Hallett, 1995). Further, their approach to work means that they can prioritise their job over their personal lives, thereby putting themselves at risk of strain and burnout (Mitchelson & Burns, 1998; Stoeber & Rennert, 2008). For managers and supervisors in the workplace, it is important to learn how to leverage the adaptive and positive aspects of a perfectionist while helping to minimise the negative impact on their own mental health, performance and productivity.

Defining features of perfectionism

In order to help managers understand perfectionism and how it manifests in the workplace below are some of the key features of perfectionism and examples of some associated and problematic workplace behaviours and implications.

Exceptionally high personal standards. Standard setting is considered the core trait of perfectionism (Frost *et al.*, 1990). Standard setting can motivate people to perform at higher levels. However, perfectionists set standards that are excessively high to the point that they are unachievable and unrealistic (Burns, 1980). Further, these standards are *rigid.* Perfectionists see things as either 'black and white' and so performance that inevitably falls short of their idealistic standards is seen as inadequate. The consequence of this in the workplace is that these excessive standards can result in inefficient time management. Perfectionists often see their work as "not good enough" and are likely to continue to revise and check their work to ensure flawlessness. For example, he/she might persist to "perfect" a relatively unimportant presentation at the cost of other, more important tasks. Some perfectionists also extend these high standards to co-workers or direct reports (Hewitt & Flett, 1991). When perfectionists hold others to their high standards, they can be intolerant to deviations from these standards. This can result in them being overly critical and providing excessive negative feedback (Houpt *et al.*, 2015). These examples reflect the paradox of perfectionism whereby striving for high quality can actually impede performance.

Need for control and organisation. Perfectionists have a strong need for control, and they have a low tolerance for situations that reduce their level of control (e.g., uncertain or ambiguous situations) (Buhr & Dugas, 2006; Wittenberg & Norcross, 2001). Perfectionists like to feel in control of situations because it reduces the likelihood of error. As you might expect, the need for control often manifests in behaviours such as micromanaging, having difficulty delegating (Burke, 2001) and an excessive focus on being organised. Perfectionists can believe that staying close to the work or even doing it themselves, will avoid the risk of the work failing to meet their standards (Houpt *et al.*, 2015). He/she might only be able to trust themselves to complete a task to their high expectations. This can be detrimental for the perfectionist because they take on more work than they need to. It can also be detrimental to their team members and productivity. Their focus on producing a perfect outcome overlooks the benefits of including others in the process such as diversity of thought, buy-in, or a sense of team pride (Houpt *et al.*, 2015). Being organised also creates a sense of control for perfectionists (Flett *et al.*, 1991). While organisation, neatness and being meticulous with details can be beneficial, perfectionists may prioritise organisation at the cost of productivity and efficiency.

A perfectionist might spend hours planning, making contingency plans for unlikely events or organising their desk and files at the expense of getting to more productive work.

Fear of failure and concerns about mistakes. Perfectionists experience a debilitating fear of failure and experience excessive concerns about making 'mistakes' or any performance that they perceive as being less than perfect (Burns, 1980; Hamachek, 1978). Research in this area suggests that failure or mistakes highlights, in the eye of the perfectionist, how his or her performance differs from their own expectations. Perhaps even more important is that perfectionists experience a sense of conditional self-worth. Their sense of self-worth is conditional on feeling worthy of admiration, respect, acceptance or appreciation (Flett, Besser, Davis & Hewitt, 2003). This means that any negative feedback or perceived failure is more detrimental psychologically to perfectionists than non-perfectionists because it has implications for their sense of self-worth (e.g. Blankstein, Flett, Hewitt & Eng, 1993; Besser *et al.*, 2008).

The fear of failure can lead to two types of behaviours. First, it can lead to excessively working to meet their high personal standards as described previously. For other perfectionists, the fear of failure can cause the individual to avoid situations that might result in a perceived failure. This might be evident in behaviours such as procrastination or prematurely stopping work on tasks or projects (Antony & Swinson, 1998; Frost *et al.*, 1990; Shafran, Cooper & Fairburn, 2002). This avoidance is believed to be a coping mechanism, allowing the perfectionist to circumvent the potential of failing. However, such behaviours only function to relieve initial apprehension regarding the quality of performance and ultimately inhibit the perfectionist's ability to achieve anything at all, thereby perpetuating their self-doubt.

Not only does a fear of failure and concern about mistake making hold perfectionists back, but so too does their own self-doubt and self-criticism. Perfectionists consistently doubt their ability to accomplish tasks (Frost *et al.*, 1990). In the workplace, this means that perfectionists might be reluctant to accept promotions or find it difficult to confidently commit to decisions.

Types of perfectionism: the adaptive and maladaptive dimensions

While there are several conceptualisations of perfectionism (e.g. Hewitt & Flett, 1991; Frost *et al.*, 1990), it is generally accepted that perfectionism has two types (Lo & Abbott, 2013): adaptive and maladaptive perfectionism. So, what is it that distinguishes these two types? First, adaptive perfectionism is characterised by *perfectionistic strivings*, which is the setting of high standards for one's own performance (see Stoeber & Otto, 2006 for a review). Maladaptive perfectionists also set high standards for themselves but, in contrast to adaptive perfectionists, they are highly self-critical about failing to meet their own high standards. Moreover, for maladaptive perfectionist's failure is taken to reflect something global and stable about themselves (e.g., "I am just no good at this job"). In contrast, adaptive per-fectionists are much more likely to think of their failure as specific and changeable (e.g., "If I work harder I can do better next time").

Adaptive perfectionism has been associated with positive psychological outcomes such as higher self-esteem, self-efficacy, positive affect, satisfaction with life and enhanced wellbeing in comparison to maladaptive perfectionists and non-perfectionists (Ashby & Rice, 2002; Chang, Watkins & Banks, 2004; Ganske & Ashby, 2007; Grzegorek et al., 2004; Rice & Slaney, 2002; Periasamy & Ashby, 2002). It is also associated with less negative outcomes such as lower levels of anxiety, depression and psychological distress (Dunkley, Blankstein, Masheb & Grilo, 2006; Egan, Wade & Shafran, 2011).

Research on these two dimensions of perfectionism in the workplace has also demonstrated that adaptive perfectionism has more positive and less negative work-related outcomes. For example, adaptive perfectionism is related to higher performance (e.g. Grzegorek et al., 2004; Bieling et al., 2003; Chang et al., 2004), conscientiousness, agreeableness, emotional stability and satisfaction with one's role or organisation (Bousman, 2007). In contrast, maladaptive perfectionism is associated with negative personal and workplace outcomes. Bousman (2007) found that maladaptive perfectionists experienced higher stress and burnout, and were more focused on preventing failure rather than seeking future success.

Dual process model of perfectionism

Slade and Owens' (1998) dual process model of perfectionism provides an explanation for why adaptive and maladaptive perfectionism lead to different outcomes. This model asserts that adaptive perfectionists are motivated to *achieve positive* outcomes. A key reason that adaptive perfectionists experience more positive outcomes and less negative outcomes than maladaptive perfectionists is because the former group *internalise their success* and experience satisfaction and a sense of accomplishment when they reach their goals (Enns, Cox & Clara, 2002; Luo et al., 2016). Further, in contrast to adaptive perfectionists who focus on what they *have achieved*, maladaptive perfectionists focus on and worry about the discrepancy between their own performance and their idealistic expectations (Stoeber & Otto, 2006). Additionally, adaptive perfectionists are confident that they will continue to *achieve future success*. Adaptive perfectionists are also more tolerant of mistakes and failures and have a less rigid and more realistic definition of success. Together, this means that adaptive perfectionists are likely to experience an increase in their sense of competence when they succeed, are more willing to try, and less likely to self-sabotage.

According to this model, maladaptive perfectionists strive to *avoid negative* outcomes, especially failure. This fear of negative consequences is often what motivates them. When people are motivated by avoiding negative outcomes (e.g., studying to avoid failure), this is called avoidance achievement motivation (Elliot & Church, 1997). In such cases, the goal is to avoid failure, rather than achieve mastery (approach achievement goals). The problem is that avoidance motivation often results in reduced performance, whereas mastery goals (e.g., studying to learn or develop) tend to promote performance. Evaluative situations, such as a promotion or probation period, are likely to heighten the fear of failure and therefore increase the avoidance motivation, potentially undermining performance.

Another key manner in which adaptive and maladaptive perfectionists differ is in their coping approaches. Research has found that adaptive perfectionists tend to deal with stress proactively via approaches to coping that deal with the stressor directly (e.g., planning, goal setting), whereas maladaptive perfectionists tend to manage stressors through avoidance or with excessive emotional responses (Dunkley, Mandel & Ma, 2014; Dunkley, Zuroff & Blankstein, 2003; Stoeber & Janssen, 2011). For example, Dunkley et al. (2014) found that adaptive perfectionism was associated with more adaptive responses to stress, in particular positive reinterpretation. On the other hand, maladaptive perfectionism was related to more avoidant coping. Further, O'Connor and O'Connor (2003) found that maladaptive perfectionist's use of avoidant coping predicted higher psychological distress. Thus, the difference in coping strategies is believed to account, in part, for why adaptive perfectionism is associated with more positive and less negative outcomes than maladaptive perfectionism.

Managing individuals with perfectionism

Being aware of stressors. The following is a list of important stressors to be aware of for perfectionists, both adaptive and maladaptive. Such situations and events can cause the perfectionist to become particularly vulnerable to experiencing psychological distress, more so than most other employees. During such times perfectionists might need additional support and resources to cope effectively.

(1) *Achievement related tasks/experiences.* Achievement related tasks and experiences are particularly stressful for perfectionists (Enns & Cox, 2005; Enns, Cox & Clara, 2002; Hewitt, Flett & Ediger, 1996). Because a perfectionist's self-worth is contingent on success (Sturman et al., 2009), such situations have the potential to provide a perfectionist with validation of their self-worth or relief regarding the avoidance of a sense of failure if they succeed, or with a sense of shame if they fall short of expectations. Achievement related tasks in the workplace might include deliverables that are being appraised, for example, preparing a proposal for review by superiors or presenting a sales pitch to potential clients.

(2) *Failure, criticism and negative feedback.* As previously mentioned, perfectionists respond particularly negatively to any perceived failure, criticism or negative feedback. This means that perfectionists will be more vulnerable to being negatively affected by demotions, receiving a pay cut or a reduction in hours, less than perfect feedback in performance reviews and even constructive feedback.

(3) *Uncertainty or loss of control.* A sense of loss of control is also associated with greater negative psychological outcomes for perfectionists (Dunkley *et al.*, 2014). You can help to create a sense of control by:

- allowing employees to have a say in how they organise their own work;
- providing opportunities for employees to have input in important decisions and to provide feedback; and
- being clear about expectations regarding their role and responsibilities.

(4) *Negative social exchanges.* Negative interactions with others are another vulnerability factor for perfectionists (Dunkley *et al.*, 2014). Negative social interactions might be as obvious as bullying behaviours but can also refer to incivility (e.g., being ignored, someone being discourteous or rude). Perfectionists might even be more sensitive to seemingly innocuous social exchanges than others. This means that workplaces that are highly political, or that have a lot of conflict or competition among team members might be particularly stressful for perfectionists.

(5) *Life stressors.* Stressful events in one's life including starting a family, buying a house, losing a parent or even taking on a new role are especially vulnerable times for perfectionists (Enns *et al.*, 2002; Flett, Hewitt, Blankstein & Mosher, 1995). While some people will experience such events and continue to thrive, perfectionists are likely to be negatively affected by such events. During particularly stressful times, check in on their wellbeing and encourage use of Employee Assistance Programs or other professional services. Be aware that perfectionists might need extra assistance to overcome such adversities.

Promote problem-focused coping and reduce avoidance coping. In Chapter 1 the importance of reducing unnecessary drains on resilience was one part of the approach to enhancing the wellbeing of employees. While managers may not be able to reduce or remove some of the stressors listed above, it is important to be aware that these sorts of situations or events can exacerbate the negative impact of perfectionism.

Importantly, a manager can assist the perfectionist with how they respond to and cope with such stressors. A key manner in which workplaces can assist perfectionists to cope with stressors is to promote problem-focused coping strategies and reducing avoidance coping strategies (Dunkley *et al.*, 2014).

When you know that there are particular stressors that could potentially cause distress, it might be useful to have a conversation with the perfectionist with the aim of encouraging a more problem-focused approach. First, take time to clarify the problem. Then work with the perfectionist to come up with possible strategies to deal with the stress, using some of the problem-focused coping approaches listed below. Help them to select a suitable and appropriate approach and then together develop a course of action. Ensure that any avoidant coping strategies listed in Table 3.1 are avoided.

TABLE 3.1 Coping strategies applied to stressors (adapted from: Carver, Scheier, & Weintraub, 1989; Karmakar & Ray, 2014)

Examples of problem-focused coping	
Active coping	Taking action to remove or prevent the stressor
Planning	Thinking about how to cope with a stressor
Suppression of competing activities	Removing or avoiding distracting activities or tasks in order to deal with the stressor
Restraint coping	Waiting for the best time to act on dealing with the stressor
Seeking instrumental social support	Seeking advice, information or assistance from others
Seeking emotional social support	Seeking moral support, understanding or sympathy from others
Positive reinterpretation and growth	Reinterpreting a situation to see it more positively
Examples of avoidance coping	
Behavioural disengagement	Decreasing efforts to deal with stressor (e.g., procrastination)
Mental disengagement	Efforts to distract from dealing with stressor
Denial	Denying there is a problem
Alcohol/drug use	Resorting to alcohol or drugs to deal with stressor

Dealing with failure. As failure and mistakes are a key concern for perfectionists, it is important to know how to help perfectionists deal with such events. Research has shown that positive reinterpretation in particular can help perfectionists deal with perceived failures (Stoeber & Janssen, 2011). Positive reinterpretation means looking for the positives or merit in a negative situation. For example, trying to see what can be learned from a particular experience ("Next time I will know what to do to get a better outcome," or "At least I now have experience preparing a sales pitch"), acknowledging any progress or achievements that were made ("Although the outcome was not as expected, at least I *was* able to finalise marketing materials that we can use again") or perhaps trying to derive meaning ("This experience will make me a better person"). As mentioned above, perfectionists tend to focus on outcome rather than process. Thus, he/she might not necessarily automatically think of the benefits of a process they embarked on if they categorise the outcome to be a failure. A manager can help the perfectionist to shift their focus and reinterpret a situation by asking them questions like:

- What do you think you could learn from this experience?
- How will this experience shape the way you approach similar situations in the future?

Provide positive feedback. Perfectionists have a high need for external validation (Flett *et al.*, 2014). They have a desire for acceptance and approval from others. Thus, providing validation may alleviate some of their stress. You can let them know that you have faith in their ability, that their hard work is appreciated, or by giving them recognition for progress, achievements, and successes.

Counselling. Perfectionism can cause significant psychological distress and it may be helpful for the employee to seek professional help. If possible, it is useful for a manager to be aware of the support systems offered to employees (e.g., employee assistant programmes) or the mechanisms by which an employee may engage support (e.g., going to see a General Practitioner for a mental health care plan).

The tyranny of impostorism

Like perfectionism, impostorism (or, the impostor phenomenon) can be highly detrimental to employee wellbeing. It can result in depressed mood, low self-esteem, social anxiety and overall poor mental health (Chrisman *et al.*, 1995; Henning, Ey & Shaw, 1998; McGregor, Gee & Posey, 2008; Sonnak & Towell, 2001). Employees also report less job satisfaction and fewer organisational citizenship behaviours (Vergauwe *et al.*, 2014). By definition, impostorism affects high achievers. Thus, impostorism has the potential to impact those who are the *most* valuable to an organisation.

Impostorism shares similar aspects to perfectionism and refers to the inability of an individual to 'own' his or her own success despite appearing outwardly accomplished. The experience was first identified by psychologists Dr. Pauline Rose Clance and Dr. Suzanne Imes in 1978 after conducting 150 interviews with female students and professionals. Throughout the interviews, the researchers noticed that many of these seemingly high achieving women expressed a feeling of being an impostor; they seemed to think they had 'tricked' those around them that they were more capable than they actually were. Since then, Dr. Clance has written a book and numerous articles on the topic. For some time, impostor beliefs were assumed to be a female specific experience, but impostorism is now understood to affect both men and women (e.g., Topping, 1983).

Defining features of impostorism

Dr. Clance and Dr. Imes identified several other thought patterns, emotions and behaviours that characterised those individuals experiencing impostorism (Clance & Imes, 1978).

Fear of being exposed. Individuals experiencing impostor beliefs harbour intense fears of being found out to be the 'impostor' they believe themselves to be, which leads to significant distress. Like perfectionists, impostors also fear failure because any performance that does not meet an impostor's exceptionally high personal standards is interpreted as indications of his or her perceived incompetence, resulting in feelings of shame and humiliation. Failure, mistakes and less than perfect performance is perceived to have the potential to expose them as a fraud (Clance, 1985). The very act of evading being "found out" as fraudulent actually increases the feelings of fear and anxiety and reinforces the cycle prior to each new evaluative event. In this regard, the "impostor cycle" may be viewed as a myriad of strategies devised to satisfy the paradox of two competing goals: the avoidance of failure and the achievement of success.

Doubt in one's own ability. Motivated by the fear of being uncovered as a fraud and of failure, impostors will worry and doubt their ability when first presented with a work or academic task that is to be evaluated. This concern about evaluation will lead to the impostor either over-preparing for the task or initially procrastinating and then overworking. Resulting success is then either credited to luck if they procrastinated or to the impostor's hard work if they have over-worked from the beginning, rather than to ability.

BOX 3.1 SIX SIGNS YOUR EMPLOYEE MIGHT BE EXPERIENCING IMPOSTORISM

Like perfectionism, there are positive and negative aspects for persons high in trait impostorism. By definition, those with impostorism are high performing. This is critical in understanding impostorism. If a person is dysfunctional or not performing at a high level, they are not classified as an impostor sufferer. There may be non-functional people who score high on the impostor phenomenon scale, but they are not impostors.

Noting this, here are some signs that your employee might be experiencing impostorism:

(1) Showing discomfort in accepting praise and positive feedback (e.g. "It was just luck", "I was just in the right place at the right time".)
(2) Being particularly sensitive to negative feedback.
(3) Either overworking and over-preparing or procrastinating and barely meeting a deadline.
(4) Reluctance to accept new leadership roles despite having the skills to carry out these roles.
(5) Discounting success achieved by hard work.
(6) Comparing oneself negatively to others by comparing one's own weakness to others perceived strengths.

Dismissive of personal accomplishment. Impostors do not recognise their own capabilities and skills (Clance & Imes, 1978) and are also resistant to accept any evidence that suggests that they are competent. This means that while impostors experience initial relief following accomplishments (as the anxiety regarding performance outcomes has subsided), they do not gain satisfaction from any resulting success, as achievements are not internalised (Clance, 1985). That is, they do not think that they themselves deserve success. Rather, they believe that their success is due to external factors such as luck or being in the right place at the right time. This means that they also worry that they can continue to work to the standards they believe others expect of them.

The impact of impostorism on employee wellbeing, career progression and the organisation

As identified previously, a key feature of impostorism is the tendency to downplay personal achievements publicly, deflect positive feedback or feel uncomfortable when provided with public positive attention. This might seem paradoxical to fearing being uncovered as an impostor, but researchers believe that those with impostorism are publicly modest to elicit support, encouragement and positive reinforcement from others (Leary *et al.*, 2000) and as a strategy to lower the expectations of others. The humility that those experiencing impostorism display can be appealing and may be strategic because they under-promise and over-deliver.

Yet, in practice, another outcome of these modest tendencies in the workplace is a lack of career progression. Those experiencing impostorism are unlikely to go for promotion unless pushed or considerably reassured by others (Parkman & Beard,2008). These employees may find themselves remaining in roles they find unchallenging and that they are very familiar and comfortable in (Clance, 1985). Impostors may not apply for alternative positions, even though these roles are well within their capability or are unwilling to accept promotions or additional responsibilities. This sort of behaviour clearly impedes on their career progression (Clance, 1985) and also means that their potential talent is not being utilised. Those with impostorism also spend more time than is necessary perfecting their work, and thus time at work is being inefficiently spent (Parkman & Beard, 2008). Finally, and similarly to perfectionists, managers who are impostors tend to hold their direct reports to excessively high standards (Parkman & Beard, 2008). Those suffering from imposterism may also micromanage and fail to delegate or share work, in an effort to avoid unnecessary judgment and scrutiny from other people. Thus, the beliefs characteristic of impostorism can result in several behaviours that can be troublesome for both the individual, but also the organisation.

Who is at risk of experiencing impostorism?

It is estimated that up to 70 per cent of individuals will experience impostorism at one point in their life (Matthews & Clance, 1985). It has been found to be common among students, particularly post-graduate students, as well as various professions including academics, medical residents, STEM-field professionals (e.g., science, technology, engineering, mathematics), senior-level administrators, CEO's, actors and librarians. It also affects persons from different cultures and countries around the world. Employees starting in a new organisation, a new role, or who have been given additional responsibilities can also be particularly prone to experiencing these feelings. According to Dr. Pauline Clance and Dr. Joan Harvey, those groups that are more prone to impostorism include:

(1) people who have experienced rapid success, for example people who have been promoted quickly in a business or managers who are younger than their peers;
(2) the first person in a family to become a professional;
(3) people with high-achieving parents;
(4) people who are in a minority in their field or workplace;
(5) people who work alone;
(6) students;
(7) people working in jobs considered atypical for their sex (either male or female); and people in creative fields.

Managing individuals with impostorism

Similar to perfectionism, many employees experiencing impostorism might actually continue to perform at high levels and experience only minimal negative emotional consequences. However, for those employees who are experiencing significant distress and whose performance is being negatively affected, support from managers and supervisors can be helpful.

It is important to note that while impostorism is not a clinical disorder, the experience is complex. Managers and supervisors cannot be relied on to "cure" it. However, there are things you can do to make work life easier for sufferers and to minimise its impact on their performance. Below are some practical tips for managing those employees experiencing impostorism.

Awareness is the first step. If you suspect a colleague or team member feels that they are "faking it" at work, you can assist by making them aware of the phenomenon. Simply learning about impostorism and putting a name to these feelings of self-doubt can be beneficial for sufferers (Clance, 1985). Further, knowing that one's experience actually has a formal name and that other people are going through the same thing helps to normalise the experience, which can be comforting (Clance, 1985; Matthews & Clance, 1985).

To help build awareness and understanding, consider the following:

(1) You could provide the employee with some information yourself.
(2) Better still, encourage them to have a search for themselves online. A useful place to start is Dr. Pauline Clance's website: www.paulineroseclance.com/. This

website gives an informative overview of the phenomenon, provides links to additional reputable articles and resources. Visitors can find a link to the Clance Impostor Scale. Completing this scale might help to develop some insight into the impostor phenomenon for those interested.

BOX 3.2 UNDERSTANDING WHY THOSE WITH IMPOSTORISM AND PERFECTIONISM FEAR FAILURE SO MUCH

Similar to perfectionists, those with impostorism hold themselves to exceptionally high standards (Thompson, Davis, & Davidson, 1998). However, high standards are not a problem in themselves. The core problem is how set-backs and failures to meet these standards are interpreted. When those experiencing impostorism or maladaptive perfectionism feel they do not reach these standards, for example if they receive less than perfect performance reviews, they interpret falling short in a particularly maladaptive way.

(1) Evidence of global inability. First, falling short of standards is considered to be more evidence of their *global* inability (e.g., "see, just more evidence that I am a complete failure"). In this way, the set-back or failure is considered by some impostors (Thompson et al., 1998; Thompson, Foreman, & Martin 2000) to reflect broader incompetence, rather than just not doing that particular task well. In contrast, an adaptive response to failure is likely to be *specific* to the behaviour or situation, rather than global (e.g., "I am not particularly good at report writing").

(2) "I cannot improve". Second, the person views the source of the failure or set-back as *unchangeable* and there are limited ways that they could improve that performance in the future (e.g., "I will always be a failure"). An adaptive response is likely to be attributed to a cause that can be changed (e.g., "I need to get more practice and mentoring").

(3) A personal cause for failure. The third aspect, is that the source of failure is *internal*. That is, for impostors and maladaptive perfectionists, failure is attributed to something about them, rather than the situation (Thompson, et al.,1998). A more adaptive response relates to considering the role of external factors (e.g., "I have had limited experience in writing reports"). In contrast to failure, impostor successes tend to be attributed to something external, like the situation (e.g., I just got lucky) (Topping & Kimmel, 1985).

These three characteristics *mean* that for perfectionists and those experiencing impostorism the fear of failure can be intense because of what it means to fail.

BOX 3.3 A MANAGER'S CONVERSATION GUIDE FOR TALKING ABOUT IMPOSTORISM

If you suspect an employee might be experiencing impostorism, here are some tips for raising it with him/her:

(1) Start by letting them know that you have noticed that despite you seeing them as a competent and high performing employee, they seem to experience some self-doubt. You could refer to some specific behaviours that you have noticed. This will help them to develop some self-awareness.

(2) Ask them if they have ever heard of impostorism. If they have, ask what their understanding of it is to open up the dialogue and gauge their undestanding. If they have not, describe it to them: *"The impostor phenomenon refers to feelings and beliefs that you have fooled other people into thinking you are more competent or intelligent than you actually are. People who feel like impostors believe that other people know a lot more than they do and that they need to work harder than their peers to achieve the same outcome. They experience a constant fear that they will be 'found out' to be the impostor they believe they are. They do not feel that they deserve any of their success, and tend to think that their achievements are due to luck, some sort of error or any other external factor."*

(3) Ask if the experience is something that they perhaps identify with. Ask them to identify whether these ways of thinking have impacted their ability to achieve valued goals in their work or personal life. This might include failure to go for promotion, keeping quiet in meetings, or the reluctance to accept additional responsibilities.

Discuss strategies that they might use to overcome the impacts of impostorism (Have you given any consideration to how you might overcome this self-doubt? What have you tried in the past?). The purpose here is for the employee to arrive at some strategies for managing their impostor beliefs that he/she might be able to try.

Encourage peer or mentor support. Finding a supportive peer, colleague or mentor to discuss impostor thoughts might enhance coping with the experience. Some initial research supports this recommendation. Sanford *et al.* (2015) found that the female participants believed that information, support and insights provided by mentors helped to build their confidence and provided necessary comfort. A second study among faculty members also identified that mentoring was helpful in dealing with the experience of impostorism (Hutchins, 2015). In particular, the participants described how mentors helped to reduce impostor thoughts by encouraging them to own their success as well as reassuring them that this sort of self-doubt was normal. Further to this, the employee could be encouraged to seek support from a professional support person (e.g., psychologist) or group therapy familiar with impostorism and its impacts. Getting validating and positive feedback from others is imperative with impostors as they are able to acknowledge only a fraction of the approval or positive regard that people feel toward them (Clance et al., 1995).

Keep a journal. In her book, *The Impostor Phenomenon: When Success Makes You Feel Like a Fake* (1985), Dr. Clance suggests that a helpful task for individuals suffering from impostorism is to keep a written record of positive feedback regarding the particular domain that they feel fraudulent in (e.g., in their role at work) as well as their own responses to the feedback. This task aims to help the individual focus on the positive feedback they receive. It also enhances awareness of the way that the individual's internal dialogue undermines their confidence.

Validation. In the first empirical study examining impostorism, Clance and Imes (1978) found that individuals suffering from this syndrome benefited from validation of their competence. Therefore, it is possible that providing positive feedback regarding performance will be beneficial for those experiencing impostorism. As was recommended for perfectionists, take opportunities to reinforce to your employees that they are capable and competent, provide positive feedback for a job well done, acknowledge their hard work and praise their efforts. It is helpful to be specific in your accolades for specific behaviours, rather than giving mere global praise. Also, encourage employees experiencing impostorism to verbally acknowledge praise by saying "thank you" or practice paraphrasing back the positive acknowledgement. These actions also help disrupt internal dialogue discounting praise.

Modelling positive behaviours. The manner in which managers respond to their own success might also influence how their team members deal with success. It is therefore important for managers to model adaptive behaviours in response to success. In their study among faculty members, Hutchins (2015) identified that when others close to them owned their own success, it helped to manage impostor thoughts. Owing your own success means being proud of accomplishments and accepting compliments graciously, rather than playing them down. It is accepting recognition for the work that you have done rather than giving undue credit to others or external circumstances.

Time and experience. For some sufferers of impostorism, it might just take time and experience for them to overcome their self-doubt. Hirschfeld (1982) posited that feelings of fraudulence would decrease over time through the accumulation of work-related observation, practice, experience and knowledge. Certainly, research suggests that experience is associated with less severe impostorism (e.g., Sanford *et al.*, 2015). Therefore, providing ample opportunities for the employee to learn and develop might be useful. As one example, help teach employees how to distinguish between what does and what does not need to be done (overly) well as a means of "safe" risk taking for growth in resiliency. For example, an interoffice memo or email may not need the same attention to detail as a major project report.

BOX 3.4 HOW TO MANAGE A MICROMANAGER

Micromanaging is something both impostors and perfectionists tend to do. It can be inefficient and impede on productivity. It can be suffocating for direct reports and disempowering. It might take the form of constant and unnecessary input, monitoring and requests for reports and updates on progress. It might help to:

(1) explain that their time is too valuable to be working so closely to their direct report's work;
(2) encourage and promote delegation;
(3) see the impact that micromanaging is having on their team, e.g. bottle-necked decision making, inefficient time management; and
(4) encourage them to relinquish some responsibility to their direct reports.

Final thoughts

In this chapter we have described two personality styles that can have negative impacts on an employee's resilience. Employees experiencing maladaptive perfectionism and impostorism can often be exceptionally hardworking, accomplished and respected by their peers, but they may also suffer from self-doubt and a fear of failure. For impostors and maladaptive perfectionists, building resilience means making a common practice of living through the discomfort of doing things not as perfectly as they would have liked to, risking failure and becoming more comfortable with not succeeding. Importantly, while impostorism and maladaptive perfectionism are individual-level characteristics the organisation and good management can have a positive impact on the experience of these employees and allow organisations to make the most of their talents.

KEY MESSAGES FROM THIS CHAPTER

- Perfectionism and impostorism are related, but are different personality styles. On one hand, they can motivate employees and even enhance performance, but this often occurs at a significant cost to the individual's wellbeing and resilience, particularly in a high-pressure workplace.
- Managers who are savvy about these personality styles and their presentation in the workplace can have a positive impact on the work lives of employees experiencing impostorism and maladaptive perfectionism.
- When managers take the time to support and nurture those experiencing impostorism and maladaptive perfectionism it is an opportunity for the organisation to make the most of their talents.
- For impostors and maladaptive perfectionists, building resilience means making a common practice of living through the discomfort of doing things not as perfectly as they would have liked to, risking failure and becoming more comfortable with not succeeding.
- This chapter highlights several key steps a manager can take to assisting employees experiencing maladaptive perfectionism or impostorism.

References

Antony, M. M. & Swinson, R. (1998). *When perfect isn't good enough: Strategies for coping with perfectionism.* Oakland, CA: New Harbinger.

Ashby, J. S. & Kottman, T. (1996). Inferiority as a distinction between normal and neurotic perfectionism. *Individual Psychology: Journal of Adlerian Theory, Research & Practice, 52,* 237–245.

Ashby, J. S. & Rice, K. G. (2002). Perfectionism, dysfunctional attitudes, and self-esteem: A structural equations analysis. *Journal of Counseling and Development, 80,* 197–203.

Besser, A., Flett, G. L., Hewitt, P. L. & Guez, J. (2008). Perfectionism and cognitions, affect, self-esteem, and physiological reactions in a performance situation. *Journal of Rational-Emotive and Cognitive-Behavior Therapy, 26,* 206–228.

Bieling, P. J., Israeli, A., Smith, J. & Antony, M. M. (2003). Making the grade: The behavioural consequences of perfectionism in the classroom. *Personality and Individual Differences, 35,* 163–178.

Blankstein, K. R., Flett, G. L., Hewitt, P. L. & Eng, A. (1993). Dimensions of perfectionism and irrational fears: An examination with the Fear Survey Schedule. *Personality and Individual Differences, 15,* 323–328.

Bousman, L. (2007). The fine line of perfectionism: Is it a strength or a weakness in the workplace? (Dissertation). University of Nebraska, Lincoln.

Buhr, K. & Dugas, M. J. (2006). Investigating the construct validity of intolerance of uncertainty and its unique relationship with worry. *Journal of Anxiety Disorders, 20,* 222–236.

Burke, R. J. (2001). Workaholism components, job satisfaction, and career progress. *Journal of Applied Social Psychology, 31,* 2339–2356.

Burns, D. D. (1980). The perfectionist's script for self-defeat. *Psychology Today*, *14*, 34–52.

Carver, C. S., Scheier, M. F. & Weintraub, J. K. (1989). Assessing coping strategies: a theoretically based approach. *Journal of Personality and Social Psychology*, *56*, 267.

Chang, E. C., Watkins, A. & Banks, K. H. (2004). How adaptive and maladaptive perfectionism relate to positive and negative psychological functioning: Testing a stress-mediation model in black and white female college students. *Journal of Counseling Psychology*, *51*, 93–102.

Childs, J. H. & Stoeber, J. (2010). Self-oriented, other-oriented, and socially prescribed perfectionism in employees: Relationships with burnout and engagement. *Journal of Workplace Behavioral Health*, *25*, 269–281.

Chrisman, S. M., Pieper, W. A., Clance, P. R., Holland, C. L. & Glickauf-Hughes, C. (1995). Validation of the Clance impostor phenomenon scale. *Journal of Personality Assessment*, *65*, 456–467.

Clance, P. R. (1985). *The impostor phenomenon: When success makes you feel like a fake.* Atlanta, GA: Peachtree Publishers.

Clance, P. R., Dingman, D., Reviere, S. L. & Stober, D. R. (1995). Impostor Phenomenon in an interpersonal/social context: Origins and treatment. *Women and Therapy*, *16*, 79–96.

Clance, P. R. & Imes, S. A. (1978). The impostor phenomenon in high achieving women: Dynamics and therapeutic interventions. *Psychotherapy: Theory Research and Practice*, *15*, 241–247.

Cox, B. J., Enns, M. W. & Clara, I. P. (2002). The multidimensional structure of perfectionism in clinically distressed and college student samples. *Psychological Assessment*, *14*, 365–373.

Crane, M.F., Phillips, J. K. & Karin, E. (2015). Trait perfectionism strengthens the negative effects of moral stressors occurring in veterinary practice. *Australian Veterinary Journal*, *93*, 354–360.

Dunkley, D. M., Blankstein, K. R., Masheb, R. M. & Grilo, C. M. (2006). Personal standards and evaluative concerns dimensions of "clinical" perfectionism: A reply to Shafran et al. (2002, 2003) and Hewitt et al. (2003). *Behaviour Research and Therapy*, *44*, 63–84.

Dunkley, D. M., Blankstein, K. R., Zuroff, D. C., Lecce, S. & Hui, D. (2006). Self-critical and personal standards factors of perfectionism located within the five-factor model of personality. *Personality and Individual Differences*, *40*, 409–420.

Dunkley, D. M., Mandel, T. & Ma, D. (2014). Perfectionism, neuroticism, and daily stress reactivity and coping effectiveness 6 months and 3 years later. *Journal of Counseling Psychology*, *61*, 616–633.

Dunkley, D. M., Zuroff, D. C. & Blankstein, K. R. (2003). Self-critical perfectionism and daily affect: dispositional and situational influences on stress and coping. *Journal of Personality and Social Psychology*, *84*, 234–252.

Egan, S. J., Wade, T. D. & Shafran, R. (2011). Perfectionism as a transdiagnostic process: A clinical review. *Clinical Psychology Review*, *31*, 203–212.

Elliot, A. J. & Church, M. A. (1997). A hierarchical model of approach and avoidance achievement motivation. *Journal of Personality and Social Psychology*, *72*, 234–252.

Enns, M. W. & Cox, B. J. (2005). Perfectionism, stressful life events, and the 1-year outcome of depression. *Cognitive Therapy and Research*, *29*, 541–553.

Enns, M. W., Cox, B. J. & Clara, I. (2002). Adaptive and maladaptive perfectionism: Developmental origins and association with depression proneness. *Personality and Individual Differences*, *33*, 921–935.

Enns, M. W., Cox, B. J. & Clara, I. P. (2005). Perfectionism and neuroticism: A longitudinal study of specific vulnerability and diathesis-stress models. *Cognitive Therapy and Research*, *29*, 463–478.

Flett, G. L., Besser, A., Davis, R. A. & Hewitt, P. L. (2003). Dimensions of perfectionism, unconditional self-acceptance, and depression. *Journal of Rational-Emotive and Cognitive-Behavior Therapy, 21,* 119–138.

Flett, G. L. & Hewitt, P. L. (2002). Perfectionism and maladjustment: An overview of theoretical, definitional, and treatment issues. In G. L. Flett & P. L. Hewitt (eds), *Perfectionism: Theory, research, and treatment* (pp. 5–13). Washington, DC: American Psychological Association.

Flett, G. L. & Hewitt, P. L. (2015). Managing perfectionism and the excessive striving that undermines flourishing: Implications for leading the perfect life. In R. J. Burke, K. M. Page & C. L. Cooper (eds), *Flourishing in life, work, and careers* (pp. 45–66). Cheltenham, UK: Elgar.

Flett, G. L., Hewitt, P. L., Blankstein, K. R. & Mosher, S. W. (1995). Perfectionism, life events, and depressive symptoms: A test of a diathesis-stress model. *Current Psychology, 14,* 112–137.

Flett, G. L., Hewitt, P. L. & De Rosa, T. (1996). Dimensions of perfectionism, psychosocial adjustment, and social skills. *Personality and Individual Differences, 20,* 143–150.

Flett, G. L., Hewitt, P. L. & Hallett, C. J. (1995). Perfectionism and job stress in teachers. *Canadian Journal of School Psychology, 11,* 32–42.

Flynn, G. (1995). Perfection can be a health hazard. *Personnel Journal, 74,* 20–22.

Frost, R. O., Heimberg, R. G., Holt, C. S., Mattia, J. I. & Neubauer, A. L. (1993). A comparison of two measures of perfectionism. *Personality and individual Differences, 14,* 119–126.

Frost, R. O., Marten, P., Lahart, C. & Rosenblate, R. (1990). The dimensions of perfectionism. *Cognitive Therapy and Research, 14,* 449–468.

Ganske, K. H. & Ashby, J. S. (2007). Perfectionism and career decision-making self-efficacy. *Journal of Employment Counseling, 44,* 17–28.

Grzegorek, J. L., Slaney, R. B., Franze, S. & Rice, K. G. (2004). Self-criticism, dependency, self-esteem, and grade point average satisfaction among clusters of perfectionists and non-perfectionists. *Journal of Counseling Psychology, 51,* 192–200.

Hamachek, D. E. (1978). Psychodynamics of normal and neurotic perfectionism. *Psychology: A Journal of Human Behaviour, 15,* 27–33.

Harvey, J. C. (1984). The impostor phenomenon: A useful concept in clinical practice. Paper presented at 92nd Annual Convention of the American Psychological Association, Toronto, Ontario, Canada.

Henning, K., Ey, S. & Shaw, D. (1998). Perfectionism, the impostor phenomenon and psychological adjustment in medical, dental, nursing and pharmacy. *Medical Education, 32,* 456–464.

Hewitt, P. L. & Flett, G. L. (1991). Perfectionism in the self and social contexts: conceptualization, assessment, and association with psychopathology. *Journal of Personality and Social Psychology, 60,* 456–470.

Hewitt, P. L., Flett, G. L. & Ediger, E. (1996). Perfectionism and depression: Longitudinal assessment of a specific vulnerability hypothesis. *Journal of Abnormal Psychology, 105,* 276–280.

Hirschfeld, M. M. (1982). The Impostor Phenomenon in successful career women (Doctoral Dissertation, Fordham University, 1982). *Dissertation Abstracts International, 43,* 1722B.

Hollender, M. H. (1965). Perfectionism. *Comprehensive Psychiatry, 6,* 94–103.

Houpt, J. L., Gilkey, R. W. & Ehringhaus, S. H. (2015). Managing personality disorders in the workplace. In J. L. Houpt, R. W. Gilkey & S. H. Ehringhaus (eds), *Learning to lead in the academic medical center* (pp. 45–50). Switzerland: Springer International Publishing.

Hutchins, H. M. (2015). Outing the imposter: A study exploring imposter phenomenon among higher education faculty. *New Horizons in Adult Education and Human Resource Development, 27,* 3–12.

Karmakar, R. & Ray, A. (2014). Adaptive and maladaptive perfectionists: Do they really differ on hardiness and using coping strategy? *International Journal of Innovative Research and Development, 3,* 380–386.

Leary, M. R., Patton, K. M., Orlando, A. E. & Funk, W. (2000). The impostor phenomenon: Self-perceptions, reflected appraisals, and interpersonal strategies. *Journal of Personality, 68,* 725–756.

Lo, A. & Abbott, M. J. (2013). Review of the theoretical, empirical, and clinical status of adaptive and maladaptive perfectionism. *Behaviour Change, 30,* 96–116.

Luo, Y., Wang, Z., Zhang, H., Chen, A. & Quan, S. (2016). The effect of perfectionism on school burnout among adolescence: The mediator of self-esteem and coping style. *Personality and Individual Differences, 88,* 202–208.

Matthews, G. & Clance, P.R. (1985). Treatment of the impostor phenomenon in psychotherapy clients. *Psychotherapy in Private Practice, 3,* 71–81.

McGregor, L.N., Gee, D.E. & Posey, K. E. (2008). I feel like a fraud and it depresses me: The relation between the impostor phenomenon and depression. *Social Behaviour and Personality, 36,* 43–48.

Mitchelson, J. K. & Burns, L. R. (1998). Career mothers and perfectionism: Stress at work and at home. *Personality and Individual Differences, 25,* 477–485.

Mor, S., Day, H. I., Flett, G. L. & Hewitt, P. L. (1995). Perfectionism, control, and components of performance anxiety in professional artists. *Cognitive Therapy and Research, 19,* 207–225.

O'Connor, R. C. & O'Connor, D. B. (2003). Predicting hopelessness and psychological distress: The role of perfectionism and coping. *Journal of Counseling Psychology, 50,* 362–372.

Ozbilir, T., Day, A. & Catano, V. M. (2015). Perfectionism at work: An investigation of adaptive and maladaptive perfectionism in the workplace among Canadian and Turkish employees. *Applied Psychology, 64,* 252–280.

Paluchowski, W. J., Hornowska, E., Haładziński, P. & Kaczmarek, L. (2013). Causes and consequences of lack of control over work – analyzing correlates of the LCWS of the Working Excessively Questionnaire (WEQ). *Polish Journal of Applied Psychology, 11,* 7–29.

Parkman, A. & Beard, R. (2008). Succession planning and the imposter phenomenon in higher education. *CUPA-HR, 59,* 29–36.

Periasamy, S. & Ashby, J. S. (2002). Multidimensional perfectionism and locus of control: Adaptive vs. maladaptive perfectionism. *Journal of College Student Psychotherapy, 17,* 75–86.

Rice, K. G., Ashby, J. S. & Slaney, R. B. (1998). Self-esteem as a mediator between perfectionism and depression: A structural equations analysis. *Journal of Counseling Psychology, 45,* 304–314.

Rice, K. G., Ashby, J. S. & Slaney, R. B. (2007). Perfectionism and the five-factor model of personality. *Assessment, 14,* 385–398.

Rice, K. G. & Slaney, R. B. (2002). Clusters of perfectionists: Two studies of emotional adjustment and academic achievement. *Measurement and Evaluation in Counseling and Development, 35,* 35–48.

Sanford, A. A., Ross, E. M., Blake, S. J. & Cambiano, R. L. (2015). Finding courage and confirmation: Resisting impostor feelings through relationships with mentors, romantic partners, and other women in leadership. *Advancing Women in Leadership, 35,* 31–48.

Shafran, R., Cooper, Z. & Fairburn, C. G. (2002). Clinical perfectionism: A cognitive – behavioural analysis. *Behaviour Research and Therapy, 40,* 773–791.

Slade, P. D. & Owens, R. G. (1998). A dual process model of perfectionism based on reinforcement theory. *Behavior Modification*, *22*, 372–390.

Slaney, R. B., Ashby, J. S. & Trippi, J. (1995). Perfectionism: Its measurement and career relevance. *Journal of Career Assessment*, *3*, 279–297.

Sonnak, C. & Towell, T. (2001). The impostor phenomenon in British university students: Relationships between self-esteem, mental health, parental rearing style and socio-economic status. *Personality and Individual Differences*, *31*, 863–874.

Spence, J. T. & Robbins, A. S. (1992). Workaholism: Definition, measurement, and preliminary results. *Journal of Personality Assessment*, *58*, 160–178.

Stoeber, J. & Janssen, D. P. (2011). Perfectionism and coping with daily failures: Positive reframing helps achieve satisfaction at the end of the day. *Anxiety, Stress and Coping*, *24*, 477–497.

Stoeber, J. & Otto, K. (2006). Positive conceptions of perfectionism: Approaches, evidence, challenges. *Personality and Social Psychology Review*, *10*, 295–319.

Stoeber, J., Otto, K. & Dalbert, C. (2009). Perfectionism and the Big Five: Conscientiousness predicts longitudinal increases in self-oriented perfectionism. *Personality and Individual Differences*, *47*, 363–368.

Stoeber, J. & Rennert, D. (2008). Perfectionism in school teachers: Relations with stress appraisals, coping styles, and burnout. *Anxiety, Stress, and Coping*, *21*, 37–53.

Stornelli, D., Flett, G. L. & Hewitt, P. L. (2009). Perfectionism, achievement, and affect in children: A comparison of students from gifted, arts, and regular programs. *Canadian Journal of School Psychology*, *24*, 267–283.

Sturman, E. D., Flett, G. L., Hewitt, P. L. & Rudolph, S. G. (2009). Dimensions of perfectionism and self-worth contingencies in depression. *Journal of Rational-Emotive & Cognitive-Behavior Therapy*, *27*, 213–231.

Thompson, T., Davis, H. & Davidson, J. (1998). Attributional and affective responses of impostors to academic success and failure outcomes. *Personality and Individual Differences*, *25*, 381–396.

Thompson, T., Foreman, P. & Martin, F. (2000). Impostor fears and perfectionist concern over mistakes. *Personality and Individual Differences*, *29*, 629–647.

Topping, M. E. H. (1983). *The impostor phenomenon: A study of its construct and incidence in university faculty members* (Unpublished dissertation). University of South Florida, Florida. *Dissertation Abstracts International*, 44, 1948–1949B.

Topping, M. E. H. & Kimmel E. B. (1985). The impostor phenomenon: Feeling phony. *Academic Psychology Bulletin*, *7*, 213–226.

Vergauwe, J., Wille, B., Feys, M., De Fruyt, F. & Anseel, F. (2014). Fear of being exposed: The trait-relatedness of the impostor phenomenon and its relevance in the work context. *Journal of Business and Psychology*, *30*, 565–581.

Wang, K. T., Slaney, R. B. & Rice, K. G. (2007). Perfectionism in Chinese university students from Taiwan: A study of psychological well-being and achievement motivation. *Personality and Individual Differences*, *42*, 1279–1290.

Wittenberg, K. J. & Norcross, J. C. (2001). Practitioner perfectionism: Relationship to ambiguity tolerance and work satisfaction. *Journal of Clinical Psychology*, *57*, 1543–1550.

4

PSYCHOLOGICAL CAPITAL

Developing resilience by leveraging the HERO within leaders

*Professor Carolyn M. Youssef-Morgan
and Jason L. Stratman*

Local and global competition is becoming more aggressive and consumer demands continue to climb worldwide. At the same time there seems to be large-scale financial system failures as debt skyrockets and economies around the world tumble. Couple this with rapid retirements and an employment culture of frequent job-hopping; it soon becomes obvious that thoughtful investments in enhancing managers' and employees' stamina in reacting to challenges, setbacks, and uncertainty in general, are necessary. Times of adversity will surface and instances of failure will occur. If adversity and failure are seen as teachable moments, one is less likely to fold under pressure and setbacks, and more likely to find ways to push oneself and others towards success. This sort of mental toughness will become more and more of a competitive advantage for organisations. The challenge to develop mental toughness must be met head on by organisational leaders.

In many ways, shying away from challenges and adversities is tantamount to waiting to be obsolete. Embracing adversity can lead to failure. However, failure can offer invaluable opportunities for learning and growth. This notion is well represented in a video called *I AM POSITIVE: Failure*, posted on YouTube by Darwin Adalia (2013). In one minute and 17 seconds, viewers are introduced to the following seven cases of failure: a girl dismissed from drama school because she was too shy to act; a band that was passed over by a recording studio because guitar music was thought to be going out of style; a failed soldier; a teenager cut from his high school basketball team; a young boy whose teacher thought he was too stupid to learn; a man fired from a newspaper for lacking imagination and a politician defeated in eight elections.

The girl was Lucille Ball. The band was The Beatles. The failed soldier was Ulysses S. Grant. The teenager cut from his high school basketball team was Michael Jordan. The boy thought too stupid to learn was Thomas Edison. The man fired from a newspaper for lacking creativity was Walt Disney. The politician defeated in eight elections was Abraham Lincoln.

Surprised? So what was it that pushed these people forward? What was it that forced them not to settle for mediocrity and drove them to be great? What kept them relentlessly pushing forward, even when adversity starred them in the face and failure had occurred? These inquiries point to psychological capital (PsyCap), an emerging concept that offers unique opportunities to capitalise on the untapped potential of positivity in managers and employees, and a paradigm shift for organisational research and practice. Like the POWER model described in Chapter 2, PsyCap is an evidence-based framework encompassing the personal resources that facilitate flourishing and resilience in the face of life's setbacks and contributes to our understanding of why there are vast individual differences in how individuals respond to stressors.

Introduction to psychological capital

The term *psychology* often evokes thoughts of college classes that focus on different forms of mental illness and coping mechanisms. This "disease model" is certainly prevalent in the field of psychology. However, the more positive areas related to improving the quality of life for "normal" people and maximising human potential have been receiving increased attention as part of an emerging stream of research and practice called "positive psychology" (Seligman & Csikszentmihalyi, 2000).

Applications of positive psychology have spread exponentially across numerous domains of life, including the workplace. For example, management scholars studied applications of positivity in organisational settings under the umbrella of "positive organisational scholarship", which they define as "a movement in organisational science that focuses on the dynamics leading to exceptional individual and organisational performance such as developing human strength, producing resilience and restoration, and fostering vitality" (Cameron & Caza, 2004, p. 731). Positive organisational behaviour is another stream of research, more focused on individual strengths, and defined as "the study and application of positively oriented human resource strengths and psychological capacities that can be measured, developed, and effectively managed for performance improvement in today's workplace" (Luthans, 2002, p. 59).

Four psychological resources fit the criteria of measurement, development, and performance impact in the workplace: *hope, efficacy, resilience* and *optimism*, summarised by the acronym "HERO". When put together, the four dimensions constitute what is now known as Psychological Capital, or *PsyCap*. Luthans, Youssef-Morgan and Avolio (2015) define PsyCap as "an individual's positive psychological state of development that is characterised by: (1) having confidence (efficacy) to take on and put in the necessary effort to succeed at challenging tasks; (2) making a positive attribution (optimism) about succeeding now and in the future; (3) persevering toward goals and, when necessary, redirecting paths to goals (hope) in order to succeed; and (4) when beset by problems and adversity, sustaining and bouncing back and even beyond (resiliency) to attain success" (p. 2).

Positive psychology, positive organisational scholarship, positive organisational behaviour, and all of the psychological resources they present, such as PsyCap, share an important emphasis. They are all characterised by the use of scientific methods to study and develop exceptional performance and a higher quality of life through accurately assessing, developing and managing positivity. This evidence-based perspective distinguishes these approaches from the many management fads and feel-good tactics that dominate the popular management and self-development literature, which primarily depend on anecdotal evidence and unsubstantiated opinions. Of course there are some notable exceptions, such as Gallup's strengths-based management models, as well as many high-quality popular resources on leadership, human capital and high-performance work practices. We encourage managers to be diligent in scrutinising and prioritising the scientific rigour of the models or practices they adopt or consider adopting. In the context of this book, this chapter proposes PsyCap as a scientific and evidence-based framework for measuring, developing and managing resilience in the workplace.

Psychological capital development and the trait-state continuum

An important characteristic of PsyCap is that research indicates it is "state-like", which means that it can be developed. The differentiation between traits and states is an important one to understand when making human capital decisions. Imagine a continuum going left to right with *traits* on the left end and *states* on the right. Personality traits are individual differences that are either genetically based or hard-wired at a very early age, and thus relatively stable. The study of personality neuroscience points to heredity as accounting for 50 per cent or more of a person's personality (Bouchard, 1994; Riemann, Angleitner & Strelau, 1997). Just like hereditary physical traits such as height and eye colour, hereditary personality traits such as general mental ability (IQ) are not open to change. However, heredity is not the sole source, and at least some personality can be attributed to the environment. Non-hereditary personality dimensions are said to be "trait-like". They are difficult to change, particularly in adults. On the trait-state continuum, trait-like dimensions come just after traits, and include conscientiousness, extraversion, agreeableness, emotional stability and openness to experience, often referred to as the "Big Five" personality traits (Murdock, Oddi & Bridgett, 2013). Because of their stable nature, development efforts targeting traits or trait-like character-istics are not wise or cost-effective investments. Desired traits and trait-like characteristics should be part of the employee selection process. In today's fast-paced economy, development efforts must focus on malleable dimensions that are open to change. These dimensions are called states or state-like resources.

On the far right of the personality continuum are states. In their purest forms, states such as transient moods and fleeting emotions are often equal to momentary feelings that are continuously changing. A common example might be the natural feeling of joy when a baby laughs or a brief bout of anger felt by a driver when abruptly cut off in traffic. After a few moments away from the situation, the momentary feeling being experienced goes away. Pure states are easy to develop. However, they are short-lived. A good example is the "high" often experienced by the audience of a motivational speaker, which quickly fizzles away at the encounter of daily life distractions or simply engaging in the next activity.

Moving closer to the middle of the continuum between states and trait-like dimensions are state-like dimensions. State-like psychological resources are malleable and open to change and development over time, but are more stable than pure states. PsyCap is a good example. Ultimately this state-like position lays the groundwork for justifying development efforts, investments and resource allocation. PsyCap strikes the balance of being malleable enough to develop, yet stable enough to allow for a reasonable amount of time to reap the benefits and returns on its development. Focusing on positive state-like resources that can be measured, developed and managed for performance improvement is what differentiates PsyCap from other approaches to managing human capital development within an organisation. Studies have yielded evidence that supports the position of PsyCap being state-like and readily open to development. Designs of evidence-based interventions to develop PsyCap in work environments have taken place with a recognised 1 to 2 per cent increase in PsyCap (Luthans *et al.*, 2006; Luthans *et al.*, 2010; Luthans, Avey & Patera, 2008). These seemingly small changes have been shown to translate into millions of dollars in perform-ance improvements and over 200 per cent return on investment (Luthans *et al.*, 2015).

A closer look at PsyCap HERO dimensions

As mentioned earlier, hope, efficacy, resilience and optimism collectively constitute PsyCap. To better understand the multi-faceted nature of PsyCap, a closer look at each dimension is warranted.

Hope. Hope has been identified as having two core components: *willpower* and *waypower*. Willpower is the motivation to pursue goals and waypower is the ability to develop pathways to those goals (Snyder, 2002). It involves the ability to act independently, make choices, stay determined, and devise alternative plans when obstacles present themselves. Snyder *et al.* (2002) explain that hope shapes perceptions of vulnerability and helplessness. Those with higher levels of hope are also likely to envision alternatives when needed versus those with low levels of hope who may feel stuck with what is in front of them. This ability to see alternative pathways to achieve goals and overcome obstacles represents an important aspect of the "waypower" component of hope.

Efficacy. Efficacy is the belief in one's ability to mobilise cognitive resources and take action to successfully execute a task (Stajkovic & Luthans, 1998). Ultimately, efficacy affects how an individual perceives and interprets events. Those with high efficacy see challenges as beatable (Avey, Luthans & Jensen, 2009; Bandura, 2008). Self-efficacy has been empirically studied and there is evidence of positive effects on desired organisational outcomes. Stajkovic and Luthans (1998) conducted a meta-analysis of 114 studies with over 20,000 subjects. A meta-analysis involves a systematic review of studies involving similar variables. Using statistical methods, results from multiple studies are combined and compared with the hope of finding points of agreement and disagreement. In other words, it involves quantitatively synthesising past research and seeking to get a sense of the overall message supported by many individual studies. Stajkovic and Luthans (1998) found a significant positive relationship between efficacy and work performance. A more recent meta-analysis by Cherian and Jacob (2013) also found that efficacy is positively related to employee performance. Beyond work performance, links to wellbeing are also identified. Shen (2009) found a positive relationship between efficacy and positive thinking and a negative relationship between efficacy and stress. Thus, developing efficacy in employees appears to lead to important improvements in both performance and wellbeing.

Resilience. Avey *et al.* (2009) argue that resilience, or the ability to bounce back from adverse events or personal setbacks, is the most important resource to navigating a troubled work environment. This is because work environments are constantly transitioning and being redesigned to meet market demands. Resilient individuals display a solid sense of reality, and are better able to handle uncertainty, more accepting of new experiences, and flexible to changing demands (Coutu, 2002; Tugade & Fredrickson, 2004). Research demonstrates a positive relationship between resilience and positive organisational outcomes, such as employee performance and organisational commitment (Luthans *et al.*, 2007; Youssef & Luthans, 2007). Resilient people are flexible, responsive to change, creative and have an ability to adapt, which allows them to readily function in the face of stress (Carolan, 2014; Marwa & Milner, 2013; Luthans, 2002; Spake & Thompson, 2013). Resilience is an admirable characteristic at all levels of an organisation and worthy of development.

Optimism. Chapter 2 presented several models where optimism was a characteristic feature of wellbeing and represents a generalised positive outlook or expectancy (Carver *et al.*, 2009). Optimism also involves an explanatory style. The concept of explanatory style helps explain why some people tend to give up under adversity, while others persist and overcome it. Explanatory style consists of people's thoughts and beliefs when explaining causes of positive or negative events (Gottschalk, 1996; Peterson & Seligman, 1984). A person with an optimistic explanatory style credits positive events to personal, permanent, and pervasive causes, and negative events to external, temporary and situation-specific ones (Seligman, 1998). Those with a pessimistic explanatory style do the opposite. For example, an optimistic employee will appropriately take credit for meeting an important project deadline, attributing this achievement to his or her knowledge, skills and hard work. A pessimistic employee may externalise this accomplishment as being lucky or the project being easy. If the deadline is not met, the pessimistic employee will likely blame himself or herself, while the optimistic employee may consider other potential causes that may have been beyond his or her control at that time or in that particular situation.

Optimism should also be realistic and flexible (Luthans *et al.*, 2015). Not all forms of optimism are equal, and undiscriminating optimism can lead to foolish behaviour. For example, overly optimistic people tend to engage in risky and unhealthy behaviours (Schneider, 2001). They may also externalise negative events that are within their control, blaming other people or situational factors. Realistic optimism allows one to take a realistic look at a situation and take personal responsibility for poor choices. Flexible optimism allows for the use of various explanatory styles, both optimistic and pessimistic (Luthans & Youssef, 2004). As Avey *et al.*, (2009) explain, flexible and realistic optimism allows one to objectively look at a situation and give him- or herself the benefit of the doubt.

The dynamics of the HERO dimensions

As explained in the previous section, each of the HERO dimensions contributes uniquely to one's wellbeing and performance. However, when they are present together, they also work to produce important synergies. These synergies emerge from both the similarities and differences between the four resources.

In a nutshell, the underlying mechanism shared between these HERO dimensions is "one's positive appraisal of circumstances and potential for success based on motivated effort and perseverance" (Luthans *et al.*, 2007, p.550). This means that the presence of each of these four resources makes a notable difference in how managers and employees perceive their situations. Each of these resources helps managers and employees see themselves and their circumstances in a more positive light, and anticipate their chances of success in achieving their goals to be more promising, which motivates them to work harder and persevere longer.

If the four HERO dimensions share these positive appraisals, does that mean that they can be interchangeable? Probably not. The reason is that beyond their similarities, there are also notable differences, and each of these differences has been shown to contribute meaningfully to positivity. One of the most notable differences is that hope, efficacy and optimism are proactive resources. They can be built and nurtured in anticipation of upcoming events, or as part of an ongoing development process. On the other hand, resilience tends to be reactive. Adversity is required to build resilience, and it is almost impossible to assess one's true level of resilience without facing setbacks. As noted in the introduction to this book, the developmental psychology literature is full of examples of at-risk children and youth who show remarkable resilience, beat the odds and become successful and well-adjusted adults. It is challenging to assess the same in children and youth who grow up in stable homes, with plenty of resources and support.

However, research also shows that hope, efficacy and optimism, as well as some of the recognised proactive processes for building them, can prepare people for resilient reactions when faced with adversities. For example, hope pathways act as contingency plans, which facilitate bouncing back from setbacks. An optimistic explanatory style can also contribute to resilience through facilitating more positive interpretations of past events and adversities. A positive outlook can promote moving on, learning and growth.

Extensive research on efficacy shows linkages to resilience. Specifically, efficacy beliefs lead to perceptions of personal control, which contribute to effective management of stress and fear. Moreover, efficacy can be built through:

(1) **Mastery experiences:** gaining a sense of mastery through repeated practice and frequent experiences of small successes, or the common adage "practice makes perfect",
(2) **Vicarious learning:** learning from observing effective role models,
(3) **Social persuasion:** gaining confidence through others' positive feedback and encouragement, a frequent "you can do it", or a metaphorical or literal "pat of the back", and
(4) **Overall physical and psychological arousal:** even if indirectly related, general health and wellbeing, both physically (e.g., through adequate sleep, regular exercise and healthy eating habits), and psychologically, can influence efficacy levels (Bandura, 1997).

These four mechanisms relate to resilience by providing asset reservoirs from which individuals draw in times of adversity (Masten *et al.*, 2009). Thus, being hopeful, confident and optimistic can prepare and equip managers and employees to react to adversities resiliently and bounce back, rather than be crushed or overwhelmed.

Benefits of PsyCap

Research related to PsyCap has greatly increased over the past decade. As a result, a recent PsyCap meta-analysis was conducted by Avey, Reichard, Luthans, and Mhatre (2011). One of the primary benefits of a meta-analysis is the ability to have a large sample size analysed uniformly. When dealing with research and statistics, the larger the sample size, the greater the possibility to generalise results across an entire population. The PsyCap meta-analysis included information from 51 independent studies and more than 12,500 employees. The authors found that higher PsyCap was related to higher performance, as well as desirable employee attitudes and behaviours. These included job satisfaction, organisational commitment, psychological wellbeing and organisational citizenship behaviours (i.e., where employees would go above and beyond their job description to help their co-workers or benefit the organisation). Low PsyCap was also found to be related to undesirable employee attitudes and behaviours, such as cynicism, anxiety, stress and deviant behaviour, such as stealing or sabotaging operations. In short, PsyCap is related to many of the desired outcomes sought by organisations, managers and human resource professionals.

PsyCap trickle-down and ripple-out. To this point, PsyCap foundations and benefits have been discussed, along with its relationship to desired organisational outcomes. What has not been discussed is how PsyCap is able to spread from person to person throughout an organisation. To understand how PsyCap moves through an organisation, two concepts are worthy of discussion; social cognitive theory and emotional contagion. Social cognitive theory is a learning theory built around the idea that part of what people learn comes from observing others. Social cognitive theory notes that environmental influences, not just past behaviour and its consequences, shape future behaviour (Bandura, 1988, 1989, 1997). In a work environment, organisational knowledge is acquired by observing how others model behaviour. Moreover, how people behave can evoke emotions, and emotions can be contagious. Schoenewolf (1990) defines emotional contagion as "a process in which a person or group influences the emotions or behaviour of another person or group through the conscious or unconscious induction of emotion states and behavioural attitudes" (p. 50). In simpler terms, emotional contagion is when emotions become transfered in some way between people (Elfenbein, 2014). This phenomenon has been studied regularly in relation to service quality between customers and employees (Lin, Huang & Chiang, 2008; Pugh, 2001). For example, if a customer enters a bank and is greeted with a smile and welcoming demeanour from the teller, the customer is also likely to smile and have positive feelings towards the encounter. If instead, the customer is greeted with a cold tone and negative demeanour, the customer will likely not smile and will have negative feelings toward the encounter. Putting social cognitive theory and emotional contagion together, people learn from other people in an organisation and if one person or group has a noticeably positive outlook and is motivated to succeed, the emotional state of others can be impacted, prompting a similar outlook and effort. To explain this further, closer examination of the interactions between leaders and followers and interactions between peers is warranted.

Leader-follower trickle-down. Perhaps one of the most effective strategies for the development of psychological resilience in employees is through leadership styles that promote the types of personal capacities reflected by PsyCap. Whether a person is in a management position currently, or aspiring to be in such a position in the future, it is important to realise that leading others has little to do with a management job title. Good leaders need to be good managers and good managers need to be good leaders. Managers certainly must pay attention to their system duties, but taking the initiative to genuinely connect on a personal level with associates is also important. Through thoughtful, transparent and genuine interactions, organisational leaders can build confidence and commitment with their associates during times of prosper or turbulence. This all begins with being a positive and authentic leader.

Similar to PsyCap, the notion of authentic leadership emerged from various positive approaches. Walumbwa and colleagues (2008) define authentic leadership as: "a pattern of leader behaviour that draws upon and promotes both positive psychological capacities and a positive ethical climate, to foster greater self-awareness, an internalised moral perspective, balanced processing of information, and relational transparency on the part of leaders working with followers, fostering positive self-development" (p. 94). As suggested in this definition, authentic leadership is comprised of four components: (1) self-awareness, which refers to an individual's understanding of his or her strengths and weaknesses and own insight; (2) relational transparency, or presenting one's true self, expressed through being open with thoughts and feelings; (3) balanced processing, displayed through objectively analysing all available information and others' input before making decisions; and (4) internalised moral perspective, a form of self-regulation guided by an individual's own moral standards and values (Walumbwa *et al.*, 2008). An authentic leader is positive, realistic, self-aware, ethical, transparent and sensitive towards the position of others (Begley, 2006; Champy, 2009; Wang *et al.*, 2014). Because these dimensions are grounded, inviting and admirable, authentic leaders are thought of as effective mentors and role models for other employees, particularly in their positivity and authenticity. Authentic leadership has been shown to directly impact creativity and PsyCap (Rego *et al.*, 2012), and to have a positive effect on individual employees' positive emotions (Zhou *et al.*, 2014). Both of these findings highlight the importance of positive and authentic leadership.

As noted earlier, the underlying mechanism for PsyCap involves a positive appraisal of circumstances and probability for success. When a leader delegates a task, a thoughtful and objective appraisal must take place. A leader first must analyse the situation, determine outcomes and identify the appropriate person or persons for whom to delegate. The level of involvement from the leader will vary from situation to situation and the initial analysis sets the tone for leader involvement. This falls in line with authentic leaders being sensitive towards the position of others. For example, if a leader is delegating a task to a subordinate for the first time, the leader should model the role of a mentor. In addition to communicating clear expectations, extra time should be afforded to guide and mentor the subordinate in constructive ways. This incorporates the positive and developmental approach of an authentic leader.

The leader's positivity and authenticity will increase the subordinate's confidence (efficacy) because the added support assures that work is progressing towards the correct goal or outcome. Through the mentoring process, a leader who explains appropriate policies and procedures and gives insight to various approaches to complete the task will build hope willpower and waypower. This highlights both the ethical and transparent nature of an authentic leader. Giving constructive feedback and recognising completed steps builds optimism because progress towards completing the expected goal is highlighted. Most importantly, when setbacks occur, a positive and authentic leader serves as a source of support and an example of perseverance to complete the task. If failure occurs, the leader should analyse root causes of shortcomings and give guidance as to how to mitigate them in the future (resilience). Both setbacks and failures become teaching and learning moments. Constructive feedback and root cause analysis depict the realistic dimension of authentic leadership. By maintaining a positive and forward-thinking perspective, authentic leaders influence the HERO dimensions of PsyCap by serving as a model of high PsyCap for their followers, as well as nurturing the followers' own PsyCap development journey. In essence, PsyCap trickles down from leader to follower through these two mechanisms. From here, progression of PsyCap can ripple out from peer-to-peer.

Peer-to-peer ripple effect. Barsade (2002) explains that expressing emotions, whether positive or negative, involves two non-verbal parameters: *energy* and *pleasantness*. Energy is related to tone and volume and pleasantness has to do with visible descriptors, such as a smile with a joyful message or pierced eyebrows with an angry message. Barsade (2002) offers some clear descriptions of how these parameters interact. An interaction that is high in energy and pleasantness is characterised as energetic, cheerful and optimistic. An interaction that is high in energy but low in pleasantness is characterised as hostile, anxious and irritable. An interaction low in energy but high in pleasantness is considered warm, serene, and pleasantly calm. Finally, an interaction low in energy and low in pleasantness is characterised as depressed, sluggish and dull. In the leader-subordinate example just presented, the subordinate left the experience with added PsyCap. Revisiting social cognitive theory and extending the example from above the worker is now completing the task with more confidence. Other co-workers witness this and now the worker acts as a role model. If a co-worker runs into a setback, the worker becomes the mentor and is now a resource to guide others through the process, thus impacting both resilience and hope. Because the setback has been overcome, the co-workers have confidence to prevent reoccurrence and optimism because they are closer to completing the task. Building on emotional contagion, the workers have experienced a shared positive emotional state. The mentor was confident, assisting the co-workers through the setback with a low energy, high pleasantness (i.e. calming) emotional interaction. Once the setback was overcome a high energy, high pleasantness (i.e. optimistic) emotional interaction occurred between co-workers as they are now closer to completing the task. Once again, modeling and positive emotional contagion lead to a rippling of PsyCap.

It goes without saying that leaders are in powerful positions. Through thoughtful assessment and modeling, leaders can develop PsyCap in their associates. Once the PsyCap drop has trickled into the pond, a rippling effect of PsyCap between employees follows.

Beginning the PsyCap journey

Understanding the benefits of PsyCap and how it moves through an organisation is all well and good, but implementing a PsyCap development intervention requires clear and intentional planning. PsyCap development cannot be done in silos and will not happen overnight. Efforts must be proactive, persistent and participatory. Whether utilising executive coaching efforts, training interventions or other forms of development, it is important to gain buy-in, conduct pre-planning and monitor progress towards goals. Presented below are key considerations to take into account.

Leadership buy-in and active participation. As mentioned earlier, PsyCap is positively related to a number of desired employee outcomes, but there is also growing research showing the close tie between PsyCap, authentic leadership and performance of employees (Caza *et al.*, 2010; Rego *et al.*, 2012; Wang *et al.*, 2014). There is an obvious value and justification at all organisational levels to develop PsyCap. As with any organisational initiative, there must be buy-in from all levels of the organisation, but particularly organisational leaders. The value must be understood by those at the executive level first. Without this level of commitment, development will be limited. Also limiting development is lukewarm participation from employees satisfied with status quo. Going through the motions is not acceptable participation. Participants need to be engaged to determine progress, but progress cannot be assessed clearly without first collecting baseline data.

Baseline data. Prior to implementing a PsyCap development programme, or any development programme for that matter, baseline data should be collected. A common saying in business is *"if you can't measure it, you can't manage it"*. There is merit to this saying. Evidence of the programme impact is a must. Without baseline data, no one will be able to determine the level of success. When developing a PsyCap intervention and considering baseline data, one must know the desired outcome variable(s). For example, is the goal to improve employee attitudes, increase their performance or reduce turnover? Once known, baseline data for both PsyCap and the outcome variable(s) should be collected.

While collection methods can vary, survey instruments with Likert rating scales or yes/no questions are commonly used. Some organisations prefer to develop instruments internally. However, this practice is discouraged because of potential bias caused by questions that are too general, not applicable, leading and a host of other potential pitfalls. When possible, survey instruments that have been scientifically validated through rigorous statistical methods are preferred. For example, the Psychological Capital Questionnaire (PCQ24), developed by Luthans *et al.* (2007), is a validated instrument used to survey individual levels of PsyCap. It is a 24-question Likert-style instrument designed to measure PsyCap components. This questionnaire has been validated in numerous business and non-business contexts, and is available through www.mindgarden.com. A shorter, 12-item version is also available. The questionnaire has been professionally translated and scientifically validated across multiple languages and cultures, also available on the same website.

Another consideration is the length of time required to complete the survey. Answering hundreds of questions will certainly yield more data, but the instruments should not be overwhelming or overly complicated to complete. Lastly, anonymity is preferred. A true representation is necessary and employees may be reluctant to give their name or other identifying information out of fear of retaliation. Once the initial baseline data is collected, the intervention programme can begin to take shape. Format of the development effort can take many forms. For instance, if formal training on PsyCap is desired, online modules and face-to-face training can be used. If a mentoring model is the mode to develop leaders and supervisors, coaching and small group discussions would fit. No matter what sort of development effort is planned, it is always important to consider what the ultimate goal is and how participants are going to be informed throughout the process.

Clear goals. Goal setting has long been recognised as a vital component to managing an organisation's human resources because goal setting leads to effective performance appraisals, coaching, training, transfer of training and self-management (Locke & Latham, 2002; 2006). Without clear goals, employees will question the purpose of taking part in training or being assigned a mentor or coach. Employees need to see the relevance in relation to their position within the organisation and how efforts eventually converge to the desired goal or outcome. Goal congruence is a term used when the same goals are shared. Recent research found a significant positive relationship between follower-leader goal congruence and job performance (Bouckenooghe, Zafar & Raja, 2015). Clarity of goals and making sure that managers' and employees' goals are aligned become important to the PsyCap development effort. Is the goal to focus on developing PsyCap in leaders to better perform as mentors or coaches to their subordinates? Is the goal to develop individual knowledge of PsyCap for all employees? Additionally, what is the desired outcome of the PsyCap intervention? In other words, goals should have value. Goals should also have clear measures of accountability and progress. Open-ended goals are to be avoided. For instance, if a goal is set that employees are to attend PsyCap training and participate in PsyCap exercises with no parameters, it is destined to fail. That is because there are no accountability measures set. How many sessions will there be? How many will attend each session and when will sessions be completed by? Who is the point-person to set up and monitor progress? Setting parameters will help determine progress and if changes need to be made. Put simply, goals need to be clear, concise and monitored for progress.

Final thoughts

Developing PsyCap can have synergistic effects because multiple positive dimensions are impacted. Additionally, development of state-like PsyCap is a sound investment compared to trait-based efforts, and as mentioned earlier, can lead to substantial returns (Luthans *et al.*, 2015; Youssef-Morgan, 2014). This is because PsyCap interventions that have been tested do not involved elaborate and lengthy training, nor are they high-dollar, feel-good workshops. In fact, PsyCap interventions have been dubbed as 'micro-interventions' and have been done in both face-to-face and online modes of delivery (Luthans *et al.*, 2006; Luthans *et al.*, 2008). In this way, PsyCap interventions are cost-effective, versatile and efficient. Moreover, research on PsyCap has demonstrated its capacity to trickle-down and ripple-out. Leadership styles that promote the types of personal capacities reflected by PsyCap can trickle-down to the behaviours and attitudes of followers. These qualities may also ripple-out across the members of the team. The combination of trickle-down and ripple-out effects contributing to the sustainability of PsyCAP interventions.

KEY MESSAGES FROM THIS CHAPTER

- Four psychological resources: *hope, efficacy, resilience* and *optimism* constitute what is known as Psychological Capital (PsyCap). These resources are malleable and can be developed to support the mental toughness and performance of employees.
- There is strong research evidence to suggest that high PsyCap is related to better performance, employee attitudes, job satisfaction, wellbeing and organisational citizenship. Conversely, it relates to lower cynicism, stress, anxiety and anti-social deviance.
- Employees and leaders high in PsyCap can enhance these PsyCap resources in others by modelling thinking styles and behaviours that are characteristic of those high in the PsyCap resources.
- There are several ways that PsyCap can be developed in employees and these principally involve modelling thinking and behavioural responses that are characteristic of the PsyCap dimensions described in this chapter.
- Authentic leadership draws from the PsyCap framework to provide an approach to leadership that is considered to foster the PsyCap resources in employees.

References

Adalia, D. (2013). I AM POSITIVE: Failure. Retrieved from www.youtube.com/watch?v=kXOx_dizgtk.

Avey, J. B., Luthans, F. & Jensen, S. M. (2009). Psychological capital: A positive resource for combating employee stress and turnover. *Human Resource Management*, *48*, 677–693.

Avey, J. B., Reichard, R. J., Luthans, F. & Mhatre, K. H. (2011). Meta-analysis of the impact of positive psychological capital on employee attitudes, behaviors, and performance. *Human Resource Development Quarterly*, *22*, 127–152.

Bandura, A. (1988). Organisational applications of social cognitive theory. *Australian Journal of Management, 13,* 275–302.

Bandura, A. (1989). Human agency in social cognitive theory. *American Psychologist, 44,* 1175–1184.

Bandura, A. (1997). *Self-efficacy: The exercise of control.* New York: Freeman.

Bandura, A. (2008). Toward an agentic theory of the self. In H. Marsh, R. G. Craven & D. M. McInerney (eds), *Advances in Self Research, Vol. 3: Self-processes, learning, and enabling human potential* (pp. 15–49). Charlotte, NC: Information Age Publishing.

Barsade, S. G. (2002). The ripple effect: Emotional contagion and its influence on group behavior. *Administrative Science Quarterly, 47,* 644–675.

Begley, P. T. (2006). Self_knowledge, capacity and sensitivity: Prerequisites to authentic leadership by school principals. *Journal of Educational Administration, 44,* 570–589.

Bouchard, T. J. (1994). Genes, environment, and personality. *Science, 264,* 1700–1701.

Bouckenooghe, D., Zafar, A. & Raja, U. (2015). How ethical leadership shapes employees' job performance: The mediating roles of goal congruence and psychological capital. *Journal of Business Ethics, 129,* 251–264.

Cameron, K. S. & Caza, A. (2004). Contributions to the discipline of positive organizational scholarship. *American Behavioral Scientist, 47,* 731–739.

Carolan, S. (2014). An online solution to employee resilience. *Occupational Health, 66,* 24–25.

Carver, C., Scheier, M., Miller, C. & Fulford, D. (2009). Optimism. In S. Lopez & C. R. Snyder (eds), *Oxford handbook of positive psychology,* 2nd edn (pp.303–312). New York: Oxford University Press.

Caza, A., Bagozzi, R. P., Woolley, L., Levy, L. & Barker Caza, B. (2010). Psychological capital and authentic leadership: Measurement, gender, and cultural extension. *Asia-Pacific Journal of Business Administration, 2,* 53–70.

Champy, J. (2009). Authentic leadership. *Leader to Leader, 54,* 39–44.

Cherian, J. & Jacob, J. (2013). Impact of self-efficacy on motivation and performance of employees. *International Journal of Business and Management, 8,* 80–88.

Coutu, D. L. (2002). How resilience works. *Harvard Business Review, 80*(3), 46–55.

Elfenbein, H. A. (2014). The many faces of emotional contagion: An affective process theory of affective linkage. *Organizational Psychology Review, 4,* 326–362.

Gottschalk, L. A. (1996). What is explanatory style? *The American Journal of Psychology, 109,* 624–630.

Lin, M., Huang, L. & Chiang, Y. (2008). The moderating effects of gender roles on service emotional contagion. *The Service Industries Journal, 28,* 755–767.

Locke, E. A. & Latham, G. P. (2002). Building a practically useful theory of goal setting and task motivation: A 35-year odyssey. *American Psychologist, 57,* 705–717.

Locke, E. A. & Latham, G. P. (2006). New directions in goal-setting theory. *Current Directions in Psychological Science, 15,* 265–268.

Luthans, F. (2002). Positive organizational behavior: Developing and managing psychological strengths. *The Academy of Management Executive, 16,* 57–75.

Luthans, F., Avey, J. B., Avolio, B. J., Norman, S. M. & Combs, G. M. (2006). Psychological capital development: Toward a micro-intervention. *Journal of Organizational Behavior, 27,* 387–393.

Luthans, F., Avey, J. B., Avolio, B. J. & Peterson, S. (2010). The development and resulting performance impact of positive psychological capital. *Human Resource Development Quarterly, 21,* 41–66.

Luthans, F., Avey, J. B. & Patera, J. L. (2008). Experimental analysis of a web-based training intervention to develop positive psychological capital. *Academy of Management Learning and Education, 7,* 209–221.

Luthans, F., Avey, J. B., Avolio, B. J. & Norman, S. M. (2007). Positive psychological capital: measurement and relationship with performance and satisfaction. *Personnel Psychology, 60*, 541–572.

Luthans, F. & Youssef, C. M. (2004). Human, social, and now positive psychological capital management: Investing in people for competitive advantage. *Organizational Dynamics, 33*, 143–160.

Luthans, F., Youssef-Morgan, C. M. & Avolio, B. J. (2015). *Psychological capital and beyond.* New York: Oxford University Press.

Marwa, S. M. & Milner, C. D. (2013). Underwriting corporate resilience via creativity: The pliability model. *Total Quality Management & Business Excellence, 24*, 835–846.

Masten, A.S., Cutuli, J. J., Herbers, J. E. & Reed, M. G. J. (2009). Resilience in Development. In S. J. Lopez & C. R. Snyder (eds), *Oxford handbook of positive psychology* 2nd edn (pp. 117–131). New York: Oxford University Press.

Murdock, K. W., Oddi, K. B. & Bridgett, D. J. (2013). Cognitive correlates of personality: Links between executive functioning and the big five personality traits. *Journal of Individual Differences, 34*, 97–104.

Peterson, C. & Seligman, M. E. (1984). Causal explanations as a risk factor for depression: Theory and evidence. *Psychological Review, 91*, 347–374.

Pugh, S. D. (2001). Service with a smile: Emotional contagion in the service encounter. *Academy of Management Journal, 44*, 1018–1027.

Rego, A., Sousa, F., Marques, C. & Cunha, M. P. E. (2012). Authentic leadership promoting employees' psychological capital and creativity. *Journal of Business Research, 65*, 429–437.

Riemann, R., Angleitner, A. & Strelau, J. (1997). Genetic and environmental influences on personality: A study of twins reared together using the self- and peer report NEO-FFI scales. *Journal of Personality, 65*, 449–475.

Schneider, S. L. (2001). In search of realistic optimism: Meaning, knowledge, and warm fuzziness. *American Psychologist, 56*, 250–263.

Schoenewolf, G. (1990). Emotional contagion: Behavioral induction in individuals and groups. *Modern Psychoanalysis, 15*, 49–61.

Seligman, M. (1998). *Learned optimism.* New York: Pocket Books.

Seligman, M. E. P. & Csikszentmihalyi, M. (2000). Positive psychology: An introduction. *American Psychologist, 55*, 5–14.

Shen, Y. E. (2009). Relationships between self-efficacy, social support and stress coping strategies in Chinese primary and secondary school teachers. *Stress and Health, 25*, 129–138.

Snyder, C. R. (2002). Hope Theory: Rainbows in the mind. *Psychological Inquiry, 13*, 249–275.

Snyder, C. R., Shorey, H. S., Cheavens, J., Mann Pulvers, K., Adams, V. H. & Wiklund, C. (2002). Hope and academic success in college. *Journal of Educational Psychology, 94*, 820–826.

Spake, M. & Thompson, E. C. (2013). Managing resilience by creating purpose. *Frontiers of Health Services Management, 30*, 14–24.

Stajkovic, A. D. & Luthans, F. (1998). Self-efficacy and work-related performance: A meta-analysis. *Psychological Bulletin, 124*, 240–261.

Tugade, M. M. & Fredrickson, B. L. (2004). Resilient individuals use positive emotions to bounce back from negative emotional experiences. *Journal of Personality and Social Psychology, 86*, 320–333.

Walumbwa, F. O., Avolio, B. J., Gardner, W. L., Wernsing, T. S. & Peterson, S. J. (2008). Authentic leadership: Development and validation of a theory-based measure. *Journal of Management, 34*, 89–126.

Wang, H., Sui, Y., Luthans, F., Wang, D. & Wu, Y. (2014). Impact of authentic leadership on performance: Role of followers' positive psychological capital and relational processes. *Journal of Organizational Behavior, 35*, 5–21.

Youssef, C. M. & Luthans, F. (2007). Positive organizational behavior in the workplace: The impact of hope, optimism, and resilience. *Journal of Management, 33*, 774–800.

Youssef-Morgan, C. M. (2014). Advancing OB research: An illustration using psychological capital. *Journal of Leadership and Organizational Studies, 21*, 130–140.

Zhou, J., Ma, Y., Cheng, W. & Xia, B. (2014). Mediating role of employee emotions in the relationship between authentic leadership and employee innovation. *Social Behavior and Personality, 42*, 1267–1278.

PART 2

Providing employee support in the workplace

5

LEADERSHIP AND MENTAL HEALTH TREATMENT SEEKING IN THE WORKPLACE

*Professor Thomas W. Britt and
Kristen S. Jennings*

A large amount of research indicates that employees are often exposed to stressors at work that result in the presence of mental health symptoms. When these symptoms begin to interfere with the work performance and quality of life of the employee, he or she may benefit from receiving mental health treatment. In addition, getting treatment when the symptoms are mild will result in a greater likelihood that the cause of the problem will be addressed, and the employee can continue functioning well. However, if employees fail to get treatment because of the stigma of how they will be perceived by others (or themselves), not having enough time to work treatment into their schedule, or because of negative attitudes they have toward mental health care, the problem will likely become more severe, and affect other areas of the employee's life (e.g. substance abuse, marital conflict).

Leaders and managers play a critical role in creating a climate within the organisation that supports employees who experience mental health problems, and that facilitates the receipt of timely treatment when necessary. Prior research has examined how leaders can either blunt or enhance the effects of work stressors on employees (Britt, Davison, Bliese & Castro, 2004). However, much less research has focused on how leaders can influence the process by which employees become aware of mental health symptoms and seek support.

In the present chapter we first address the issue of mental health problems among employees, and the barriers employees face in receiving necessary treatment for these difficulties. Critically, we discuss the importance of leaders in promoting the psychological health of employees, and how leaders and managers can reduce the barriers associated with the timely receipt of mental health treatment and create a supportive climate for employees getting help. This chapter then addresses how early treatment for mental health problems is consistent with an organisational climate promoting resilience among employees. As is pointed out in Chapter 1, support seeking does not mean that one's personal resilience has failed – quite the opposite – early support seeking is part of a resilient person's tool kit for managing situational demands and such behaviours should be encouraged. The chapter concludes with practical recommendations for how leaders and managers can create an organisational climate supportive of treatment seeking.

Mental health problems among employees and treatment seeking behaviour

A large amount of research has documented the negative mental health consequences arising from employees being exposed to high levels of stress (Barling, Kelloway & Frone, 2005; Cooper, Dewe & O'Driscoll, 2001). Sources of stress at work that can cause mental health problems include acute traumatic events (e.g. witnessing or being a victim of an act of violence at work) as well as chronic interpersonal and workplace stressors, such as interpersonal conflict and work overload (Maslach, Schaufeli & Leiter, 2001). Research conducted by the World Health Organisation has found that mental disorders account for a substantial number of missed work days (Alonso *et al.*, 2011), and that employees with a mental illness earn one-third less than the median for a given country.

Although a great deal of research has documented the relationship between stressful work conditions and mental health problems, surprisingly little research has investigated the percentage of employees who get treatment for these problems, and the reasons for not getting help. Worldwide, only a minority of individuals experiencing a mental health problem get treatment for their difficulties (Mojtabai *et al.*, 2011). Many organisations include mental health services as part of their employee assistance programme (EAP) and yet very little research has examined the determinants of whether employees utilise these programmes (see Cooper, Dewe & O'Driscoll, 2011).

Prior authors have noted a lack of information on the percentage of employees who utilise mental health treatment services, or the amount of time that elapses between when employees recognise they have a problem and make the decision to seek treatment (Bamberger, 2009). Some prior research has examined the percentage of employees who utilise their organisation's EAPs. French, Dunlap, Roman and Steele (1997) reported that 11 per cent of their sample utilised the EAP at their workplace. However, the authors did not document the percentage of the sample that was experiencing a mental health problem. In addition, EAPs offer services other than mental health treatment, so EAP utilisation by itself is not informative regarding the use of mental health services in particular. Therefore, the question of how many employees in typical organisational settings need treatment but do not seek it remains largely unanswered.

The most informative research on mental health concerns associated with work demands thus far has been conducted among employees in high stress occupations. The recent combat operations in Iraq and Afghanistan have resulted in the US military identifying the number of service members experiencing mental health problems and the percentage of those with problems receiving mental health treatment. Research among this sample of employees documents that up to one-third of US service members screen above clinical cutoffs for post-traumatic stress disorder, depression, anxiety or alcohol abuse (Hoge et al., 2004; Thomas et al., 2010). However, only a minority of military personnel get treatment for mental health problems that are clearly the result of severe stressors encountered at work (Castro & Adler, 2011; Kim et al., 2010; Thomas et al., 2010).

Is supporting mental health treatment consistent with an emphasis on resilience?

Above we noted the large amount of research that has documented the relationship between exposure to different workplace stressors and the development of mental health problems among employees. These studies support the argument that mental health problems are often the result of occupational hazards, and that employees should not feel like a failure for developing symptoms that may be negatively affecting their health and performance, and for getting treatment for these symptoms. Britt and McFadden (2012) argued that in traditional discussions of the tripartite model of prevention (Ivancevich et al., 1990), the receipt of mental health treatment is seen as a tertiary level of prevention, as the development of significant symptoms represents a failure of primary and secondary prevention.

The argument that mental health treatment represents a "last ditch" effort to stem the negative consequences of work-related stressors likely discourages employees from getting help when their symptoms are relatively mild. Recent research suggests that early treatment for mental health problems can help prevent the more negative long-term consequences that occur when individuals wait until problems become severe to get treatment (Boulos & Zamorski, 2015). Therefore, the early receipt of mental health treatment by employees is completely consistent with an organisational emphasis on the resilience of employees. The timely receipt of mental health treatment helps employees to return to their baseline functioning more quickly (Lagerveld et al., 2012; Kröger et al., 2015), and may even elevate the employee's ability to address additional work demands.

Furthermore, the receipt of needed mental health treatment can co-occur with other resilience training initiatives being conducted by the organisation. Employees should be encouraged to view resilience training and mental health treatment as two different but compatible strategies for addressing the consequences of demands encountered in the workplace in order to maintain their health, wellbeing and performance. As we will discuss in this chapter, leaders can play a critical role in shaping the attitudes and beliefs that their employees have towards treatment. If leaders proactively highlight treatment as a way to prevent small problems from becoming larger, and therefore as a tool to enhance the resilience of employees, employees should be much more likely to get help proactively. The early receipt of treatment will then enhance the resilience of the employee and ultimately the organisation.

Barriers to care: why do employees not get treatment for mental health problems?

Research has identified a number of barriers that discourage individuals from seeking mental health treatment in general, including not having access to care, financial concerns about the cost of treatment, the lack of a perceived need for treatment, wanting to handle the problem oneself, stigma resulting from a fear of negative career repercussions, concerns about differential treatment by others and an individual's own perceived weakness at needing treatment (Corrigan, 2004; Jennings et al., 2015; Mojtabai et al., 2011; Sareen et al., 2007; Vogel, Wade & Haake, 2006).

Many of these factors are also present when examining an employee's decision to report mental health problems in the workplace and to get treatment for these problems (Toth & Dewa, 2014). Regarding civilian employees, one of the primary areas of research examining mental health problems in the workplace involves the determinants of whether employees disclose having a mental health problem to their supervisor and/or co-workers. Brohan et al. (2012) conducted a systematic review of 48 different studies examining the disclosure of mental health problems in the workplace, and found that expectations or experiences of discrimination by supervisors and co-workers was the most frequent theme identified for not disclosing a mental health problem. The authors found other major reasons for non-disclosure included employees wanting to keep the problem private and not believing they needed to disclose the problem in order to effectively do their job.

Regarding the use of EAPs, French et al. (1997) examined the predictors of EAP utilisation and found that employees who tended to perceive that services were confidential were also more likely to use EAPs. Moreover, Milne, Blum, and Roman (1994) also found that the extent to which employees trusted the EAP was related to their propensity to use it if needed. Together these results suggest that like the general public, employees are concerned about the potentially negative consequences of others finding out about the need for mental health treatment.

Research on the determinants of treatment seeking for work-related problems has been primarily conducted in military settings. Ouimette et al. (2011) examined the perceived barriers to care held by patients of the Department of Veterans Affairs (VA) and found that stigma-related barriers, such as discomfort with help-seeking and concerns about social consequences, were rated as more salient barriers than institutional barriers to care (e.g., not being able to get an appointment). Britt et al. (2015a) found that career-related concerns, concerns about differential treatment by fellow unit members and the self-stigma of feeling weak and inefficacious for needing treatment were all associated with a reduced likelihood of soldiers with a problem reporting the receipt of treatment. Because individuals in the military place a high emphasis on being resilient and self-sufficient, Britt and McFadden (2012) noted that it might be particularly difficult for these personnel to admit to having a mental health problem as a result of exposure to stressful working conditions (e.g., combat). As indicated above, employees in civilian work contexts may also be concerned about the stigma associated with admitting a psychological problem and seeking mental health treatment.

In addition to the stigma associated with mental health treatment, employees may also have doubts about the effectiveness of treatment, and instead prefer to deal with the problem without resorting to therapy. Adler *et al.* (2015) conducted a longitudinal investigation of treatment seeking among military personnel with an identified mental health problem, and found that the main predictors of future treatment seeking were having positive attitudes toward mental health treatment, and having low values on a preference for self-managing psychological problems. These results suggest that in order to increase employees utilising treatment for mental health problems when necessary, employees need to believe in the effectiveness of treatment, and recognise when attempting to handle a problem oneself is no longer working (i.e. when the problem is not getting better or is in fact getting worse).

In summary, prior research indicates that many employees suffer from psychological problems that result from stressors encountered at work, yet only a minority of employees seek treatment to address these difficulties. The failure of employees to get needed treatment not only results in negative consequences for the employee, but also affects the ability of the employee to perform effectively for the organisation, resulting in negative consequences for the performance of the organisation. A salient barrier identified by past research is the perception of confidentiality and the social implications of treatment seeking. In the next section, we address the role of leaders and managers in creating a workplace environment that is supportive of employee mental health and treatment seeking.

The role of leaders in employee mental health and treatment seeking

Britt and McFadden (2012) highlighted the importance of leaders in high-risk occupations being supportive of employees accessing mental health treatment for problems that are often created by exposure to traumatic events. However, leaders and managers of all employees are in a unique position to influence an employee's decision to address mental health symptoms that are negatively affecting their health and job performance. Britt, Wright, and Moore (2012) recently demonstrated that military leader behaviours were directly related to treatment seeking perceptions in personnel. These authors showed that when leaders were perceived by employees to treat team members fairly there was also lower reported stigma regarding getting treatment for mental health problems and lower reported practical barriers associated with treatment (e.g., not being able to fit treatment into their work schedule). In contrast, negative behaviours such as showing favouritism to some team members was related to more stigma and more reported practical barriers. Britt and colleagues also examined reported leader behaviours from both the soldiers' Non-Commissioned Officers (NCOs, who are their immediate supervisors) and from their Commissioned Officers (COs; the leaders in charge of their entire unit). The purpose of this was to determine whether the proximity of the leadership to the team members was important in influencing stigma and treatment seeking. These researchers found that positive and negative leadership behaviours had a stronger effect on stigma and getting treatment when these behaviours were exhibited by the immediate supervisor (NCO). The relationship of leader behaviour to treatment seeking outcomes was less strong for more distant leadership (CO). Thus, the most immediate supervisor appeared to have the strongest impact on stigma and barriers to care. Applied to civilian organisations, the findings of this research demonstrate the critical impacts that both positive and negative immediate manager behaviours can have on two determinants of treatment seeking among employees: (1) the perceived stigma of getting treatment and (2) the practical barriers to accessing care.

Researchers have also noted that leaders can directly influence an employee's decision to seek mental health treatment. Pfeiffer *et al.* (2012) conducted interviews with 30 National Guard soldiers who had experienced a combat deployment regarding the barriers soldiers encounter in getting treatment and how peers might influence engagement in treatment. The authors found that leadership support for treatment seeking was mentioned by soldiers as being critical for programmes designed to get military personnel into treatment. Zinzow *et al.* (2013) also examined the role of leadership as a barrier and facilitator of treatment seeking by conducting qualitative research with two samples of active duty military personnel: focus groups of soldiers of different ranks and interviews with soldiers who made the decision to seek treatment while on active duty. Problems with leaders being a barrier to treatment seeking emerged in 11 of the 12 focus groups, and in 21 of the 32 interviews. In the focus groups, soldiers noted concerns with a lack of confidentiality within the unit, not trusting leaders, leaders being too busy with operational matters to recognise soldier problems or provide support, and leaders being uncertain regarding the implications of treatment for performance and mission accomplishment. Many of these same problematic aspects of leadership were mentioned in the interview sample of personnel who had sought treatment, along with additional concerns of being seen as malingering to get out of work and not receiving support from one's leaders and colleagues once in treatment. On the other hand, soldiers in the two samples also reported that leader behaviours could be important facilitators of treatment seeking. In the focus group sample, 11 of the 12 groups identified supportive leaders behaviour as important facilitators of treatment seeking, including leaders allowing soldiers to have time off for treatment, allowing work flexibility around the treatment schedule, being generally supportive of treatment seeking, leaders being role models by discussing their own treatment seeking when applicable, and leaders providing information on when and where to get treatment. In the interview sample, 19 of the 32 soldiers who had sought treatment mentioned many of these same facilitators, including the importance of the leader's approval for seeking treatment and the leader treating the soldier the same after they received treatment.

These qualitative studies highlight the importance of leadership as both a facilitator and inhibitor of treatment seeking among employees. Although most of the qualitative research on leadership and treatment seeking that we are aware of has involved military personnel, we believe that leadership is also likely to be an important determinant of treatment seeking among employees more generally. The importance of the leader in treatment seeking can be understood within the context of the Theory of Planned Behavior (Ajzen, 1985). According to this theory, one important factor in whether an individual will engage in any behaviour is the subjective norms that exist in regard to performing that behaviour. Subjective norms refer to the individual's belief that others who are important to the individual would be supportive of the individual performing the behaviour. Within the context of employees getting treatment for mental health problems, the support of leaders increases the employee's perception of the subjective norms for engaging in the behavior of treatment seeking, which makes treatment seeking more likely.

Britt *et al.* (2011) examined subjective norms and other determinants of treatment among a sample of reserve component veterans. Perceptions of leader support for treatment seeking were included in the assessment of subjective norms, along with perceptions of support from fellow unit members, friends and family. Among veterans screening positive for a mental health problem, overall subjective norms regarding treatment seeking were associated with whether soldiers indicated receipt of treatment. Veterans who perceived more positive social norms for treatment seeking were more likely to report getting treatment in the past six months.

In addition to leaders influencing employee treatment seeking through their influence on subjective norms for engaging in a behaviour, leaders are also influential in the climate they create within an organisation or unit for treatment seeking. Prior research has demonstrated that leadership attitudes to safety is an important determinant of safety climate within an organisation, the interactions the leader has with employees regarding performing safety behaviours sets expectations employees have for the importance placed on safety (Zohar, 2010). Leadership attitudes to treatment seeking are likely to have much the same impact on the treatment seeking behaviour of employees as they do on safety behaviour. In fact, Britt and McFadden (2012) argued that leaders likely influence employee treatment seeking through similar processes. If leaders do not show an interest in the mental health of their subordinates, or an interest in their subordinates getting help for mental health problems, employees are unlikely to perceive a climate within the organisation or unit that is supportive of treatment seeking. Similar to employees performing safety-related behaviours (Zohar, 1980), employees should be more likely to get mental health treatment when key leaders in the organisation indicate their support for such behaviour. Supporting this argument, Milne *et al.* (1994) found that employee perceptions of both top management and their direct supervisor support for the use of EAPs were associated with the employee's confidence in the effectiveness of the EAP, which predicted the propensity of employees to actually use the EAP. Together this research suggests that leaders and managers have a critical role in influencing employee treatment seeking behaviour.

Training managers to be more supportive of employee mental health and treatment seeking

Given the influence of leaders and managers on employee health and treatment seeking decisions, a natural question that emerges is whether leaders and managers can be trained to increase their level of support. Dimoff, Kelloway, and Burnstein (2016) recently examined the effects of Mental Health Awareness Training (MHAT) for leaders in the workplace. The MHAT that was examined in the study was modeled after the training of Kitchener and Jorm (2002) that was designed to increase mental health awareness and how to respond to individuals with mental health problems in the general public. Ultimately, the training is designed to improve individuals' knowledge and attitudes towards those experiencing mental health problems, and supporting individuals with problems. Kitchener and Jorm (2004) examined the effectiveness of MHAT in an occupational setting among employees in general, and found that the training resulted in employees demonstrating more accurate beliefs about effective treatment for two disorders, decreased social distance toward individuals with the disorders, and increased their own mental health.

In tailoring the MHAT for leaders, Dimoff *et al.* (2016) developed a 3-hour training programme that was administered to managers and supervisors on a single day. The training consisted of two lecture based modules focused on: (1) improving knowledge of mental health among employees and risk factors for the development of mental health problems, and (2) enhancing the confidence of the leader in promoting mental health in the workplace. The training also included a discussion of two different case studies, where leaders applied what they had learned in the lectures to depictions of employees experiencing mental health symptoms that indicated the presence of a potential problem. The authors found that compared to a wait-list control group, leaders who received the MHAT demonstrated significant increases in knowledge and confidence toward promoting mental health in the workplace. The authors also found that the length of disability claims for mental health problems was shorter in the months following the leader MHAT training in comparison to the months before the training. Finally, the authors also compared the frequency and duration of mental health claims of disability in four provinces (Canadian) where leaders received MHAT training to two provinces where leaders did not receive the training. The provinces where leaders had been trained in MHAT reported fewer and shorter disability claims than the control provinces. These results indicate that leaders can be trained to be more knowledgeable and supportive of mental health problems in the workplace. Even more important, the MHAT was translated into actual reduced costs associated with employees being out of work and compensation claims.

Our research team recently examined the effectiveness of unit and leader training to improve support for mental health treatment seeking among military personnel (Britt *et al.*, 2015b). The leader training was two hours in duration, and addressed many of the same areas as those in the MHAT, with an additional focus on supporting the decision of military personnel to get mental health treatment, and to create a unit climate where support is included. In addition, the training focused on the importance of not assuming soldiers are malingering when they get mental health treatment, and the role of leaders in reducing the barriers and enhancing the facilitators associated with treatment seeking. Leaders were also encouraged to consider getting treatment themselves if experiencing mental health problems, and sharing their treatment experiences with fellow soldiers when appropriate. Finally, at the end of the training unit leaders developed specific goals for improving the climate of support for treatment seeking within their units.

Evaluation of the leader training is underway, but initial evidence suggests that leader evaluations of the training were positive, and that the training resulted in increased knowledge and awareness of mental health treatment. In addition, the training was effective in decreasing negative leader perceptions, such as that soldiers seek mental health treatment in order to get out of work. All leaders also indicated that they planned to implement changes in their unit based on the training.

Applying the lessons from research to management practices

As discussed frequently throughout this chapter, leaders and managers are in a unique position to create a climate of psychological health and a climate of safety for employees getting help for mental health problems when necessary. In this section, we identify a number of recommendations for practical applications of the chapter material. Appendix 5.1 contains a summary of these recommendations in the form of a self-assessment tool addressing the extent that your current leader behaviours are promoting psychological health and support for treatment seeking.

Given the recent emphasis on the importance of leadership for employee wellbeing, it is important for you as a leader to have an understanding of the current mental health needs of your employees. Organisations frequently administer anonymous survey measures to assess job attitudes such as satisfaction and engagement, but are less likely to assess the mental health of their employees. Conducting an anonymous survey of the mental health and wellbeing of employees within an organisation can provide the leader or manager with an overall assessment of the organisation. If the survey results indicate a generally high presence of mental health symptoms (e.g. depression, anxiety, sleep difficulties), the leader can take action to address the demands in the work environment that may be producing the symptoms, and then re-assess the mental health of employees following such actions.

A general measure of mental health/distress that could be administered to employees is the K10, which is a 10-item measure designed to assess the presence of psychological distress (Kessler *et al.*, 2002, 2003). Participants are asked how often they have had certain feelings in the past 30 days. Sample items include "tired for no good reason" and "nervous". In addition to identifying mental health concerns among your employees, it will also be useful to assess whether employees are using resources that are available to them for addressing work demands (Bakker & Demerouti, 2007), and to encourage the utilisation of resources that are infrequently used.

As a leader or manager, it is also important that you ensure that employees have an accurate understanding of information about disclosure of mental health symptoms and resources that are available to employees who could benefit from mental health treatment. Many employees are unaware of resources that are available within an organisation related to getting help for mental health problems. A manager can increase awareness of the resources available (e.g., EAPs, counseling services covered with employment benefits) by discussing the availability of these resources with your employees, or by bringing in representatives from EAPs or other programmes to provide information. EAP programmes may be available, but employees are unlikely to utilise the programmes without leaders reinforcing the importance of utilising these programmes before mental health symptoms become severe. Furthermore, the importance of utilising these programmes should be emphasised when the employee first arrives at the organisation, and be part of any new-hire orientation. Moreover, such manager communications implicitly communicate support of treatment seeking. As discussed earlier, supervisor support is a critical factor in whether employees disclose mental health problems in the workplace. You can also encourage support seeking by letting employees know there will not be discrimination or repercussions based on having a mental health problem (with a clear statement of exceptions such as threats of harm to self, harm to others or safety concerns). In addition, when employees disclose a mental health problem, be sure to maintain confidentiality of the disclosure in order to build the employee's trust in how the organisation addresses mental health concerns.

Given the variation that exists among leaders in the extent to which they engage in transformational or positive behaviours, leaders likely also differ in the extent to which they are inclined to focus on their employee's mental health. Dimoff *et al.* (2016) recently showed that leaders' knowledge, attitudes and support of mental health in the workplace can be increased through MHAT. Therefore, organisations should consider MHAT as a component of leader training and development. Dimoff *et al.* (2016) showed that benefits of MHAT for leaders could be obtained with the administration of a single 3-hour training session. Therefore, organisations can enhance their leaders' understanding of mental health among their employees with a relatively small investment of time and resources. This training could also highlight how positive leader behaviours can reduce the stress employees are exposed to and/or reduce the impact of inevitable stressors that are encountered in the workplace.

In addition to training highlighting the overall importance of leaders being attuned to the mental health of their subordinates, we also recommend training that facilitates leaders building trusting relationships with employees so they feel comfortable coming forward about stress-related issues. In addition, leaders need to be aware of the signs that mental health symptoms are interfering with the employee's wellbeing and work performance, and to actively encourage the early receipt of mental health treatment. Encouraging open conversations about mental health can also reduce the stigma employees feel about developing mental health symptoms and potentially getting treatment, as well as misperceptions about the nature of mental health treatment and those who seek treatment. We would encourage managers to also communicate common signs of mental health symptoms to their work unit to promote a culture of looking out for the mental health of one another. Because co-workers may have more daily contact with fellow employees than the manager, they can be an important resource in recognising mental health concerns and either encouraging the individual to seek help or confidentially reporting concerns to the manager.

Finally, it is important that organisations evaluate the effectiveness of these types of leader training programmes, and fine tune the training based upon feedback from those leaders participating in the training. Depending on the culture within an organisation, different types of exercises or training formats may be more or less effective. For example, talking about mental health with high-risk occupations such as military personnel, police officers and firefighters faces the challenge of acknowledging the presence of symptoms within a culture that emphasises resilience in the face of extreme work demands. Within these types of occupations, it may be especially helpful for leaders to highlight the importance of employees addressing mental health symptoms early in order to enhance their operational readiness and ability to contribute to the unit's mission.

Final thoughts

From the previous discussion, the importance of manager support for treatment seeking is a critical determinant of whether employees seek support when they need it. Managers should endeavour to communicate their interest in the wellbeing of employees, support for employees who take positive steps to engage in treatment, as well as try to eliminate any practical barriers to receiving support. Managers who fail to do these things may be impacting their employee's willingness to take positive steps to supporting their own resilience and wellbeing.

KEY MESSAGES FROM THIS CHAPTER

- Leader and manager attitudes to mental health problems and treatment seeking play an important role in whether or not employees will engage support when necessary.
- Leaders are in a unique position to both support the psychological health of their employees, and facilitate employee treatment seeking.
- Discrete positive (e.g., fairness) or negative (e.g., favouritism) leader behaviours can enhance or discourage the treatment seeking of employees.
- Recent studies suggest that leaders can be trained to be more attuned to the mental health needs of their employees, and to be more knowledgeable and supportive of employees experiencing mental health problems.

> • Such training will allow leaders to enhance the resilience of the employees and the organisation by encouraging employees to address mental health symptoms before they become debilitating.

References

Adler, A. B., Britt, T. W, Kim, P. Y., Riviere, L. A., & Thomas, J. L. (2015). Longitudinal determinants of mental health treatment seeking for U.S. soldiers. *British Journal of Psychiatry*, *207*, 346–350.

Ajzen, I. (1985). From intentions to action: A theory of planned behavior. In J. Kuhl & J. Beckman (eds), *Action control: From cognition to behavior* (pp. 11–39). Heidelberg: Springer.

Alonso, J., Petukhova, M., Vilagut, G., Chatterji, S., Heeringa, S., Üstün, T. B. & . . . Kessler, R. C. (2011). Days out of role due to common physical and mental conditions: Results from the WHO World Mental Health surveys. *Molecular Psychiatry*, *16*, 1234–1246.

Bakker, A. B. & Demerouti, E. (2007). The Job Demands-Resources model: State of the art. *Journal of Managerial Psychology*, *22*, 309–328.

Bamberger, P. (2009). Employee help-seeking: Antecedents, consequences and new insights for future research. *Personnel and Human Resources Management*, *28*, 49–98.

Barling, J., Kelloway, E. K. & Frone, M. R. (eds) (2005). *Handbook of work stress*. Thousand Oaks, CA: Sage.

Boulos, D. & Zamorski, M. (2015). Do shorter delays to care and mental health system renewal translate into better occupational outcome after mental disorder diagnosis in a cohort of Canadian military personnel who returned from an Afghanistan deployment? *BMJ Open*, 5:e008591.

Britt, T. W., Bennett, E. A., Crabtree, M., Haugh, C., Oliver, K., McFadden, A. & Pury, C. L. S. (2011). The theory of planned behavior and reserve component veteran treatment seeking. *Military Psychology*, *23*, 82–96.

Britt, T. W. & Bliese, P. B. (2003). Testing the stress-buffering effects of self engagement among soldiers on a military operation. *Journal of Personality*, *72*, 245–265.

Britt, T. W., Davison, J., Bliese, P. D. & Castro, C. A. (2004). How leaders can influence the health consequences of stressors on soldiers. *Military Medicine*, *169*, 541–545.

Britt, T. W., Jennings, K. S., Cheung, J. H., Pury, C. L. S. & Zinzow, H. M. (2015a). The role of different stigma perceptions in treatment seeking and dropout among active duty military personnel. *Psychiatric Rehabilitation Journal* (Special Issue: Self-Stigma and Mental Illness), 38, 142–149.

Britt, T. W., Jennings, K. S., Cheung, J. H., Pury, C. L. S. & Zinzow, H. M. (2015b). Evaluation of leader training to improve the unit climate of support for treatment seeking. *Unpublished Manuscript*, Clemson University, Clemson, SC.

Britt, T. W. & McFadden, A. (2012). Understanding mental health treatment seeking in high stress occupations. In J. Houdmont, S. Leka & R. Sinclair (eds), *Contemporary occupational health psychology: Global perspectives on research and practice* (pp. 57–73). Hoboken, NJ: Wiley-Blackwell Publishers.

Britt, T. W., Wright, K. M. & Moore, D. (2012). Leadership as a predictor of stigma and practical barriers toward receiving mental health treatment: A multilevel approach. *Psychological Services*, *9*, 26–37.

Brohan, E., Henderson, C., Wheat, K., Malcolm, E., Clement, S., Barley, E. A., Slade, M. & Thornicroft, G. (2012). Systematic review of beliefs, behaviours and influencing factors associated with disclosure of a mental health problem in the workplace. *BMC Psychiatry*, *12*, 1–14.

Castro, C. A. & Adler, A. B. (2011). Reconceptualizing combat-related posttraumatic stress disorder as an occupational hazard. In Adler, A. B., Bliese, P. D. & Castro, C. A. (eds), *Deployment psychology: Evidence-based strategies to promote mental health in the military*. (217–242). Washington, DC, US: American Psychological Association.

Cooper, C. L., Dewe, P. J. & O'Driscoll, M. P. (2001). *Organizational stress: A review and critique of theory, research, and applications*. London, Sage Publications.

Cooper, C. L., Dewe, P. J. & O'Driscoll, M. P. (2011). Employee assistance programs: Strengths, challenges, and future roles. In J. C. Quick & L. E. Tetrick (eds), *Handbook of occupational health psychology* (2nd edn, pp. 337–356). Washington, DC.

Corrigan, P. (2004). How stigma interferes with mental health care. *American Psychologist*, *59*, 614–625.

Dimoff, J. K., Kelloway, E. K. & Burnstein, M. D. (2016). Mental Health Awareness Training (MHAT): The development and evaluation of an intervention for workplace leaders. *International Journal of Stress Management*, *23*, 167–189.

Dollard, M. F. & Bakker, A. B. (2010). Psychosocial safety climate as a precursor to conducive work environments, psychological health problems, and employee engagement. *Journal of Occupational and Organizational Psychology*, *83*, 579–599.

French, M. T., Dunlap, L. J., Roman, P. M. & Steele, P. D. (1997). Factors that influence the use and perceptions of employee assistance programs at six worksites. *Journal of Occupational Health Psychology*, *2*, 312–324.

Hall, G. B., Dollard, M. F. & Coward, J. (2010). Psychosocial safety climate: Development of the PSC-12. *International Journal of Stress Management*, *17*, 353–383.

Hoge, C. W., Castro, C. A., Messer, S. C., McGurk, D., Cotting, D. I. & Koffman, R. L. (2004). Combat duty in Iraq and Afghanistan, mental health problems, and barriers to care. *New England Journal of Medicine*, *351*, 13–22.

Idris, M. A., Dollard, M. F., Coward, J. & Dormann, C. (2012). Psychosocial safety climate: Conceptual distinctiveness and effect on job demands and worker psychological health. *Safety Science*, *50*, 19–28.

Ivancevich, J. M., Matteson, M. T., Freedman, S. M. & Phillips, J. S. (1990). Worksite stress management interventions. *American Psychologist*, *45*, 252–261.

Jennings, K. S., Cheung, J. H., Britt, T. W., Goguen, K., Jeffirs, S., Peasley, A. & Lee, A. (2015). How are perceived stigma, self-stigma, and self-reliance related to treatment seeking? *Psychiatric Rehabilitation Journal* (Special Issue: Self-Stigma and Mental Illness), *38*, 109–116.

Kelloway, E. K., Weigand, H., McKee, M. C. & Das, H. (2013). Positive leadership and employee well-being. *Journal of Leadership and Organizational Studies*, *20*, 107–117.

Kelloway, E. K., Turner, N., Barling, J. & Loughlin, C. (2012). Transformational leadership and employee psychological well-being: The mediating role of employee trust in leadership. *Work and Stress*, *26*, 39–55.

Kessler, R. C., Barker, P. R., Colpe, L. J., Epstein, J. F., Gfroerer, J. C., Hiripi, E., Howes, M. J., Normand, S-L. T., Manderscheid, R. W., Walters, E. E. & Zaslavsky, A. M. (2003). Screening for serious mental illness in the general population. *Archives of General Psychiatry*, *60*, 184–189.

Kessler, R. C., Andrews, G., Colpe, L. J., Hiripi, E., Mroczek, D. K., Normand, S.-L. T., Walters, E. E. & Zaslavsky, A. (2002). Short screening scales to monitor population prevalence and trends in nonspecific psychological distress. *Psychological Medicine*, *32*, 959–976.

Kim, P. Y., Thomas, J. L., Wilk, J. E., Castro, C. A. & Hoge, C. W. (2010). Stigma, barriers to care, and use of mental health services among active duty and National Guard soldiers after combat. *Psychiatric Services, 61*, 572–588.

Kitchener, B. A. & Jorm, A. F. (2002). Mental health first aid training for the public: Evaluation of effects on knowledge, attitudes and helping behavior. *BMC Psychiatry, 2*, doi:10.1186/1471-244X-2-10.

Kitchener, B. A. & Jorm, A. F. (2004). Mental health first aid training in a workplace setting: A randomized controlled trial [ISRCTN13249129]. *BMC Psychiatry, 4*, doi:10.1186/1471-244X-4-23.

Kröger, C., Bode, K., Wunsch, E., Kliem, S., Grocholewski, A. & Finger, F. (2015). Work-related treatment for major depressive disorder and incapacity to work: Preliminary findings of a controlled, matched study. *Journal of Occupational Health Psychology, 20*, 248–258.

Lagerveld, S. E., Blonk, R. B., Brenninkmeijer, V., Wijngaards-de Meij, L. & Schaufeli, W. B. (2012). Work-focused treatment of common mental disorders and return to work: A comparative outcome study. *Journal of Occupational Health Psychology, 17*, 220–234.

Maslach, C., Schaufeli, W. B. & Leiter, M. P. (2001). Job burnout. *Annual Review of Psychology, 52*, 397–422.

Mojtabai, R., Olfson, M., Sampson, N. A., Jin, R., Druss, B. . . . & Kessler, R. C. (2011). Barriers to mental health treatment: results from the National Comorbidity Survey Replication. *Psychological Medicine, 41*, 1751–1761.

Milne, S. H., Blum, T. C. & Roman, P. M. (1994). Factors influencing employees' propensity to use an employee assistance program. *Personnel Psychology, 47*, 123–145.

Ouimette, P., Vogt, D., Wade, M., Tirone, V., Greenbaum, M. A., Kimerling, R. & . . . Rosen, C. S. (2011). Perceived barriers to care among veterans health administration patients with posttraumatic stress disorder. *Psychological Services, 8*, 212–223.

Pfeiffer, P. N., Blow, A. J., Miller, E., Forman, J., Dalack, G. W. & Valenstein, M. (2012). Peers and peer-based interventions in supporting reintegration and mental health among National Guard soldiers: A qualitative study. *Military Medicine, 177*, 1471–1476.

Sareen, J., Jagdeo, A., Cox, B. J., Clara, I., ten Have, M., Belik, S. & . . . Stein, M. B. (2007). Perceived barriers to mental health service utilization in the United States, Ontario, and the Netherlands. *Psychiatric Services, 58*, 357–364.

Thomas, J. L., Wilk, J. E., Riviere, L. A., McGurk, D., Castro, C. A. & Hoge, C. W. (2010). Prevalence of mental health problems and functional impairment among Active Component and National Guard soldiers 3 and 12 months following combat in Iraq. *Archives of General Psychiatry, 67*, 614–623.

Toth, K. E. & Dewa, C. S. (2014). Employee decision-making about disclosure of a mental disorder at work. *Journal of Occupational Rehabilitation, 24*(4), 732–746.

Vogel, D. L., Wade, N. G. & Haake, S. (2006). Measuring the self-stigma associated with seeking psychological help. *Journal of Counseling Psychology, 53*, 325–337.

Zinzow, H., Britt, T., Pury, C., Raymond, M. A., McFadden, A. & Burnette, C. (2013). Barriers and facilitators of mental health treatment-seeking among active duty Army personnel. *Military Psychology, 25*, 514–535.

Zohar, D. (1980). Safety climate in industrial organizations: Theoretical and applied implications. *Journal of Applied Psychology, 65*, 96–102.

Zohar, D. (2010). Thirty years of safety climate research: Reflections and future directions. *Accident Analysis and Prevention, 42*, 1517–1522.

APPENDIX 5.1: LEADER SELF-ASSESSMENT FOR PSYCHOLOGICAL HEALTH AND SUPPORT CLIMATE

(1) Do I act quickly to correct problems/issues that affect employee's psychological health?[1]

(2) Do I act decisively when a concern of an employees' psychological status is raised?[1]

(3) Do I show support for stress prevention through involvement and commitment?[1]

(4) Do I make the psychological wellbeing of my staff a priority?[1]

(5) Do I consider the psychological health of employees to be of great importance?[1]

(6) Do I consider the psychological health of my employees to be as important as productivity?[1]

(7) Do I encourage good communication in my unit/organisation about psychological safety issues that affect employees?[1]

(8) Do I listen to employee contributions to resolving occupational health and safety concerns?[1]

(9) Do I encourage employees to become involved in psychological safety and health matters?[1]

(10) Do I know when my employees may be experiencing a mental health problem?

(11) Am I aware of the resources that exist to support employees who are experiencing mental health problems?

(12) Am I encouraging employees to come talk with me when they are having mental health concerns?

(13) Do I help employees get mental health treatment when necessary?

(14) Do I support employees when they are in mental health treatment?

(15) Do I support employees when they return to my organisation after completing treatment?

Note. [1] = item modified from Hall et al. (2010).

6

ENHANCING THE RESILIENCE OF EMPLOYEES THROUGH THE PROVISION OF EMOTIONAL, INFORMATIONAL AND INSTRUMENTAL SUPPORT

Kristen S. Jennings and
Professor Thomas W. Britt

Organisational scholars recognised the importance of support and demonstrating concern for employees as a responsibility of good leaders in some of the earliest research on leadership. Some of the initial (and still supported) conceptualisations of leadership came down to two over-arching components of helping employees stay on task and providing support for them (Fleishman, 1953; Fleishman, Harris & Burtt, 1955; Judge, Piccolo & Ilies, 2004). Social support can be a particularly useful tool for a manager to use to help employees be resilient in the face of job stress. Yet, social support comes with several caveats on when it is most useful and how it should be implemented. How managers provide support to employees can impact their ability to demonstrate resilience under difficult work conditions. Although the overwhelming majority of studies have reported positive associations between social support at work and measures of health and wellbeing, this is not always the case. Other studies have failed to find a positive relationship, or even found a negative relationship. This may be a result of several factors, such as providing support that amplifies the stressful nature of the situation or not providing the supportive behaviour an individual really needs. Researchers from various fields are still working to understand the complexities of support and how it may be best used as a resource to enhance employee wellbeing. However, without doubt, it can be troubling when an employee lacks support in the context of stressful work and non-work lives.

Many jobs today involve a high level of employee stress, whether it be balancing a large number of complex tasks, enduring intense physical environments, or making high-stakes decisions involving large financial costs or even human lives. In these situations, it is important that employees be resilient to the obstacles that may impact their health, wellbeing and ability to perform their jobs. In most cases, it is hard for an individual to do this without the help of others in some form. Support from an employee's manager and workgroup can be critical resources in helping employees to thrive amidst these challenging circumstances. Although providing support seems like a basic concept that is relatively obvious to enact, researchers have found that social support is much more complicated and can have a wide range of effects on employees.

Take this example. A researcher at a private firm has a helpful and outgoing supervisor, with whom he works on a regular basis. He enjoys working with her and acknowledges that she is exceptionally helpful, competent and an overall great leader. Oftentimes he experiences some difficulty completing more complex statistical analyses and goes to his supervisor for help on this. She quickly volunteers to do the tasks for him, to help him out. While he is relieved to have the help, he often feels discouraged and incompetent that she has to take over. So while his supervisor has positive intentions to help him, this type of support may undermine his confidence and efforts to learn.

As another example, consider a construction worker who loves his job and his manager, who has become a close friend and helpful resource for getting his work done. One day, the worker injured his back while lifting some heavy materials. He experienced a lot of pain that lasted several days. Instead of reporting the incident and taking time to visit a doctor, he decided to work through the injury because the job had to get done and he did not want to disappoint his manager. In this case, not wanting to let the manager down led the employee to act in ways that could limit his performance and harm his health.

In both of these cases the leader or manager had good intentions to support his or her employee; however, this support had some unintended negative consequences. Situations such as these may arise in the workplace more often than one would expect, where managers have good intentions, but need more information on how to best support their employees in various circumstances. Managers and co-workers alike should be informed on how to best support a variety of employee needs, whether that is offering an ear to listen to a problem or more tangible resources to help solve a problem. Knowing the most appropriate steps is critical in ensuring that the support offered is effective in helping employees build resilience and thrive in these complex work environments.

In this chapter, we provide a brief overview of the research that has been conducted in the area of social support. We focus on definitional aspects of support, including types of supportive behaviours and sources of support, how support can be helpful in stressful conditions, and when support can actually result in negative outcomes. Importantly, the second part of the chapter will shift to a practical focus on what managers can do to provide support to their employees.

What is social support?

Social support has long been an interest of social researchers, who conducted an extensive amount of research in a relatively short amount of time (Barrera & Ainlay,

1983). However, the surge in this research led to some very different conceptual-isations of social support, making a single, clear definition difficult. Social support has been defined in broad terms as an individual providing resources to another to enhance his or her wellbeing, or the perception that assistance would be avail-able if it was needed (Langford *et al.*, 1997; Shumaker & Brownell, 1984). The resources provided can include tangible assistance, like helping complete a task or giving someone money, or can be more emotionally oriented, like offering an ear to listen to a concern about a work task or providing advice.

Researchers have made several distinctions in social support, including: (1) whether the support is specified as perceived or enacted, (2) the different behaviours that constitute support, and (3) the different sources of support in a person's social network. Recognising these distinctions can be important to gaining a greater awareness of effective ways managers can support their employees.

(1) Perceived or enacted support. The first distinction is that social support can be perceived or enacted. Perceived support means that an individual acknowledges that support would be available if needed, which may or may not accurately reflect the availability of resources. Enacted support is when someone actually performs a supportive behaviour (Haber *et al.*, 2007). While enacted support seems to better capture the reality of supportive behaviours, researchers have actually found evidence that perceived support is more consistently related to health outcomes (Haber *et al.*, 2007). Further, some would argue that actual supportive behaviours may only be helpful if they are perceived by the person receiving support as satisfactory or necessary (Dunkel-Schetter & Bennett, 1990; Sarason, Sarason & Pierce, 1990).

These distinctions between perceived and enacted support may be important for managers to consider. Even if managers do not necessarily feel they have the capacity to tangibly provide assistance to all employees, making it known that they can be available to help employees as needed may be a more important foundation. In addition, the behaviours managers engage in to support their employees may not be beneficial if employees do not actually perceive those behaviours as supportive, either because the behaviour is not obvious or the intent is unclear. Managers may therefore need to evaluate whether the supportive behaviours they engage in match the employee's perceived support needs by seeking regular feedback from employees.

(2) The different functions of support. A second distinction is in the types of supportive behaviours, which can serve very different functions. Most researchers distinguish four major categories of supportive behaviours: (1) emotional, (2) instrumental, (3) informational, and (4) appraisal (e.g., Cutrona & Russel, 1990; House, 1981; Langford *et al.*, 1997). Emotional support is what typically comes to mind when thinking of social support. That is, providing emotional care for someone, such as by listening to a concern or conveying that the individual is valued and cared for (House, 1981). Perceiving emotional support has been associated with positive health and wellbeing outcomes in a broad range of stressful conditions

(Cutrona & Russel, 1990). A major concern about emotional support, however, is that it depends heavily on the perception of the individual receiving support (House, 1981). For example, a boss may demonstrate care for an employee under high demands through offering words of encouragement, but the employee may not acknowledge the encouragement or misinterpret it as unhelpful or insincere. Thus, it may be harder for managers to gauge whether or not an employee feels emotionally supported in his or her job role.

Instrumental support is provided when someone engages in a behaviour that directly addresses the recipient's need, such as providing tangible goods or services (House, 1981). Broadly, this may be giving someone money, food or a ride when a person is in need. In a workplace, this may include actually performing work duties for another person or providing supplies needed to perform a task. Instrumental support can be very useful and has been related to positive health outcomes under stressful circumstances (Cutrona & Russell, 1990). Many readers can probably think of specific examples where a co-worker, boss, or other individual provided encouraging words when they were stressed about a task, but what they really needed was someone to help get the work done. Using instrumental support speaks to the idea that actions can sometimes speak louder than words, especially in stressful work environments.

The provision of instrumental support can be problematic if it is not perceived in a positive manner. For example, an employee may interpret his or her manager jumping in to help complete a project as a signal that the individual is not competent to do the job alone. Another common example of the slippery slope of providing instrumental support is with providing money to someone, which could signal that they are in need of money and dependent on other people to help them. Practically speaking in these examples, being too quick to offer instrumental support could also prevent employees from gaining job-relevant skills that could be acquired through further training or instruction. Overall, however, when applied appropriately, instrumental support can be helpful and results in positive outcomes under stressful conditions.

Informational support is when an individual provides information or advice that helps to solve a problem (Cutrona & Russel, 1990). Providing information to "help someone help themselves" can sometimes be a better alternative than providing emotional or instrumental support. Informational support means helping an employee to better handle a situation, without risking reduced efficacy or feelings of inadequacy that may result from directly intervening. Informational support provided in stressful situations has been associated with outcomes such as higher positive affect and lower levels of depression symptoms (Cutrona & Russell, 1990). In the workplace, examples might include providing information about organisational resources that are available, providing training opportunities for an employee, or giving contact information for technical support. Some of these informational support behaviours may take more time than a brief word of encouragement or just doing a task oneself, but could have long-term benefits for the employee and organisation, particularly in the case of developing more resilient employees.

Lastly, appraisal support is similar to informational support, where information is provided in regards to self-evaluation (House, 1981). Appraisal support is typically shown through statements or behaviours that affirm that an individual is doing a good job or engaging in an appropriate behaviour in the given context (Langford et al., 1997). In the workplace, this may include feedback or recognition from a supervisor that the employee performed a task well, or even telling a new employee that it is ok to feel overwhelmed at first and to validate concerns he/she may be experiencing. These forms of support can be very important in boosting an employee's self-worth, and especially for new employees, letting them know that they are on the right track.

Recognising the different types of supportive behaviours can be valuable in determining the best ways to support employees. In particular, understanding any unintended consequences of presumably supportive behaviours can help to identify the optimal ways to support employees to be more resilient. These considerations will be examined in more detail in the later discussion of ways support may actually be associated with negative outcomes in the workplace.

(3) Sources of support. The third feature of support is who is providing the support. The source of the support may also impact individual and organisational outcomes. While this chapter is intended to focus on the manager's role as a source of support, other individuals can serve a vital role in supporting employee needs. There are several other important sources of support, such as co-workers or family and friends outside of work, who may be more impactful in helping employees to cope with different job demands. Considering a more holistic view of support from a variety of sources may not only provide more useful information for making employees more resilient, but may also allow more realistic recommendations. Most managers must balance a wide range of responsibilities, and trying to support every employee in specific ways may not always be feasible. However, promoting an overall culture of support, such as through supportive co-workers, can create more resources for employees to turn to when managers are unable to fulfill all of the needed support roles.

Specifically, in relation to employee stress, support from managers and co-workers has been found to have unique influences on employee outcomes. At times, support from a manager may be more critical for employees because of the control a manager has over factors like the tasks an employee performs or the resources that are available. For example, studies have found that supervisor support, but not co-worker support, was associated with lower levels of psychological distress and symptoms of depression (Akerboom & Maes, 2006; Dormann & Zaph, 1999). As another example, Halbesleben (2006) found that employee feelings of being burned out were differentially impacted by support from people in and outside the workplace. Support from those at work was associated with less experience of exhaustion, likely because exhaustion is closely tied to the particular work demands. However, support from those outside of work was more closely related to an employee's feelings of depersonalisation (i.e., feeling detached from or cynical toward work and/or work-related relationships) or personal accomplishment. Thus, those outside of work may contribute to these more personal, emotional experiences associated with work stress.

As a final example, some sources of support may not only matter for an employee's wellbeing, but could contribute to important behaviours in organisations. In a study of Taiwanese employees, Chiu, Yeh, and Huang (2015) found that co-worker support, but not supervisor support, was associated with a lower likelihood of engaging in deviant behaviours toward other employees. Interestingly, when employees rated co-worker support as high, they were less likely to engage in deviant behaviours, even as their stress from balancing multiple roles increased. These examples highlight that managers are important sources of support, but are not the only important source of support.

Seeking to promote an organisational climate with high co-worker support could be valuable for a number of reasons. First, employees may feel more comfortable accepting support from co-workers. Many times, individuals can feel uneasy when they receive support, but feel they have nothing they can give in return. Buunk and colleagues (1993) found that employees reported they could more equally reciprocate help received from colleagues compared to help received from supervisors. Further, employees may feel it reflects poorly on them to go to a supervisor for help, while the costs are much less intimidating to ask a peer. As a second consideration, co-workers may simply spend more time with one another as compared to the time the manager gets to spend with employees. Therefore, a co-worker may better be able to perceive when an employee has a need for support or may be more familiar with what resources are most needed in specific work situations.

Leaders should not, however, use supportive co-workers as an opportunity to step out of their support role, but as an invaluable supplement to the unique ways a leader can support his or her employees. Leaders may also need to initiate efforts to encourage employees to support one another. Research from the field of occupational health has demonstrated that leaders play a major role in creating the overall climate within a workgroup. For example, research on safety at work has noted leadership as a primary influence on the climate related to safe practices in a workplace (Zohar, 2010). Therefore, the leader may be highly influential in setting the precedent for supporting fellow employees. As an applied example, having high task demands and individualised incentives may move employees to be very independent of one another in their work (and potentially even promote competition). However, encouraging collaboration and making schedules with some room to back-up or support a co-worker in need creates a more optimal foundation for supportive co-worker relationships to form.

Support is *not* always helpful: avoiding harmful forms of support

Although most researchers and anecdotal experiences would suggest that support from others is helpful, not all research has had the same promising findings. Some studies find either no effect of social support on improving employee health, or even an opposite relationship where support was associated with harm to an employee's wellbeing. Under certain conditions social support has been related to negative outcomes. For example, Ray and Miller (1994) found that nursing home employees experiencing high amounts of stress reported more exhaustion and burnout as co-worker support increased. Others have found that social support was associated with increased mental health symptoms such as psychosomatic complaints, anxiety and depression under some stressful situations (Frese, 1999). Even in the case of traumatic stress, some forms of support may not reduce the impact of experiencing trauma on physical and mental health outcomes (e.g., Stephens & Long, 2000). Lastly, studies have found that support may not always serve as a buffer to stressful circumstances. For example, support did not buffer the negative effects of stress on job satisfaction in a study by Ducharme and Martin (2000).

Empirically speaking, many of the inconsistent relationships may be due to issues with the study design or the way support was actually measured. Many researchers use the term "social support" for a measure that may or may not be capturing support well. For instance, some researchers measure support as the number of close relationships possessed by the individual, while some better capture the quality of relationships, and others focus on specific aspects of support, such as the content of conversations in a supportive relationship (e.g., Stephens & Long, 2000). Some researchers have also argued that plausible explanations for correlations between negative outcomes and support are that those with a higher need seek out more support to begin with or that individuals receiving support when they do not want it, experience negative reactions (e.g., Barrera, 1986; Deelstra et al., 2003). The claim that those with higher needs seek more support has not been clearly tested in empirical studies. However, Deelstra and colleagues (2003) did consider the relationships between need for support and responses to support in a lab study, finding that having a high need was not associated with more positive reactions to receiving support.

Cohen and Wills (1985) argued that the type of stress and support offered must adequately match in order to find an effect where support reduces the impact of stress on relevant outcomes. Therefore, support may not be helpful if it does not adequately fit the demand or the problem the employee is experiencing. For instance, employees experiencing a stressor of a social nature (e.g., an interpersonal conflict) may benefit from more emotional support. If the demand is a practical need (e.g., help completing a task), the employee may need instrumental support to reduce the demand and the impact on his or her health.

As briefly noted in the provision of instrumental support, sometimes supervisors or co-workers can have good intentions to help an individual that have unintended consequences. Therefore, it is important that managers are aware of the most appropriate forms of support to fit an employee's need, and recognise how some supportive behaviours could potentially harm a person or situation. Beehr, Bowling, and Bennett (2010) provided three specific examples where support could actually be harmful.

(1) Increasing one's focus on the stressor. The first example is when the type of support brings more attention to the stressful circumstance than would normally occur. As an example, Kaufmann and Beehr (1989) argued that this potentially accounted for a reverse-buffering effect they found in a sample of police officers. These authors found that high perceptions of instrumental support, specifically that others were available to help with work as needed, was associated with experiences of increased strain when under high stress. They argued that in this case, the instrumental support may have re-affirmed the stressful nature of the officer's job, rather than reducing strain responses. Most readers can probably personally recall an instance of this phenomenon where the more they discussed a stressful event with others, the more stressful the experience became. The employee may normally just face these circumstances, with little or no stress, but the additional attention unnecessarily highlights aspects that unsettle them. Optimally, providing support should never make a worker feel worse than they did before an encounter.

Bringing additional attention to work-related problems may have also been a factor in the unexpected findings of Hahn (2000). These researchers found that emotion-focused social support was associated with higher reports of anger when employees experienced interpersonal conflict. In this case, confiding in others and seeking emotional support could unintentionally cause an employee venting about a problem to dwell on it and see it as more stressful. Similarly, Iwata and Suzuki (1997) found that the relationship between role stress and mental health symptoms was stronger for Japanese bank workers who reported high emotional support from co-workers. Thus, these employees may all have been more likely to dwell on their stressful experiences when receiving support, exacerbating the negative effects.

(2) Support as a threat to competence. The second example provided by Beehr *et al.*, (2010) is when helping poses a threat to the employee's perceived ability or self-image. The manager who takes on the "let me do it for you" attitude when a task seems complicated, rather than helping someone to help themselves, typifies this example. Such behaviour can make an employee feel inferior and incapable of completing their job, and could even be embarrassing if it is a task he/she should be able to do. Peeters, Buunk, and Schaufeli (1995) found evidence of this dynamic in their study of correctional officers. Officers who received instrumental support at work reported higher negative affect at the end of the day. The authors proposed, as other researchers have as well, that this type of support in this context may have been associated with feelings of inferiority.

(3) "If I want your support I will ask for it". The third and final example is trying to support someone who does not want support. Employees may feel frustrated when a co-worker or supervisor intervenes when help is unwanted. Therefore, it is important to gauge the extent to which support is needed before being too eager to help someone who may not actually need help. In a sample of university employees, Beehr and colleagues (2010) found evidence that some of these types of attempted social support can be associated with higher levels of emotional

exhaustion and even physical health symptoms, particularly when those behaviours are coming from supervisors. Deelstra and colleagues (2003) also found that getting unwanted support for a clear task was associated with higher negative affect.

Application: what should I do?

As a manager, you are in an optimal position to support employees in a variety of different situations. Based on the research evidence, we provide several recommendations for being a supportive supervisor that promotes resilience in employees. These include understanding the employee's demands, matching their demands with appropriate forms of support, and forming a supportive climate within the workgroup you supervise. These recommendations are discussed in more detail in the final section of this chapter, and are also summarised in a self-assessment format in Appendix 6.1.

Making it clear that support is available. A problematic assumption that can be made by supportive managers is that the employees know that support is available if they need it. Ensuring routinely that employees know where and how they can access support is important, particularly for newer team members who might not be aware of various avenues for accessing support. Thus, it may be helpful to clearly convey that managers are available to help employees with different problems (e.g., getting the resources they need, talking about any difficulties in completing work), rather than making the assumption that the employees know he/she can come to them when needed.

Building an awareness of employee needs. As with most duties of a manager, being supportive will most likely begin with coming to a better understanding of the employee's needs. It is hard to know how to be appropriately supportive without knowing what the employee's demands look like. Building an awareness of employee needs may come from prior experience in the role of the employee, if the manager was promoted from the same job. Alternatively, a manager may have to invest more time in observing employees or talking with them about their job. This can be difficult within the constraints of a manager's busy schedule, but even talking with employees about specific tasks that are difficult, time-consuming or in general stressful, can provide some useful information in knowing what to do to support them. Free programmes are also available where a manager could create an anonymous survey to administer to his or her workgroup to get feedback on where employees could use more support (e.g., Google forms; Survey Monkey).

Anticipating and mitigating stressor. A good manager may be able to prevent some stressful experiences altogether by providing resources needed or altering job duties. For example, if a company was introducing new software for tracking sales, the manager could provide step-by-step training on how to use the software to avoid the stressful situation of not knowing what to do (and not to mention adding learning the programme to their normal job duties). Managers should not under-estimate the amount of stress that can be caused to employees with the introduction of new systems and software. Poor support to complement such changes can create not only harm to the employees, but also lowers morale and productivity. Prevention is better than trying to cure a problem after it occurs. Therefore, an important role of a manager in maintaining employee resilience is to anticipate the stress that can be created by change or other stressors and to develop strategies to prevent it.

Changing the way employees think about stressors. When stressful events are inevitable, as is the case in most jobs, a manager can help the employee to adjust their perspective on the event as a whole. For example, a nursing supervisor can emphasise that though a patient is difficult, the nurse is able to serve a vital role in helping his or her health improve or potentially saving a life. Such reframing can help employees to take a new perspective on the stressful event to make it less threatening.

Considering how to best provide support. After understanding the demands an employee experiences, a manager should consider how to best support that employee. In the opening of the chapter, some examples were provided on when a manager may have good intentions of supporting an employee, but the supportive behaviour does not match the employee's actual need. Some common issues that employees may find frustrating might be managers who always provide encouragement through conversation and communicating concern, but do not provide tangible resources or information that an employee actually needs to solve a problem. Another concern that has not received much research attention, and is likely hard to detect, could be if a manager is very supportive and the employees form a loyalty to them that can result in negative outcomes. This is likely a higher concern in jobs with high physical (or psychological) demands that could result in workplace injuries that warrant professional help. If an employee does not seek treatment because he or she does not want to disappoint their manager, it could have negative long-term outcomes.

In determining the optimal form of support, managers may want to think through a few questions, such as: (1) "What is the source of this stressor?" (2) "Do I have any power to change if the employee experiences the stressor?" and (3) "Do I have any power to change how the employee perceives the stressor?" In reference to the first question, the manager may consider if the stressor is something that is more social or practical in nature. If it is an interpersonal or social issue, emotional support may be critical, while instrumental or informational support may be more helpful in addressing practical concerns. In reference to the second and third questions, managers should consider if they could change aspects of the job or work environment as a practical way to provide support instrumentally. If they cannot, they may still be able to provide emotional support or informational support to help the employee overcome the demand or perceive it in a more positive manner.

As a final consideration, a manager should think about any unintended consequences of the type of support that is provided. This is highlighted in the checklist and many of the examples throughout the chapter. Anytime a manager is seeking to help an employee they should consider factors like, whether they are jumping in too soon to offer help, if the help might make the employee feel incompetent, if the employee is missing out on learning a new skill because of their support, or if the help is over-emphasising an event as stressful. This issue may also be uncovered through seeking feedback from employees as to whether or not they feel supported appropriately.

Build a workplace environment that emphasises support. While managers are in an optimal position to support employees in many ways, they simply cannot do it all. Even good managers with good intentions have a lot of tasks that they must get done and will not always be able to know everything that is going on for their employees. With these limitations, an important tool is to build up a work-group environment that emphasises support. Co-worker support has been demonstrated to uniquely relate to positive occupational health and organisational outcomes (e.g., Biron, 2013; Chiu *et al.*, 2015), and may benefit employees in ways that support from a manager cannot (i.e., because the manager cannot offer the same behaviours or they are less impactful coming from the manager). Other benefits of a supportive unit climate are that employees may actually get enjoyment out of helping one another! A study by Brown and colleagues (2003) found that providing support may be more beneficial than receiving support.

In order to achieve this, managers can consider how they can proactively set up supportive networks among work units before stressful events ever occur. Examples could include mentoring programmes between experienced and novice employees so new employees can learn more about what to expect on their job or even strategies that have been successful (or perhaps more importantly, unsuccessful) for the more experienced employees. Other examples may be training programmes on how to manage stress, information on how to receive help if experiencing a mental or physical health problem, or even how to detect when a co-worker is experiencing a problem and how to support them in that circumstance.

Practical steps may be necessary in the work context to allow enough time and resources for employees to help one another. For example, managers should be aware if an employee's job is so demanding that they simply do not have time to help their co-workers or form supportive relationships in general. They could also improve on resources available to provide help, such as potential training programmes discussed, on how to recognise and help a co-worker who may be experiencing a problem. This might also mean adjusting some of the structure of the work environment and job tasks with more flexibility and/or interdependent tasks to make it a natural and easy behaviour for co-workers to help one another as needed. Rigid schedules with little autonomy will allow less freedom for employees to foster such relationships where they can meaningfully provide support.

Reacting in a supportive way. While recognising employee needs for support and creating a unit climate of support are more proactive measures, managers may also want to consider how to react in a supportive way after employees experience a stressful situation. In helping employees cope after a stressor has occurred, it may be important to talk about resources available or even discuss the event as a group. For example, Sattler, Boyd, and Kirsch (2014) found that participating in debriefings after critical incidents was associated with lower levels of post-traumatic stress and higher levels of post-traumatic growth for firefighters who had been exposed to trauma. This may also be an opportune time to notice signs that a co-worker may be experiencing a problem, and how to help the co-worker cope with any mental health symptoms that may result. While this may be especially important in high-risk jobs that involve traumatic events, debriefing could also be a useful practice during busy or stressful seasons in less risky work environments.

Encouraging employees to proactively seek the support they need. Lastly, it may also be important to encourage employees to be proactive in seeking support for work problems themselves. Again, supervisors cannot feasibly be aware of all employee needs at all times, so it is important that employees are aware and encouraged to seek out the resources they need, whether it be from the manager, from a co-worker, or from an outside source. One study found that employees who had emotional resources available and who were likely to seek out emotional support when needed were less likely to experience emotional exhaustion from their work (van de Ven, van den Tooren & Vlerick, 2013). Therefore, making employees aware of resources and how to access them may be a vital tool in promoting employee resilience.

Final thoughts

There is a long history of research in social support and its impacts on wellbeing. However, it seems that not all support can yield good outcomes. Thus for managers wishing to provide good support to employees the landscape is extremely complex and it may be very difficult for them to provide support to employees in their job. Managers should be informed on how to best support a variety of employee needs, whether that is offering an ear to listen to a problem or more tangible resources to help solve a problem. This insight can come from spending the time to identify what employees would find most useful when it comes to support. Moreover, while managers are central to supporting their employees they cannot do it all. Thus, it is important to invest time in developing a supportive culture within the team or organisation. At another level, employees should be actively encouraged to proactively seek and access the support they need whether that be from managers, colleagues or professional support (e.g. mental health providers; counselors). Understanding the importance and nature of support required in your workplace and having appropriate support resources in place is critical in ensuring that the support offered is effective in helping employees build resilience and thrive in complex work environments.

KEY MESSAGES FROM THIS CHAPTER

- Not all forms of support are helpful and a manager needs to carefully consider the type of support provided to staff members.
- Inappropriate support that undermines an employee's worth, is unwanted, or that brings unnecessary attention to the stressful nature of a work situation may have some unintended consequences.
- Seeking to promote an organisational climate with high co-worker support is valuable for supporting the mental health and resilience of staff. Managers have an important role in influencing the culture of co-worker support.
- Managers can seek to build an awareness of employee support needs and offer support that matches these needs, encourage a supportive atmosphere among co-workers, anticipate stressor events and proactively initiate support and make efforts to ensure that employees know how to seek out resources when needed.

References

Akerboom, S. & Maes, S. (2006). Beyond demand and control: The contribution of organizational risk factors in assessing the psychological well-being of health care employees. *Work and Stress, 20,* 21–26.

Barrera, M. (1986). Distinctions between social support concepts, measures, and models. *American Journal of Community Psychology, 14,* 413–445.

Barrera, M. & Ainlay, S. L. (1983). The structure of social support: A conceptual and empirical analysis. *Journal of Community Psychology, 11,* 133–143.

Beehr, T. A., Bowling, N. A. & Bennett, M. M. (2010). Occupational stress and failures of social support: When helping hurts. *Journal of Occupational Health Psychology, 15,* 45–59.

Biron, M. (2013). Effective and ineffective support: How different sources of support buffer the short- and long-term effects of a working day. *European Journal of Work and Organizational Psychology, 22,* 150–164.

Brown, S. L., Nesse, R. M., Vinokur, A. D. & Smith, D. M. (2003). Providing social support may be more beneficial than receiving it: Results from a prospective study of mortality. *Psychological Science, 14,* 320–327.

Buunk, B. P., Doosje, B. J., Jans, L. G. J. M. & Hopstaken, L. E. M. (1993). Perceived reciprocity, social support, and stress at work: The role of exchange and communal orientation. *Journal of Personality and Social Psychology, 65*(4), 801–811.

Chiu, S., Yeh, S. & Huang, T. (2015). Role stressors and employee deviance: the moderating effect of social support. *Personnel Review, 44,* 308–324.

Cohen, S. & Wills, T. A. (1985). Stress, social support, and the buffering hypothesis. *Psychological Bulletin, 9,* 310–357.

Cutrona, C. E. & Russel, D. W. (1990). Type of social support and specific stress: Toward a theory of optimal matching. In B. R. Sarason, I.G. Sarason & G. R. Pierce (eds), *Social Support: An interactional view* (pp.319–366). New York: Wiley.

Deelstra, J. T., Peeters, M. W., Schaufeli, W. B., Stroebe, W., Zijlstra, F. H. & van Doornen, L. P. (2003). Receiving instrumental support at work: When help is not welcome. *Journal of Applied Psychology, 88*, 324–331.

Dormann, C. & Zapf, D. (1999). Social support, social stressors at work, and depressive symptoms: Testing for main and moderating effects with structural equations in a three-wave longitudinal study. *Journal of Applied Psychology, 84*, 874–884.

Ducharme, L. J. & Martin, J. K. (2000). Unrewarding work, coworker support, and job satisfaction a test of the Buffering Hypothesis. *Work and Occupations, 27*, 223–243.

Dunkel-Schetter, C. & Bennett, T. L. (1990). Differentiating the cognitive and behavioral aspects of social support. In B. R. Sarason, I.G. Sarason & G. R. Pierce (eds), *Social Support: An Interactional View*, pp. 267–296. New York: Wiley.

Fleishman, E. A. (1953). The description of supervisory behavior. *Journal of Applied Psychology, 37*, 1–6.

Fleishman, E. A., Harris, E. F. & Burtt, H. E. (1955). Leadership and supervision in industry; an evaluation of a supervisory training program. Ohio State University. *Bureau of Educational Research Monograph, 33.*

Frese, M. (1999). Social support as a moderator of the relationship between work stressors and psychological dysfunction: A longitudinal study with objective measures. *Journal of Occupational Health Psychology, 4*, 179–192.

Haber, M. G., Cohen, J. L., Lucas, T. & Baltes, B. B. (2007). The relationship between self-reported received and perceived social support: A meta-analytic review. *American Journal of Community Psychology, 39*, 133–144.

Hahn, S. E. (2000). The effects of locus of control on daily exposure, coping and reactivity to work interpersonal stressors: A diary study. *Personality and Individual Differences, 29*, 729–748.

Halbesleben, J. R. (2006). Sources of social support and burnout: a meta-analytic test of the conservation of resources model. *Journal of Applied Psychology, 91*(5), 1134.

House, J. S. (1981). *Work stress and social support.* Reading, Massachusetts. Addison-Wesley Publishing Company.

Iwata, N. & Suzuki, K. (1997). Role stress-mental health relations in Japanese bank workers: A moderating effect of social support. *Applied Psychology: An International Review, 46*, 207–218.

Judge, T. A., Piccolo, R. F. & Ilies, R. (2004). The forgotten ones? The validity of consideration and initiating structure in leadership research. *Journal of Applied Psychology, 89*, 36–51.

Kaufmann, G. M. & Beehr, T. A. (1989). Occupational stressors, individual strains, and social supports among police officers. *Human Relations, 42*, 185–197.

Langford, C., Bowsher, J., Maloney, J. & Lillis, P. (1997). Social support: a conceptual analysis. *Journal of Advanced Nursing, 25*, 95–100.

Peeters, M. C., Buunk, B. P. & Schaufeli, W. B. (1995). Social interactions and feelings of inferiority. *Journal of Applied Social Psychology, 25*, 1073–1089.

Ray, E. B. & Miller, K. I. (1994). Social support, home/work stress, and burnout: Who can help? *The Journal of Applied Behavioral Science, 30*, 357–373.

Sarason, B. R., Sarason, I. G. & Pierce, G. R. (1990). Traditional views of social support and their impact on assessment. In B. R. Sarason, I.G. Sarason & G. R. Pierce (eds), *Social Support: An interactional view*, pp. 9–25. New York: Wiley.

Sattler, D. N., Boyd, B. & Kirsch, J. (2014). Trauma-exposed firefighters: relationships among posttraumatic growth, posttraumatic stress, resource availability, coping and critical incident stress debriefing experience. *Stress and Health, 30*, 356–365.

Shumaker, S. A. & Brownell, A. (1984). Toward a theory of social support: closing conceptual gaps. *Journal of Social Issues, 40*(4), 11–36.

Stephens, C. & Long, N. (2000). Communication with police supervisors and peers as a buffer of work-related traumatic stress. *Journal of Organizational Behavior, 21*, 407–424.

van de Ven, B., van den Tooren, M. & Vlerick, P. (2013). Emotional job resources and emotional support seeking as moderators of the relation between emotional job demands and emotional exhaustion: A two-wave panel study. *Journal of Occupational Health Psychology, 18*, 1–8.

Zohar, D. (2010). Thirty years of safety climate research: Reflections and future directions. *Accident Analysis and Prevention, 42*, 1517–1522.

APPENDIX 6.1: CONSIDERATIONS FOR MANAGERS PROVIDING SUPPORT

(1) Do I engage in supportive behaviours toward my employees?

(2) Do my employees actually perceive my behaviours as supportive?

    a   Do they comment on whether they do or do not feel supported?

    b   Do I have enough information on this? If not, consider an anonymous employee survey or conversations about how you can support them during performance appraisals or other interactions.

(3) What types of behaviours do I use to support my employees?

    a   Emotional
    b   Instrumental
    c   Informational
    d   Appraisal

(4) Do these behaviours match their greatest needs?

    a   Do I know what their greatest needs are? If not, try to find out.
    b   Are there any unintended outcomes that could come from the type of supportive behaviour I provide?

(5) Am I the right person to be providing this support?

    a   Can I feasibly help with this problem?
    b   Could I train co-workers to support this need?
    c   Is this something that I should bring up to upper management to initiate broader organisational changes?

PART 3

Managing organisation factors that erode resilience

7

HOW WORK DESIGN CAN ENHANCE OR ERODE EMPLOYEE RESILIENCE

Dr. Ben J. Searle

Jill and Jen are twin sisters who work as accountants. During their university years they felt invulnerable. It didn't seem to matter what they did: pulling all-nighters to finish course assignments, staying out late at parties, or working late shifts at the local supermarket; they never felt wiped-out for long. Nor were they particularly overwhelmed by stressful life events, such as break-ups with boyfriends or the time a fire destroyed the building where they shared an apartment. In many ways, Jill and Jen were prime examples of resilient individuals.

However, six years out from university things look quite different for Jill. She was much more distressed than Jen when the apartment they were renting was sold, and they had to move out. Three months after the move, Jen is perfectly content with their new place, but Jill is still upset. Jill often worries about losing her job, and about never earning enough money to buy her dream house. Jill also regularly moans to Jen about her job, her co-workers, or her supervisor.

So what changed? Jill and Jen work for different organisations, so it could well be something about the work context that has impacted Jill's capacity for resilience.

Jill works for a major international finance company, in a well-paid job with regular international travel assignments. While she was initially thrilled to get her job, she feels overwhelmed with the challenges she faces in her role. She feels that the quality of her work is undermined by the political manoeuvring of several managers in her department, as well as feeling constantly obstructed by complicated bureaucratic requirements that often change several times per year. The resulting confusion has led Jill to clash with co-workers about who is responsible for which tasks and outcomes. Jill also feels intimidated by her current supervisor, who sometimes yells at people when he is stressed, and who is still making jokes about a suggestion that Jill made in a meeting that happened nearly a year ago. One consequence of this is that Jill is reluctant to make decisions without her supervisor's formal approval.

By comparison, Jen continues to be resilient, perhaps because the company where she works places a high value on its employees. This is a smaller company than Jill's, but Jen has a high level of control over her work processes. She is required to work hard — sometimes she works longer hours than Jill — but Jen seems to thrive on the challenging assignments she is allocated. Jen's achievements and contributions to the company are often publicly recognised. Jen is not as well-paid as Jill, and there is no travel, but as a reward for her achievements she gets a small annual budget to spend on her skill development.

The case of Jill and Jen illustrates how individual resilience is not a quality that exists independently of the environment. Resilient employees may cope well with difficult situations for a while, but few people can endure them indefinitely without being affected. It would be foolish for an organisation to overlook problems endemic to their workplace in a desire to achieve employee resilience through selection and/or training. Indeed, establishing a supportive work environment may help not only to attract resilient, capable employees, it may even enhance resilience among existing staff.

For these reasons, an examination of wellbeing and resilience in the workplace would be incomplete without a consideration of work design. Work design (also known as job design) is all about job characteristics. These characteristics relate to job content (the activities performed, such as writing reports), job processes (such as the way reports are allocated and reviewed), job resources (such as the amount of feedback provided on draft reports), and, to an extent, the job context (such as the information and equipment used to prepare reports, and the work environment in which they are written). The term "work design" could be interpreted as suggesting that jobs are carefully *designed* by planners who try to balance the organisational objectives of a new work role with the need to create a positive work experience for each employee. While such a proactive approach would be ideal, it is rare! Instead, the term "work design" simply refers to the current set of characteristics of a given job.

Work design has been linked to many psychological outcomes over the past 40 years: satisfaction, motivation, stress, burnout, engagement, self-efficacy and more. There are many reasons why work design has such a powerful impact on psychological phenomena, such as:

- **Work is a core aspect of life.** We derive so much from work: direction to our lives, structure to our day, a sense of who we are, opportunities to learn and grow, and more. Work is the common factor linking many of the people in our lives. For many adults, half their waking lives revolve around work, including not just work time but commuting, phone calls and emails, and more. Consequently, characteristics of work have the potential to have a powerful impact.
- **The characteristics of work design are continuously influential.** Unlike events (either negative ones, such as harassment or positive ones, such as promotions), the characteristics of one's work are present day after day. This means their influence is experienced on an almost-daily basis. Positive aspects of work can

provide regular stimulants to our self-esteem, sense of personal achievement, and feelings of self-determination. Negative aspects of work can erode and undermine these sensations. The process is gradual, but implacable.

The psychological phenomenon of *resilience*, as it is currently conceptualised, is relatively new, and there has been less attention to the relations between work design and resilience than, for example, between work design and burnout. Nevertheless, many of the 'outcomes' of work design are also correlates of resilience, suggesting a relationship between the two is likely. Furthermore, from the few studies that have explicitly examined this relationship, the results are clear: if you want employees to be resilient, it pays to invest in good work design.

This chapter describes several models of work design, along with work design characteristics in broad or narrow categories, in order to clarify how they can affect employee wellbeing in general, as well as how they relate to employee resilience in particular.

Exploring models of work design

Herzberg's Two-Factor Model. Herzberg's Two-Factor Model (or Two-Factor Theory) is one of the earliest models describing the psychological impacts of job characteristics, yet it is still referenced in modern research in this field. In short, it categorises job characteristics into two factors to address two different psychological processes. This takes a little explaining.

If you are willing to accept that job characteristics influence wellbeing, it would be easy to assume that these characteristics could be arranged on a continuum from beneficial (such as rewards and recognition) through to harmful (such as interpersonal conflict and job insecurity). Yet if this were genuinely the case, then the psychological harm associated with undesirable job characteristics (such as bullying or physical danger) could be balanced out by providing enough desirable characteristics (such as a high salary). A moment of reflection on these examples should highlight the problems with such an assumption: many people find exposure to undesirable work characteristics distressing, even if they also have access to plenty of desirable work characteristics.

Concerns about such assumptions were part of the motivation for Herzberg, Mausner, and Snyderman (1959) to propose that different work features are important for meeting different needs, and that the extent to which these different needs are met has psychological implications. Influenced by Maslow's (1943) needs hierarchy, Herzberg and his colleagues believed that people experience two distinct levels of needs: lower-level needs (which they called *hygiene*), which related to basic needs for safety, security, sustenance etc.; and higher-level *motivational* needs, comprising needs for things like personal growth and achievement. From this, Herzberg reasoned that different work characteristics were important for fulfilling different needs. Work characteristics such as safety, job security and reasonable pay were all seen as essential contributors to the basic hygiene needs, thereby preventing the emergence of employee dissatisfaction. Work characteristics such as recognition for achievement, opportunities for skill development and the chance to solve interesting and challenging problems were seen as meeting needs necessary for higher-level motivation, thereby increasing satisfaction. The work characteristics within each factor are quite diverse, but are united by the nature of the needs they fulfil.

Herzberg and colleagues (1959) argued that characteristics important for hygiene needs were necessary in order to avoid negative outcomes such as employee dissatisfaction, but they were not sufficient to ensure that employees felt motivated. As with the saying, "Money can't buy you happiness", the principle of the Two-Factor Model was that a different group of work characteristics was required to meet each need. Thus an organisation would not only need to provide reasonable pay and conditions, but would also need to invest in personal development and recognition for achievement, in order to maximise positive aspects of employee wellbeing as well as minimising negative aspects.

Think about Jill and Jen. Compared to Jen, Jill is paid more and gets to travel for work, but Jen's benefits are more than sufficient to meet her hygiene needs. In terms of motivational factors, Jen has more responsibility, better recognition, and more support for skill development than does Jill, resulting in Jen having a substantially better psychological experience of work.

Having said all that, let's look at the evidence. It should be acknowledged that the predictive power of Herzberg's model has been criticised (e.g., Hulin & Smith, 1967; King, 1970). Not every work characteristic fits only one of the two factors: for example, opportunities to interact with other people at work may be critical to meet hygiene needs, but an interactive social environment could also motivate people. Similarly, the characteristics in one factor may not influence only one type of outcome: for example, skill development opportunities, recognition for excellence and interesting work are considered motivators, but they may also play a role in diminishing dissatisfaction. Nevertheless, others have praised the model, particularly for its early recognition that achievement, recognition and growth contribute more to positive aspects of wellbeing than does salary (e.g., Sachau, 2007). Herzberg's theory was also one of the first to recognise the potential psychological benefits of enhancing challenge within work roles (Paul, Robertson & Herzberg, 1969), which influenced several more contemporary theories, such as the challenge-hindrance stressor framework[1] (Cavanaugh et al., 2000).

Herzberg's model has relevance to the relationship between work design and resilience. If some fundamental work characteristics have to be met in order to meet an employee's basic hygiene needs (and if the absence of these characteristics is likely to cause pronounced dissatisfaction), such aspects may be important for the maintenance of resilience. It may be that employees whose hygiene needs are met through ongoing safety, security and adequate remuneration at work will be more capable of handling the challenges of personal or organisational change. By contrast, work environments lacking key hygiene characteristics may undermine employees' capacity for resilience. Supporting this notion is evidence that employees experiencing long-term job insecurity use less effective stress coping strategies (e.g., venting and avoidance; Roskies, Louis-Guerin & Fournier, 1993) than do employees in more secure job roles, indicative of job insecurity diminishing resilience.

Based on the Herzberg Two-Factor Model, managers are advised to identify the basic needs you can meet for your employees. Are your pay, insurance and other conditions of employment adequate to meet those needs? Are you doing enough to provide a safe environment, one that is free of physical violence, sexual harassment and bullying? Do you offer as much job security as can be achieved within your sector? Without these things, it may not be reasonable to expect resilience from your staff.

Job Characteristics Model. A later model in this field that had an almost immediate impact (and which continues to influence modern research and practice) is Hackman and Oldham's (1976) Job Characteristics Model. Unlike Herzberg's two large and diverse factors, this model focuses on five specific job characteristics:

- *skill variety* (the opportunity to apply a range of different skills in your job);
- *task identity* (the extent to which your work activities contribute to an identifiable outcome, such as doing a small project all by yourself instead of contributing a small part to a big project);
- *task significance* (doing work that has personal meaning, possibly even making the world a better place);
- *autonomy* (the freedom to decide which goals to focus on, how to achieve them, and possibly even what your goals will be); and
- *feedback* (including written and spoken feedback from others, as well as being able to observe whether your actions are facilitating or inhibiting your success).

In addition to identifying these as some of the most psychologically-critical work design characteristics, Hackman and Oldham (1976) also specified the mechanisms by which they should have their effects on motivation and performance. They argued that feedback works by clarifying relations between cause (work actions) and effect (the impact of those actions), that autonomy works by creating a sense of responsibility for one's decisions, and that variety, significance and identity work by making one's job seem more meaningful. Hackman and Oldham argued that increasing levels of these five job characteristics in a job (a process known as *job enrichment*) would activate these mechanisms, resulting in higher levels of intrinsic work motivation.

Meta-analytic studies have supported the core propositions of the job characteristics model, showing the five job characteristics collectively relate to motivation, and to a lesser extent, work effectiveness (Fried & Ferris, 1987; Loher et al., 1985). Meta-analyses have also identified experienced meaningfulness as the most important mediating factor, and one that can be influenced by all five job characteristics (Humphrey, Nahrgang & Morgeson, 2007). Research has also supported links between the five job characteristics and such psychological states such as job satisfaction (Loher *et al.*, 1985; Saavedra & Kwun, 2000), vigor and enthusiasm (Saavedra & Kwun, 2000; Shraga & Shirom, 2009), flow (Saks, 2006), and even self-efficacy beliefs (Parker, 2003). Of the five job characteristics, autonomy and task significance are typically identified as having the greatest impact on psychological outcomes (Searle & Parker, 2013).

There are also suggestions that different work characteristics influence different psychological outcomes. For example, Saavedra and Kwun (2000) found that autonomy and significance mainly influenced relatively activated positive emotions (e.g., enthusiasm, excitement), while also reducing fatigue. Task feedback (i.e., whether the task is being performed well) had positive effects on emotions across the activation spectrum, enhancing both enthusiasm and relaxation. By contrast, skill variety was associated with less relaxation and more nervousness (despite positive effects on wellbeing being recorded in many of the studies described above). These results are consistent with the notion that different characteristics influence different processes.

Hackman and Oldham's (1976) job characteristics model has some valuable implications for supporting employee resilience. First, it introduces the job characteristic of autonomy as a key factor in the psychological experience of work. All major work design models after this point also included autonomy, as it so reliably predicts so many psychological and behavioural outcomes. To some extent, this is for the reason outlined by Hackman and Oldham: the process of making our own decisions conveys on us a sense of responsibility and accountability – you chose to do it this way, so if it doesn't work out that's your fault. However, it is now widely accepted that autonomy fulfils a critical psychological need for freedom and self-determination (Deci & Ryan, 1985), so its absence can be psychologically harmful. Beyond this, there are other benefits attributed to work autonomy, such as the way that making one's own decisions encourages active forms of coping (Karasek, 1979) and can stimulate learning (Leach *et al.*, 2005) and self-efficacy (Parker, 2003). Thus, while a sense of responsibility may not be play a major role in enhancing resilience, autonomy at work can fulfil important psychological needs and enhance confidence, learning, and coping, which are known to be important in the development of resilience (Hammond, 2004).

Something that differentiates the job characteristics model from many of the work design models before or since is the central placement of task features, such as significance. Involvement in work that seems broadly valuable and important, by activating a sense of meaningfulness, gives employees a reason to care about what they do. Employees who find their jobs meaningful may be better able to overlook some of the difficulties they face and focus on their work objectives because they see their work from a broader perspective. Consistent with this speculation, studies have shown higher levels of task significance to be associated with less psychological strain and more self-efficacy (Jex & Bliese, 1999) in correlational studies, and contribute to better work dedication and performance (Grant, 2008) in experimental studies.

Based on the job characteristics model, managers are advised to consider the levels of skill variety, task identity, task significance, autonomy and feedback in the roles performed by your employees. Can these aspects of work be enriched, to create a more motivating work experience? In particular, are there ways you can give employees more freedom over their day-to-day actions, or ways you can increase their level of involvement in higher-level decisions? Can you enhance the real-world significance of the work they do, find ways to draw attention to that significance? Such actions could be effective in developing resilience among your staff.

Demands-Resources And Challenge-Hindrance Models. The Job Demands-Resources Model (Demerouti *et al.*, 2001) is arguably the dominant work design model influencing research and practice today. Like Herzberg's model, it categorises job characteristics into two broad factors. However unlike Herzberg, the characteristics within each factor are united not only by their effects but because they share a common feature: *demands* refers to any job characteristics that require effort and/or attention (including time pressure, physical labour, complex problems, or interpersonal conflict), whereas *resources* refers to any job characteristics that facilitate the effective handling of work demands (such as work autonomy, support from peers and supervisors and opportunities for skill development). The simple predictions of the model are that (a) demands are psychologically harmful, and so they contribute to burnout; (b) resources are psychologically beneficial, and so they contribute to engagement.[2]

Research broadly supports the notion that these different categories of work characteristics affect different psychological mechanisms and even different work behaviours (Bakker & Demerouti, 2007). For example, demands contribute to exhaustion, which diminishes in-role job performance (e.g. timely task completion), whereas resources contribute to engagement, which enhances extra-role job performance (e.g. helping others; Bakker, Demerouti & Verbeke, 2004). Similarly, demand-induced burnout appears to diminish workplace safety behaviour, whereas resource-induced engagement appears to enhance safety (Nahrgang, Morgeson & Hofmann, 2011).

One implication of the model is that in order to mitigate the negative effects of demands, one could draw upon many different types of resources (depending on what is available and suitable within a given work context). However, inconsistent findings indicate that it is not so simple. It may be, for example, that the demand-buffering effect of resources depends on the suitability of a specific resource for a specific demand. Solutions have been proposed for the effective matching of resources to demands (most notably the DISC model by De Jonge & Dormann, 2006). However, there are other limitations to the model, such as the inconsistent effects of demands on engagement. Nevertheless, given the simplicity of the model, its predictive power in the research literature is strong, and its application principles are very clear.

In another popular two-category model, Cavanaugh and colleagues (2000) focused primarily on demanding work characteristics, and further differentiated these demands based on whether they supported one's goals (*challenge* demands) or whether they obstructed goal attainment (*hindrance* demands). Table 7.1 provides a comprehensive list of both challenge and hindrance demands often present in organisations. The purpose of dividing demands in this way was to address an underlying problem with stressor-strain models of wellbeing: that some aspects of work can be stressful, at least in the short-term, and yet can still lead to psychological benefits. By lumping together all of the demanding characteristics of work, we may be missing the psychological benefits associated with a subset of these demands.

The Challenge-Hindrance Model predicts that although hindrance demands should only be harmful, challenge demands have the potential to be beneficial. In their original study (Cavanaugh *et al.*, 2000), challenging work demands were associated with more satisfaction and less intention to leave, whereas hindering demands were associated with less satisfaction and more intention to leave. Other research has supported this differentiation of demand types. LePine, LePine and Jackson (2004) found challenge demands had stronger effects on learning motivation, whereas hindrance stressors had stronger effects on exhaustion. Meta-analyses by LePine, Podsakoff and LePine (2005) and Podsakoff, LePine and LePine (2007), which re-classified numerous earlier work design studies to apply the challenge-hindrance distinction, showed a consistent pattern: both types of

TABLE 7.1 Challenge demands versus hindrance demands

Challenge demands		Hindrance demands	
Example	*Why goal-supportive*	*Example*	*Why goal-obstructive*
Workload	High workload pushes people to achieve more within less time, contributing to a greater sense of achievement	Role ambiguity	Less clarity about who does what to what standard leads to time wasted on unnecessary tasks, improving substandard work, or extra communication.
Responsibility	High responsibility carries higher status, more control over decisions, and a greater sense of achievement	Role conflict	Incompatibility between different expectations (e.g. quality & quantity) means that people feel unable to adequately fulfil stated goals
Complexity	More complex work draws on more skills, with operators providing a higher level of value to the organisation, creating a greater sense of achievement	Bureaucratic processes	More steps of administrative tasks and more layers of approval can delay the execution of more critical aspects of work

demand appeared to increase psychological strain (consistent with predictions from the Job Demands-Resources Model), but challenge demands were associated with improved job satisfaction, motivation, commitment and even performance. Conversely, hindrance stressors were associated with worse attitudes and outcomes.

Research exploring the ideas proposed in the Challenge-Hindrance Model was initially conducted separately from research exploring the Job Demands-Resources Model. However, in recent years the merits of combining these theories has been examined. Crawford, LePine, and Rich (2010) presented a meta-analysis[3] showing that research into work design the data better where job resources were included alongside demands, yet demands were differentiated into challenges and hindrances. This Three-Category Model of job characteristics, called the differentiated Job Demands – Resources Model, presented several clear findings. First, resources increased engagement and reduced burnout, consistent with the Job Demands – Resources Model. Also consistent with the Job Demands – Resources Model, both types of demands increased burnout,[4] although the effect of hindrances was stronger than the effect of challenges. Finally, consistent with the challenge – hindrance model, hindrance demands reduced engagement, but challenge demands increased engagement.

The differentiated Job Demands – Resources Model has implications for supporting employee resilience. The effects of challenge and hindrance demands on resilience are addressed in the next section, so I will focus on resources and resilience. However, we have already addressed (above) the benefits of autonomy for resilience, and the role of social support was addressed in Chapter 5. Therefore, I will instead draw on Hobfoll's (1988) conservation of resources theory to explain why resources *as a whole* are valuable for resilience.

According to conservation of resources theory, people are motivated to identify, accumulate and protect resources, since this provides an evolutionary advantage. Hobfoll talks about resource maintenance and resource gain spirals, whereby the possession of some resources (e.g. time, money, fitness, friends) facilitates the preservation of existing resources, and even the accumulation of more resources through effective resource investment. Hobfoll describes how this also leads to the aggregation of multiple types of resources, rather than simply the accumulation of a single resource type, particularly in collective settings where resources can be exchanged. This may help explain why people with above-average resource levels are more resilient: they would likely have many types of resources to choose from and invest in to maintain their wellbeing in times of crisis.

This means that resource diversity seems to be critical. Managers are advised to consider not just autonomy, but the wide range of work resources available to your employees. What actions are being taken to maintain or improve peer support and co-worker relationships? Are there mechanisms and processes that encourage collaboration and teamwork? Are leaders given the training, feedback, and recognition they need to be able to support their teams effectively? Are information systems, equipment and other structural resources adequate to facilitate effective work? Does everyone have the time they need, not only to handle their own work demands but to anticipate future needs, or offer assistance to others? Such resources are important for people to build their resilience.

The role of challenge stressors in building resilience

Crane and Searle (2016) conducted a longitudinal study to investigate how different aspects of work design influence resilience over time. Using an online survey procedure, they measured challenge demands, hindrance demands, resilience and symptoms of stress (strain) in 208 working adults, with a three-month gap in between two measurement periods. What they found, results that are illustrated in Figure 7.1, highlights the importance of a sophisticated approach to work design in the maintenance and development of employee resilience.

First, Crane and Searle found that, as expected, resilience predicted strain over time. Those employees who initially felt resilient were likely to report less strain three months later. Hindrance demands also influenced strain over time, such that those who were initially experiencing high levels of hindrance demands were likely to report more strain three months later. More importantly though, for our under-standing of resilience, was that work design influenced resilience levels three months later. Specifically, for those who initially reported above-average challenge demands, resilience levels had increased three months later. However, for those who initially reported above-average hindrance demands, resilience levels had decreased three months later. Exposure to challenges helped to enhance employee resilience, while exposure to hindrances eroded employee resilience.

This is the most direct evidence yet that work design is critical to employee resilience. It shows that where work environments consistently hinder employees through bureaucratic obstacles, conflicting priorities, or unclear goals, this will

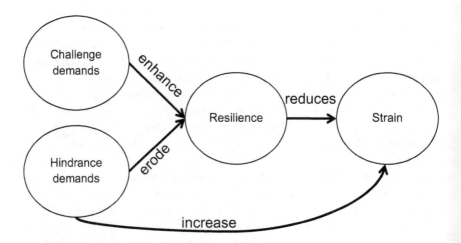

FIGURE 7.1 Relations between challenge and hindrance demands, resilience and strain

TABLE 7.2 Self-assessment and response tool

Resilience-Enhancing Features	Resilience-Eroding Features	Improvement Options
☐ Tasks make an obvious contribution to a meaningful outcome	☐ Work allocations seem arbitrary, unconnected, and meaningless	☐ Clarify how tasks affect bigger goals. Involve staff in more elements of a project so they see their impact
☐ Staff understand how their role fits alongside the roles of their peers	☐ Role boundaries are ambiguous	☐ Clarify responsibilities, priorities, and expectations, especially wherever there may be mixed messages
☐ Objectives are clearly stated and, once set, change rarely	☐ Objectives are unclear, and tend to change mid-project	☐ Set and explain goals, and try to keep these goals stable for as long as possible
☐ Considerable decision-making freedom exists over methods used to achieve objectives	☐ Staff are expected to follow set procedures and guidelines for the majority of their tasks	☐ Provide opportunities for staff to take control of their own workspaces, to determine their priorities, and to choose appropriate methods for achieving set goals
☐ Process improvements and other new ideas are encouraged	☐ Innovation is discouraged. Changes require multiple levels of approval.	☐ Actively encourage suggestions, creativity and displays of initiative. Support new approaches.
☐ Existing skills can be enhanced, new skills can be learned	☐ Little support for skill development	☐ Encourage staff to develop skills and pursue personal learning goals. Support where possible.
☐ Opportunities exist to apply a wide variety of skills	☐ Tasks are simplified to minimise error and to maximise staffing flexibility	☐ Allow staff to broaden their roles to apply a wider variety of skills. Promote development opportunities.
☐ Opportunities exist to take on higher-stakes responsibilities	☐ Higher-stakes responsibilities can only be accessed following promotion	☐ Where staff display capability, find ways for them to attempt tasks or roles involving greater responsibility
☐ Social environment is positive – staff can form relationships of mutual gain with people who respect them	☐ Social environment is negative, with incivility and disrespect (if not outright harassment) and little mutual support	☐ Model positive social behaviour by showing respect and support for all staff. Seek and challenge anyone who disrespects others. Reward cooperation.
☐ Excellence and achievement are well recognised, as is citizenship	☐ Excellence/ achievement are rarely recognized; citizenship is ignored	☐ Publicly recognise staff who help improve the work environment as well as those achieving excellence

eventually undermine employees' resilience. However, provided hindrances are kept to a minimum, exposing employees to complex projects, high levels of responsibility and stretch goals has the potential to enhance their resilience.

Clearly, Crane and Searle's work has two messages for managers. First, unless managers are doing whatever they can to minimise or eliminate factors that keep employees from doing their jobs, then – all else being equal – the workplace may be contributing to a steady decline in employee resilience. Second, if such hindrances are kept under control, and if appropriate resources are in good supply, then employees have the potential to get personal and professional benefits (including enhanced resilience) from exposure to appropriate work challenges.

Final thoughts

Now it is your turn. Does your workplace support employee resilience? Or does the environment drain the wellbeing from employees? And if the environment is not ideal, what can you do about it?

Complete the checklist (shown in Table 7.2) for either your own job or for the team you supervise. Which resilience-enhancing features are you lacking? Which resilience-eroding features require some attention? In each case, there may be actions that you, as a manager, can take to convert a less-than-ideal workplace into an environment that promotes engagement and resilience.

KEY MESSAGES FROM THIS CHAPTER

- Resilience is not just about what an individual brings to the organisation, but also the characteristics of the job.
- Managers and leaders have an important role to play in managing these job characteristics.
- Models of job design have been helpful in highlighting some of the broad categories of job characteristics that can support or erode resilience.
- Managers can help support their staff by trying to eliminate or reduce *hindrances*, those aspects of work that obstruct the accomplishment of meaningful goals.
- Managers also need to make available a broad array of *resources* that employees will be able to use to meet the demands that they face.
- If hindrances are kept to a minimum, and appropriate resources are available, managers can also help their staff become *more* resilient by providing appropriately suitable and meaningful work *challenges*.

Notes

1   This was the basis of Crane and Searle's (2016) study of work design and resilience (described later in this chapter).
2   Depending on the level of complexity you want to add, resources have also been shown to reduce burnout and even (in some studies) to mitigate the effects of demands on burnout (Bakker, Hakanen, Demerouti & Xanthopoulou, 2007).
3   A systematic review of research studies that examine similar variables, using statistics to synthesise findings into broad patterns of consistent effects across multiple studies.
4   There are some doubts about the consistency of this effect. For example, when van den Broeck, De Cuyper, De Witte & Vansteenkiste (2010) tested the same model, challenge demands did not affect burnout.

References

Bakker, A. B. & Demerouti, E. (2007). The job demands-resources model: State of the art. *Journal of Managerial Psychology, 22*, 309–328.

Bakker, A. B., Demerouti, E. & Verbeke, W. (2004). Using the job demands-resources model to predict burnout and performance. *Human Resource Management, 43*, 83–104.

Bakker, A. B., Hakanen, J. J., Demerouti, E. & Xanthopoulou, D. (2007). Job resources boost work engagement, particularly when job demands are high. *Journal of Educational Psychology, 99*, 274–284.

Cavanaugh, M. A., Boswell, W. R., Roehling, M. V. & Boudreau, J. W. (2000). An empirical examination of self-reported work stress among U.S. managers. *Journal of Applied Psychology, 85*, 65–74.

Crane, M. & Searle, B. J. (2016). Building resilience through exposure to stressors: The effects of challenges versus hindrances. *Journal of Occupational Health Psychology*.

Crawford, E. R., LePine, J. A. & Rich, B. L. (2010). Linking job demands and resources to employee engagement and burnout: a theoretical extension and meta-analytic test. *Journal of Applied Psychology, 95*, 834–848.

Deci, E. L. & Ryan, R. M. (1985). *Intrinsic motivation and self-determination in human behavior.* New York, NY: Plenum Publishing.

De Jonge, J. & Dormann, C. (2006). Stressors, resources, and strain at work: a longitudinal test of the triple-match principle. *Journal of Applied Psychology, 91*, 1359–1374.

Demerouti, E., Bakker, A. B., Nachreiner, F. & Schaufeli, W. B. (2001). The job demands-resources model of burnout. *Journal of Applied Psychology, 86*, 499–512.

Fried, Y. & Ferris, G. R. (1987). The validity of the job characteristics model: A review and meta-analysis. *Personnel Psychology, 40*, 287–322.

Grant, A. M. (2008). The significance of task significance: Job performance effects, relational mechanisms, and boundary conditions. *Journal of Applied Psychology, 93*, 108–124.

Hackman, J. R. & Oldham, G. R. (1976). Motivation through the design of work: Test of a theory. *Organizational Behavior and Human Performance, 16*, 250–279.

Hammond, C. (2004). Impacts of lifelong learning upon emotional resilience, psychological and mental health: fieldwork evidence. *Oxford Review of Education, 30*, 551–568.

Herzberg, F., Mausner, B. & Snyderman, B. (1959). *The Motivation to Work.* New York, NY: John Wiley.

Hobfoll, S. E. (1988). *The ecology of stress.* New York, NY: Taylor & Francis.

Hulin, C. L. & Smith, P. A. (1967). An empirical investigation of two implications of the two factor theory of job satisfaction. *Journal of Applied Psychology, 51*, 396–402.

Humphrey, S. E., Nahrgang, J. D. & Morgeson, F. P. (2007). Integrating motivational, social, and contextual work design features: a meta-analytic summary and theoretical extension of the work design literature. *Journal of Applied Psychology, 92*, 1332–1356.

Jex, S. M. & Bliese, P. D. (1999). Efficacy beliefs as a moderator of the impact of work-related stressors: a multilevel study. *Journal of Applied Psychology, 84*, 349–361.

Karasek, R. (1979). Job demands, job decision latitude, and mental strain: Implications for job redesign. *Administrative Science Quarterly, 24*, 285–306.

King, N. (1970). Clarification and evaluation of the two-factor theory of job satisfaction. *Psychological Bulletin, 74*, 18–31.

Leach, D. J., Wall, T. D., Rogelberg, S. G. & Jackson, P. R. (2005). Team autonomy, performance, and member job strain: Uncovering the teamwork KSA link. *Applied Psychology: An International Review, 54*, 1–24.

LePine, J. A., LePine, M. A. & Jackson, C. (2004). Challenge and hindrance stress: Relationships with exhaustion, motivation to learn, and learning performance. *Journal of Applied Psychology, 89*, 883–891.

LePine, J. A., Podsakoff, N. P. & LePine, M. A. (2005). A meta-analytic test of the challenge stressor-hindrance stressor framework: An explanation for inconsistent relationships among stressors and performance. *Academy of Management Journal, 48*, 767–775.

Loher, B. T., Noe, R. A., Moeller, N. L. & Fitzgerald, M. P. (1985). A meta-analysis of the relation of job characteristics to job satisfaction. *Journal of Applied Psychology, 70*, 280–289.

Maslow, A. H. (1943). A theory of motivation. *Psychological Review, 50*, 370–396.

Nahrgang, J. D., Morgeson, F. P. & Hofmann, D. A. (2011). Safety at work: a meta-analytic investigation of the link between job demands, job resources, burnout, engagement, and safety outcomes. *Journal of Applied Psychology, 96*, 71–94.

Parker, S. K. (2003). Longitudinal effects of lean production on employee outcomes and the mediating role of work characteristics. *Journal of Applied Psychology, 88*, 620–634.

Paul, W. J., Robertson, K. B. & Herzberg, F. (1969). Job enrichment pays off. *Harvard Business Review, 47*, 61–78.

Podsakoff, N. P., LePine, J. A. & LePine, M. A. (2007). Differential challenge stressor-hindrance stressor relationships with job attitudes, turnover intentions, turnover, and withdrawal behavior: a meta-analysis. *Journal of Applied Psychology, 92*, 438–454.

Roskies, E., Louis-Guerin, C. & Fournier, C. (1993). Coping with job insecurity: How does personality make a difference? *Journal of Organizational Behavior, 14*, 617–630.

Saavedra, R. & Kwun, S. K. (2000). Affective states in job characteristics theory. *Journal of Organizational Behavior, 21*, 131–146.

Sachau, D. A. (2007). Resurrecting the motivation-hygiene theory: Herzberg and the positive psychology movement. *Human Resource Development Review, 6*, 377–393.

Saks, A. M. (2006). Antecedents and consequences of employee engagement. *Journal of Managerial Psychology, 21*, 600–619.

Searle, B. J. & Parker, S. K. (2013). Work design and happiness: An active, reciprocal perspective. In S. A. David, I. Boniwell & A. Conley Ayers (eds) *Oxford handbook of happiness*, pp. 711–732. Oxford: Oxford University Press.

Shraga, O. & Shirom, A. (2009). The construct validity of vigor and its antecedents: A qualitative study. *Human Relations, 62*, 271–291.

van den Broeck, A., De Cuyper, N., De Witte, H. & Vansteenkiste, M. (2010). Not all job demands are equal: Differentiating job hindrances and job challenges in the Job Demands – Resources model. *European Journal of Work and Organizational Psychology, 19*, 735–759.

8

WORK, REST AND PLAY

The importance of brief and daily rest for employee resilience

Frances McMurtrie and Dr. Monique F. Crane

The concept of work, rest and play is well known. Nearly every role imaginable has specific working hours, and traditionally, the time outside of those hours were the employees' to enjoy. However, with the introduction of the internet, and ability for people to work remotely, the boundary between work and the remainder of employees' days have become blurred. Now the average working week is no longer constrained to 40 hours Monday to Friday, and employees can be reached at any time of the day, any day of the week thanks to mobile phones and email. This might sound great from a productivity perspective. After all, what's wrong with having a workforce available at all hours of the day for the same cost as a traditional 9 to 5 role? The problem is that this way of working neglects employees' need for recovery from the strain of the workday, and this has serious implications for their personal wellbeing, and their employment performance.

Prior research shows that recovery during daily respite, such as in evenings and weekends, is associated with enhanced wellbeing, work engagement and next-day job performance (Sonnentag, 2003; Totterdell *et al.*, 1995). Conversely, failure to recover frequently from stressors leads to the chronic accumulation of stress and has implications for longer-term physical and mental health (e.g., Brosschot, Gerin & Thayer, 2006; Geurts & Sonnentag, 2006). Taken together, the above research suggests that daily respite periods are an important opportunity to facilitate psychological resilience by assisting employees regularly recover from daily work stress. Fortunately, it is not the time available for the rest that matters, but rather the *quality* of the rest experience (Westman & Eden, 1997). Given the increasingly limited time available for daily rest it is critically important to maximise the psychological benefit gained from daily respite for the management of chronic job stress. In this chapter, we will review the factors that contribute to effective recovery from work, and practical steps employers and employees can take to maximise the effectiveness of rest periods experienced by employees.

The importance of recovery and psychological detachment from work

Recovery from work refers to the process of reducing the physical, mental and emotional strain that is caused by job stressors (Craig & Cooper, 1992). This means that an individual's resources that are normally called upon during work are given time to be revived during non-work time (Meijman & Mulder, 1998; Zijlstra & Sonnentag, 2006). Research investigating how well employees are able to recover from work has demonstrated that the quality of this recovery process has important impacts on wellbeing and job-related behaviours. It may seem like common sense that time spent resting after or between work periods is beneficial and worthwhile for employees. What is less understood; however, is how this time 'recovering' from work should be spent to most effectively support an individual's wellbeing, and also their performance in their employment.

A particularly important aspect of the recovery process during leisure time appears to be psychological detachment from work. The notion of psychological detachment from work was introduced by Sonnentag and Bayer (2005) in an effort to describe ideal circumstances for recovery from work strain. Psychological detachment means that the employee is able to completely refrain from any work-related activities and not even think about job-related activities (Sonnentag & Fritz, 2015). It might be useful at this point to consider how often you are psychologically detached your work. If psychological detachment from work is not something that you are achieving often when not physically at work then it may be the same for your employees.

Psychological detachment from work is a critical aspect of the recovery process and means more than simply not being at work. The effect of a bad day at work can impact how employees feel after the workday is complete. For example, an employee may find that if they experience a particularly stressful day at work, when they arrive home their mood will be low as a result of their difficult day. This can have carry-over effects whereby the individual may experience difficulties with their family or friends, or feel unable to effectively 'switch-off' from their difficult day as a result of their low mood. The challenge is that greater job stress is actually thought to reduce the ability to become psychologically detached from work (Sonnentag, Kuttler & Fritz, 2010). The lack of psychological detachment is then likely to mean that there is limited recovery. Experiencing an evening like this will further contribute to the employee's low mood, and will prevent them from achieving high quality recovery time from their workday. This lack of recovery will then negatively impact the employee's ability to perform well at work the following day (Sonnentag & Binnewies, 2013). Most people have probably experienced feeling worried or pre-occupied about their work after the workday is complete. You might not really engage with your family during the evening, or spend the night sleeping poorly as a result of your work worries. This is what happens when employees fail to detach effectively from work at the end of each day. Even though they are no longer at work, they continue to think about it after hours. This thinking stops them from fully engaging with their life outside of work, and from achieving effective recovery. This is a negative cycle whereby a difficult day at work can lead to a difficult night, which in turn leads to fatigue, low mood and disengagement in work the following day, and so this pattern will continue. Perhaps this is a cycle that seems familiar. It is for this reason that achieving high quality recovery time from work is incredibly important. To do so, employees must be able to successfully "detach" themselves from their workday.

There is extensive research regarding the importance of detachment from work, and how this improves employee mood and engagement after hours, and work performance the following day. Effective psychological detachment during breaks and after work has been shown to assist employees with managing job demands, and in protecting their well-being and work engagement (Sonnentag, Binnewies and Mojza, 2010). For instance, Sonnentag, Binnewies, and Mojza (2010) found that low psychological detachment from work during non-work time predicted greater emotional exhaustion over the course of one year. Hahn, Binnewies, and Haun (2012) identified that when psychological detachment over a weekend was low there was an increase in the employee's negative emotional state. Furthermore, achieving psychological detachment between or after work shifts is positively associated with employee engagement and proactive behaviour the following day (Sonnentag, 2003). The consequences of not achieving psychological detachment during work breaks are also well established. Poor psychological detachment can lead to high levels of emotional exhaustion and physical illness. These in turn can increase the need for effective recovery from work, which cannot be achieved without psychological detachment. In summary, recovery and psychological detachment from work has important benefits when it is achieved, but can lead to health and performance problems when it is not.

"But, I am always working and I am totally fine"

At this point some readers might be thinking, "but I am always working and I am totally fine!". If this is you, then it is possible that your work gives you an enormous sense of mastery, meaning, and satisfaction. These experiences are also important for wellbeing and resilience as well, but we cannot assume that our employees experience them to the same extent.

How to make rest effective

We have established so far in this chapter that: (1) rest between work periods is important for employee wellbeing and performance and (2) psychological detachment from work is necessary in order for employees to engage in effective rest. We will now look at factors that make the rest period itself effective. There are four main factors that need to be taken into account in order to optimise the effectiveness of rest: (1) enjoyment, (2) home environment, (3) work characteristics and (4) timing.

(1) Enjoyment. First, the activities undertaken during the rest period must be enjoyed by the employee. A break in and of itself is not enough, the employee must be engaged in something they personally find enjoyable to facilitate effective recovery. Interestingly, even if the employee is engaged in work-related activities during their break, if this is something they find personally enjoyable he/she will still benefit from the break period. Equally, if they engage in something typically considered to be enjoyable (i.e. social activities) but do not have a good time, this will actually negatively impact on the effectiveness of their break (Oerlemans, Bakker & Demerouti, 2014). Furthermore, it is understood that employee enjoyment in both their work and non-work activities is important for recovery. The combination of enjoyable work and enjoyable non-work activities is positively associated with high quality recovery. A combination of unpleasant and effortful work negatively impacts on an employee's quality of recovery (van Hooff *et al.*, 2011).

(2) Home environment. The home environment of the employee and in particular with whom they share their home appears to affect psychological detachment from work. Research demonstrates that ability to detach is affected by the ability of the employee's partner to also detach and achieve effective rest. In this scenario, a person may be feeling reasonably detached from their work, however when their partner arrives home from what could have been a stressful day, they will want to discuss this with the first person, and ruminate on the issues they experienced at work throughout the evening. Through this interaction, the first person is likely to reflect on their own workplace to relate their partner's stories to their own experience. In this way, if the employee's partner has difficulty detaching from their work then it is likely that this will affect the ability of the employee to also detach. What is interesting however is that when children are present in this environment, the interaction effect between the partner's failure to detach is minimised. This may be because children require their parents' attention, and thus the adults are unable to remain fixated on work for the evening and inadvertently achieve detachment (Hahn & Dormann, 2013).

It has also been shown that the activities each partner engages in after work will impact on their own and each other's ability to recover. Women who engage in more housekeeping activities after work will experience higher stress levels than if they had engaged in more social or leisure activities. However, if their spouses engage in more housekeeping than social or leisure activities, women's stress levels actually decrease (Saxbe, Repetti & Graesch, 2011), thus promoting higher recovery quality (at the expense of their partners' recovery!).

(3) Work characteristics. The impact of work characteristics on recovery requires some special attention because this is where managers can really take matters into their own hands. Research has demonstrated that the characteristics of an individual's employment also affect their ability to recover effectively. Aspects like the number of work hours, hours of overtime, and time pressure tend to reduce the capacity for psychological detachment (e.g., Burke, Koyuncu & Fiksenbaum,

2009; Kinnunen, Feldt & Siltaloppi, 2011; Sonnentag & Bayer, 2005). Moreover, jobs that are highly complex and require complex decision making or focused attention are also associated with a lack of psychological detachment (Oosthuizen, Mostert & Koekemoer, 2011). Emotional demands at work may also make detachment difficult, this includes where jobs require a display of an emotion other than the one actually felt (e.g., flight attendant) or where the role is emotionally taxing (e.g., counsellor, university employees) (Sonnentag et al., 2010; Oosthuizen et al., 2011). These aspects of a role are often fairly difficult to change and are likely to be intrinsic to the job-role. In these situations, as a manager it is useful to be aware that as a consequence of these factors it is likely that employees are going to be less likely to detach from work, therefore it may be prudent to focused on helping employees with their ability to detach (e.g., mindfulness training). Moreover, managers need to be more mindful of any tendencies they have to engage employees in work in non-work time (e.g., emails, phone-calls, text messaging).

In contrast to the above work characteristics, there are other characteristics that a manager is likely to have a direct impact on. Some research has identified a relationship between role ambiguity (i.e., the employee is not quite sure what their role requires) and lower detachment from work (Sonnentag & Fritz, 2007). This is more likely to be the case for those employees new to the organisation or employees who are early in their career. Social stressors like workplace interpersonal conflict are also associated with less detachment (Demsky, 2012). Moreover, work-related activities using email or phone during non-work time are also unsurprisingly related to less detachment (Park, Fritz & Jex, 2011). These are all aspects of the job role that managers can do something about. For example, role ambiguity can be managed by providing clear guidance to employees about their job-requirement, goals, role and reports. For early career or new employees this could be extended to coaching or mentorship as they become adjusted to their role and the organisation. Moreover, providing constructive feedback to employees can also help to resolve ambiguity. In terms of interpersonal conflict, managers can empower employees to address these issues by providing appropriate training in handling challenging conversations and negotiation skills. Where necessary, managers can also intervene to mediate interpersonal conflict between team members, and support them to identify and follow appropriate resolution steps that protect the interests of both parties. When it comes to establishing boundaries regarding work-related activities in the home, Park and colleagues (2011) found that a strong work team culture in favour of separating work and home life was associated with higher detachment from work. Thus, a manager can establish clear boundaries for work and non-work time.

There are also some job characteristics that can actually improve the ability to detach from work. Employees offered work-related learning and opportunities for personal development are more likely to report higher levels of recovery and relaxation (Jalonen et al., 2015). Higher levels of autonomy and control over one's work can also contribute to effective recovery (Oosthuizen et al., 2011). In this regard, managers can work closely with their team members to build their skills in core decision-making areas of their roles, until the employee is able to demonstrate competence in acting on their judgement alone. It is recommended that managers start small with this approach by not providing employees with direction for any given situation or task, but instead asking the employee what they themselves would do. When the employee provides their response, the manager can give them feedback if their response is not at the level of judgement required and direction can be given as needed. Once the employee is consistently responding with appropriate judgement calls, the manager can then empower the employee to apply their own judgement without first checking with the manager if their approach is correct. Some employees need support with regards to confidence in this area before they can experience role autonomy, but once established, will feel a greater sense of control and ownership of their role.

(4) Timing. The fourth factor that contributes to effective recovery is the timing of activities and breaks. In relation to activities, employees who completed activities they preferred earlier in their work shift experience higher levels of recovery (Hunter & Wu, 2015). In relation to breaks, frequent short breaks help sustain an employee's resources throughout the day. The earlier in the day they are taken, the more effective these breaks are (Hunter & Wu, 2015).

Practical strategies to help employees recover effectively

A large health services provider had a large cohort of staff who repeatedly requested structured 'Rostered Days Off' (RDOs) to be allowed, in order to counteract the perceived high potential for burn-out associated with their roles. The organisation was not in a position to pay for this, and the shift-work nature of the organisation's activities did not align well to an RDO model. When questioned about their request, the staff involved stated that they would likely use the extra day off each fortnight to complete activities such as going to the bank, taking their family members to appointments, and catching up on personal administration. Even if the organisation had been in a position to support RDOs, if this was how the employees intended to spend their extra time off, it is quite clear that no real recovery was likely to occur (unless they really enjoyed admin tasks!). Instead, the organisation would have been better placed to introduce some of the following strategies to help improve employee's recovery from work and reduce the need for additional time off each fortnight.

Education. The first step in helping employees to use their rest time effectively for recovery is to provide education about the importance of effective recovery. Without this, any policies or processes put in place to support effective recovery will not be fully understood or appreciated, and the full benefit will not be realised for the employees or the organisation. As explained throughout this chapter, recovering from work is not just about not physically being at work. Supporting employees to understand this will greatly enhance their wellbeing. An education programme could take several forms, including formal training sessions, e-learning or a mentoring programme. Whichever model is selected the recovery education programme should provide employees with the following information:

1   The importance of effective recovery for their wellbeing and employment performance
2   The importance of effective detachment from work each day
3   How to achieve effective recovery through:

  •   Engaging in enjoyable activities during time away from work
  •   Prioritising enjoyable work activities earlier in the work day
  •   Supporting family members to also effectively detach from their work day

Organisational policy and practice

Supporting effective recovery can also be achieved through organisational policy and practice. Here are some steps that an organisation can take:

Electronic sundown. To support effective detachment, organisations must look for ways to counter the ever-connectedness we now experience thanks to technology. One way to achieve this is to establish communication boundaries for employees by setting an Electronic Sundown policy, which states no work communications are to occur outside of business hours. This reduces the pressure felt by employees to always be available, and will help them to detach effectively as they will not always be waiting for the next email or phone call from their boss each evening and weekend.

Agreed after-hours communication times. If an Electronic Sundown does not suit the organisation's operating model, consider negotiating with employees about when they are willing to be reached after hours. It may be that they do not wish to be contacted in the evenings after work, but they are happy to be available for a few hours each Saturday. Establishing agreed after-hours communication times provide the employees with control over their working hours. As aforementioned, control over one's work contributes to effective recovery.

Break targets. As we have established, taking frequent breaks and engaging in enjoyable activities during breaks is imperative to effective recovery and work performance. An initiative that supports this is to establish suitable break targets for each employee. By requiring each employee to take a minimum of three effective breaks throughout the day, an organisation will benefit from their workforce's improved productivity and effectiveness in their roles, compared to if no breaks were taken. As mentioned, control is an important aspect of supporting effective recovery. It is important that break targets for each employee are established with their input. Finding out when will best suit each employee to take a break, and what enjoyable activities they will engage in during their break will respect the importance of each employee having control over their work environment.

Job crafting and career progression. A common theme throughout the research regarding effective recovery is that of enjoyment. It is important for effective recovery that employees enjoy their work, and enjoy their time away from work. Managers can aid this by supporting employees to focus on aspects of their employment they most enjoy through job crafting and career progression opportunities. This can be practically achieved through the formal performance appraisal system whereby at each review, employees are asked to specify which aspects of their role they find most enjoyable, and collaboratively set targets for the subsequent review period in these areas. Further, career progression goals can be aligned to these key areas of enjoyment for each employee, and thereby tailored to each employee's preferences.

Alternatively, if the organisation does not utilise a formal performance appraisal system, managers can support their employees to craft their role to their areas of interest and enjoyment through other means. Establishing a framework for managers to speak to their team members about what they enjoy most about their role, and minimum frequencies for these conversations to take place will provide the organisation with the information they need to offer each employee opportunities aligned to their interests and areas of enjoyment.

Accountability for recovery. It is vital that employees are supported to take responsibility for their own effective recovery, in order to ensure that any recovery oriented policies and practices are supported by the workforce. A 'buddy system' for effective recovery is one way to achieve this. This system requires each employee to be allocated or to choose a buddy. The buddies will be accountable to one another for their recovery activities each week. For example, a buddy pair may meet each week to discuss their recovery activities undertaken that week, and to agree to recovery activity goals for the week ahead. The following week, those goals can be reviewed and discussed. Moreover, group based recovery sessions are also applicable for break periods during work hours, with both relaxation and physical activities found to increase the effectiveness of time spent in recovery from work (Coffeng *et al.*, 2015).

Final thoughts

It is hoped that by understanding the high importance of effective recovery for employees, and incorporating some of these suggested strategies into the organ-isation managers will have the tools to support their workforce to value their rest. This in turn will protect employee wellbeing, and provide the organisation with greater levels of productivity and effectiveness.

KEY MESSAGES FROM THIS CHAPTER

- Employees who recover effectively from their workday have greater wellbeing, work engagement and performance.
- Managers play an important role in establishing a work environment that enables employees to achieve effective recovery.
- Successful recovery from work requires employees to effectively detach from their jobs.
- Effective detachment involves first disengaging from the work environment (both physical and online) and then actively engaging in an enjoyable activity.
- Regular breaks throughout the workday can also support recovery from work strain, as long as the employee achieves detachment during each break.

References

Brosschot, J. F., Gerin, W. & Thayer, J. F. (2006). The perseverative cognition hypothesis: A review of worry, prolonged stress-related activation, and health. *Journal of Psychosomatic Research, 60*, 113–124.

Burke, R. J., Koyuncu, M. & Fiksenbaum, L. (2009). Benefits of recovery after work among Turkish manufacturing managers and professionals. *Education, Business and Society: Contemporary Middle Eastern Issues, 2*, 109–122.

Coffeng, J., van Sluijs, E., Hendriksen, I., van Mechelen, W. & Boot, C. (2015). Physical activity and relaxation during and after work are independently associated with the need for recovery. *Journal of Physical Activity and Health, 12*, 109–115.

Craig, A. & Cooper, R. E. (1992). Symptoms of acute and chronic fatigue. In A. P. Smith & D. M. Jones (eds), *Handbook of human performance* (Vol. 3, pp. 289–339). London: Academic Press.

Demsky, C. A. (2012). Interpersonal conflict and employee well-being: The moderating role of recovery experiences. *Dissertations and Theses*. Paper 766.

Geurts, S. A. E. & Sonnentag, S. (2006). Recovery as an explanatory mechanism in the relation between acute stress reactions and chronic health impairment. *Scandinavian Journal of Work, Environment, and Health, 32*, 482–492.

Hahn, V., Binnewies, C. & Haun, S. (2012). The role of partners for employees' recovery during the weekend. *Journal of Vocational Behavior, 80*, 288–298.

Hahn, V. & Dormann, C. (2013). The role of partners and children for employees' psychological detachment from work and well-being. *Journal of Applied Psychology, 98*, 26–36.

Hunter, E. M. & Wu, C. (2015). Give me a better break: choosing workday break activities to maximize resource recovery. *Journal of Applied Psychology, 101*, 302–311.

Jalonen, N., Kinnunen, M.-L., Pulkkinen, L. & Kokko, K. (2015). Job skill discretion and emotion control strategies as antecedents of recovery from work. *European Journal of Work and Organizational Psychology, 24*, 389–401.

Kinnunen, U., Feldt, T., Siltaloppi, M. & Sonnentag, S. (2011). Job demands – resources model in the context of recovery: Testing recovery experiences as mediators. *European Journal of Work and Organizational Psychology*, *20*, 805–832.

Meijman, T. & Mulder, G. (1998). Psychological aspects of workload. In P. J. Drenth & H. Theirry (eds), *Handbook of work and organizational psychology: Vol. 2. Work psychology* (pp. 5–33). Hove, England: Psychology Press.

Oerlemans, W. G. M., Bakker, A. B. & Demerouti, E. (2014). How feeling happy during off-job activities helps successful recovery from work: A day reconstruction study. *Work and Stress*, *28*, 198–216.

Oosthuizen, J., Mostert, K. & Koekemoer, F. (2011). Job characteristics, work-nonwork interferences and the role of recovery strategies among employees in a tertiary institution. *SA Journal of Human Resource Management*, *9*, 1-15, retrieved from: www.sajhrm.co.za/index.php/sajhrm/article/view/356

Park, Y., Fritz, C. & Jex, S. M. (2011). Relationships between work-home segmentation and psychological detachment from work: the role of communication technology use at home. *Journal of Occupational Health Psychology*, *16*, 457–467.

Saxbe, D. E., Repetti, R. L. & Graesch, A. P. (2011). Time spent in housework and leisure: Links with parent's physiological recovery from work. *Journal of Family Psychology*, *25*, 271–281.

Sonnentag, S. (2003). Recovery, work engagement, and proactive behavior: A new look at the interface between nonwork and work. *Journal of Applied Psychology*, *88*, 518–528.

Sonnentag, S. & Bayer, U. (2005). Switching off mentally: predictors and consequences of psychological detachment from work during off-job time. *Journal of Occupational Health Psychology*, *10*, 393–414.

Sonnentag, S. & Binnewies, C. (2013). Daily affect spillover from work to home: Detachment from work and sleep as moderators. *Journal of Vocational Behavior*, *83*, 198–208.

Sonnentag, S., Binnewies, C. & Mojza, E. J. (2010). Staying well and engaged when demands are high: The role of psychological detachment. *Journal of Applied Psychology*, *95*, 965–976.

Sonnentag, S. & Fritz, C. (2015). Recovery from job stress: The stressor_detachment model as an integrative framework. *Journal of Organizational Behavior*, *36*, S72-S103.

Sonnentag, S. & Fritz, C. (2007). The recovery experience questionnaire: development and validation of a measure for assessing recuperation and unwinding from work. *Journal of Occupational Health Psychology*, *12*, 204–221.

Sonnentag, S., Kuttler, I. & Fritz, C. (2010). Job stressors, emotional exhaustion, and need for recovery: A multi-source study on the benefits of psychological detachment. *Journal of Vocational Behavior*, *76*, 355–365.

Totterdell, P., Spelten, E., Smith, L., Barton, J. & Folkard, S. (1995). Recovery from work shifts: How long does it take? *Journal of Applied Psychology*, *80*, 43–57.

van Hooff, M. L. M., Geurts, S. A. E., Beckers, D. G. J. & Kompier, M. A. J. (2011). Daily recovery from work: The role of activities, effort and pleasure. *Work & Stress*, *25*, 55–74.

Westman, M. & Eden, D. (1997). Effects of a respite from work on burnout: Vacation relief and fade-out. *Journal of Applied Psychology*, *82*, 516–527.

Zijlstra, F. R. & Sonnentag, S. (2006). After work is done: Psychological perspectives on recovery from work. *European Journal of Work and Organizational Psychology*, *15*, 129–138.

PART 4

Creating a resilient team

9

TEAM RESILIENCE

Shaping up for the challenges ahead

Professor Jill Flint-Taylor and
Professor Sir Cary L. Cooper

Introducing the idea of team resilience

The term "team resilience" is not widely used, although it appears to be more common now than it used to be – reflecting an upsurge of interest in the general topic of resilience in the workplace. When it does appear, for example when the stated aim of a training intervention is to improve team resilience, it often refers to the combined personal resilience of the individual team members. Yet, team resilience is not synonymous with personal resilience (Alliger *et al.*, 2015). Consider a scenario where your team recruits a new member to replace someone who has left. This is a situation that we are likely to all be familiar with. Arguably if team resilience were simply made up of the personal resilience of team members, then it would increase or decrease in a straightforward way depending on whether the new team member was more or less resilient than the person who left. However, what if this team member exhibited behaviour that undermines other team members and challenges the morale of the team? In this scenario, there would be a negative impact on team resilience above and beyond the change in individual-level resilience, especially if the team's manager fails to act quickly to address the issue. We see team resilience as a useful concept that incorporates, but goes beyond, the collective personal resilience of individuals that make up a team to include a number of other factors that strengthen the team's response to pressure. Team resilience is also distinct from related concepts such as performance, effectiveness, wellbeing or engagement in the team.

The distinction between personal and team level resilience is central to our approach and to our discussion here. In our previous research, we have described personal resilience as "being able to bounce back from setbacks and to keep going in the face of tough demands and difficult circumstances, including the enduring strength that builds from coping well with challenging or stressful events" (Cooper, Flint-Taylor & Pearn, 2013, p.15). We agree that such definitions can equally be applied to teams and other groups (West, Patera & Carsten, 2009, p.253). That is, teams can also bounce back from setbacks or difficulties that impact the team as a whole and can develop as a result the team-based qualities that allow the capacity for resilience.

We also see team resilience as distinct from organisational resilience. There are many models of organisational resilience from the perspective of disaster recovery and the sustained functioning of organisational systems and processes (e.g. Somers, 2009). While in principle these models and related research findings may be applied to groups smaller than whole organisations, the general approach has limited relevance to the kind of group that constitutes a team.

Defining team resilience

In view of the many different definitions of personal resilience and the general move away from a trait-based perspective towards defining resilience in terms of process and outcome (Reich, Zautra & Hall, 2010), it can be useful to treat "resilience" as an umbrella term rather than as a unitary construct (Peterson & Seligman, 2004). This is also a useful principle to apply to "team resilience". Nevertheless, we need to be clear that team resilience is distinct from, and provides added value over and above, related constructs such as that of the high performing team.

For our broad, "umbrella" definition of team resilience we apply the process and outcome view, and refer to the processes of managing pressure effectively across the team as a whole, and the outcomes of doing so that further strengthen the capacity of the team to deal with future challenges and adversity. As with personal resilience, the management of pressure and adversity are integral to the construct of team resilience. So, while team resilience and team performance are related, they are not the same thing. For example, while it is to be hoped that building a team's resilience will help to improve the team's performance, there will be situational factors unrelated to the management of pressure that influence performance outcomes. Similarly, a team may be seen as high performing at one point in time, but fail to sustain this performance in the face of a market downturn or other adverse conditions. A team that performs well even in the face of adversity, experiencing relatively slight reductions in performance despite hardship as well as growing stronger in the process, could be considered to be demonstrating and building team resilience. Seen in this way, team resilience may be considered a "capacity of the team – something a team may possess, whether or not a challenge is present" (Alliger et al., 2015, p. 178).

Research on team resilience in a nutshell

Over the past ten years or so, the concept of team resilience has been put forward and explored from several different perspectives. These include a systems approach (Edson, 2012), positive psychology (West et al., 2009) and the management of posttraumatic stress (Paton, 2003). Nevertheless, it is still very early days in the study of team resilience, with relatively little progress since Bradley West and his colleagues observed that: "The question of how to maintain and sustain resilient team performance via effective workforce development strategies remains under-researched in the literature" (West *et al.*, 2009, p.254). Their own investigation of the issue explored team optimism, team resilience and team efficacy ("team level positive psychological capacities"), as distinct predictors of team outcomes (e.g. cohesion, cooperation, coordination, conflict, and team satisfaction). To measure team resilience, West and colleagues used a direct adaptation of an individual resilience measure, the PsyCap questionnaire (Luthans *et al.*, 2007), producing items such as: "Our team usually manages difficulties one way or another when working". The results of their study showed a significant relationship between team resilience and better team functioning with respect to all the outcomes they measured.

While West and colleagues developed their constructs and measures of team resilience through extrapolation from the study of individual resilience, Blatt (2009) extrapolated a different set of team resilience constructs and measures from inferences made by group researchers who had not set out to study resilience directly. In reviewing the "antecedents of team resilience", Blatt cites the example of an inference made by a group of researchers about the positive impact that accumulated knowledge and variety in group composition could be expected to have on the group's resources and efficacy. For her own study on entrepreneurial teams, Blatt drew on her review of these "antecedents" and adapted items from related questionnaires to produce the following team resilience survey items: (1) we talk about mistakes and ways to learn from them; (2) when unexpected challenges occur, we discuss how we could have prevented them; (3) we look for creative ways to alter difficult situations; (4) regardless of what happens to us, we can control our reaction to it; (5) we can grow in positive ways by dealing with difficult situations; and (6) we actively look for ways to overcome the challenges we encounter. These items reflect the presence of certain resilient team behaviours such as learning from past difficulty and challenges and collective re-appraisal of difficulties as team growth opportunities. These approaches to adversity are embedded in *team norms* (i.e., an endorsed set of rules or standards that direct team behaviour; Turner, 1991). Sometimes team norms are referred to as 'team culture', but basically it amounts to group behaviours that allow the capacity for resilience to set the scene for team resilience. The work of West and colleagues and that of Blatt helped to operationalise the construct of team resilience and to provide evidence in support of the view that team resilience is not simply the aggregated personal resilience of individual team members.

More recent findings include: the importance of developing collective positive emotions to help teams to foster team resilience and improve their performance (Meneghel, Salanova & Martínez, 2016); the identification of four main resilient characteristics of elite sport teams (Morgan, Fletcher & Sarkar, 2013); the way a group of individuals with a similarly positive disposition benefits team effectiveness in a crisis situation (Kaplan, LaPort & Waller, 2013).

One of the most recent and comprehensive accounts of team resilience to date (Alliger *et al.*, 2015) describes what the authors refer to as the "three behavioural strategies" and also as the "three team resilience strategies" that resilient teams use to deal with pressures, stressors and difficult circumstances. The three strategies are labelled "*minimise, manage, and mend*", and are illustrated by the authors through reference to several specific behaviours associated with each. Alliger and colleagues also set out four sets of actions that leaders can take: (1) ensure access to the right tools and documents (e.g. guides); (2) run team resilience training/facilitated sessions; (3) conduct post-challenge debriefs and (4) create the right "team resilience" culture. The themes from these research studies will be expanded on later in this chapter.

Team resilience: the manager's role

One of the most important differences between team and individual resilience lies in the temporary nature of teams. Personal resilience tends to be relatively stable over time, although it can be improved or undermined by specific circumstances or interventions. Team resilience, on the other hand, is often more transient in nature. For example, as alluded to earlier, the entry or departure of a single individual can have a significant impact on the climate and behaviour of a team. This is particularly the case when that individual is the manager. Our view is that a manager holds the primary responsibility for ensuring that their team as a whole is in good shape and able to bounce back, although of course everyone has a part to play. When it comes to developing the personal resilience of team members, it is the other way round. The onus is on each individual and the manager's role is a support one.

A central theme of this book is the essential part that managers play in building resilience. Chapter 1 set the scene for this by reporting two important conclusions from recent research and organisational practice. First, there is no doubt that employees' experience of stress is significantly affected by management practices and process. This has been well understood for many years, and has been the subject of many studies, policies and practical interventions, leading to comprehensive, evidence-based frameworks such as the UK Health and Safety Executive's 'management standards' approach (Yarker *et al.*, 2008). Second, a newer research trend has established that by targeting the way managers shape the work environment, organisations can go beyond stress management to build resilience for the longer term (Piccolo & Colquitt, 2006).

Fundamentally, this is a particular angle on good management practice. There is no doubt that it is valuable for managers to develop their specific understanding of stress and personal resilience. However, by far the greatest impact, whether positive or negative, derives from the way teams and organisations are managed overall. This in turn depends on a wide range of skills related to developing capability, managing performance, creating a positive team climate, and so on. Another critical factor is leadership style, both at the level of the individual leader, and at the level of the leadership team. Later in this chapter we explore the relationship between leaders' personality and style on the one hand, and how they manage pressure for themselves and for their teams, on the other.

A framework for building team resilience

We turn now to a framework for understanding and managing some of the elements and processes that help to build team resilience, and for describing the outcomes that result and that in turn serve to strengthen the team's capacity to respond in a resilient way in the future. This framework is based on a review of the literature, as well as on our own study of workplace pressure and its relationship to wellbeing and performance at the team and organisational levels (Flint-Taylor & Cooper, 2014).

It is well established that the management of certain factors in the work environment has a major influence on whether pressure is experienced as positively energising or unduly stressful. These factors are known as the sources of workplace pressure. In a team where they are managed well, the process of establishing a healthy level of pressure ensures that wellbeing and performance move together towards an optimal level (Figure 9.1). This in turn has a major positive impact on the team's ability to respond in a resilient way to future challenges and adversity.

Our framework (Figure 9.2) outlines a practical approach to building team resilience by assessing and managing the sources of workplace pressure (Table 9.1). It is not intended as a comprehensive guide to strengthening team resilience, but it is an evidence-based approach that has proved valuable in our own organisational practice. Also included is a description of outcomes, both in terms of the main elements that make up the team's capacity for resilience and the resilient response that results. The capacity outcomes are described as Confidence, Purposefulness,

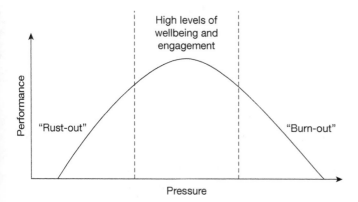

FIGURE 9.1 The relationship between pressure, performance and wellbeing

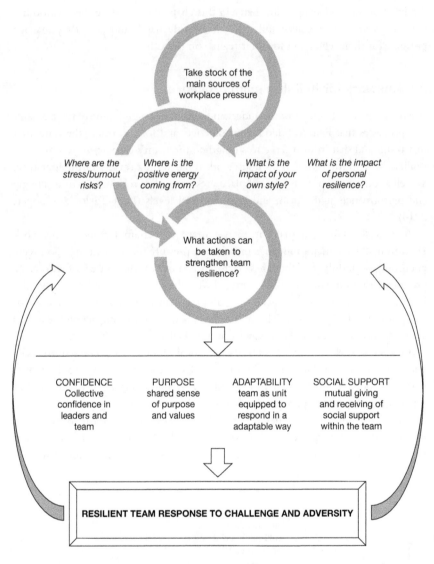

FIGURE 9.2 A framework for building team resilience

Adaptability, and Social Support. These categories are drawn from our study of the literature on personal resilience, and the model we developed to describe what we refer to as personal resilience resources. Figure 9.2 summarises how we have extrapolated these categories to apply to team resilience. The next section explores in detail each component of this framework beginning with taking stock of the main sources of workplace pressure.

Taking stock of the main sources of workplace pressure

We became interested in the concept of team resilience through helping leaders and their teams to understand and respond to the results of organisation-wide stress/wellbeing audits and employee attitude/engagement surveys. These measures are specifically designed to help managers and organisations take stock of important indicators related to employee wellbeing and organisational performance. Common to all is a recognition of the close relationships between mental health, employee engagement, and the performance of individuals and organisations (Macleod & Clarke, 2009). Although the primary unit of measurement is individual employee perceptions and attitudes, the purpose is to identify trends at the team, department and organisational levels and to link these where possible to organisational performance. This link is powerfully illustrated by a study of nearly 8,000 separate business units in 36 companies, in which employee wellbeing and engagement scores were found to be correlated with several measures of business unit performance, including sickness-absence, customer satisfaction, productivity, and employee turnover (Harter, Schmidt & Keyes, 2003).

It is the tradition of stress auditing, now expanded to include other measures of wellbeing, which focuses specifically on taking stock of the sources of workplace pressure. Within this approach there is a high level of agreement regarding the nature of these factors, although they have been described and categorised in various ways. For our purpose here we use six categories (Table 9.1), in an adaptation of the ASSET model (Faragher, Cooper & Cartwright, 2004). These categories incorporate all the main sources of workplace pressure identified by a large body of research (HSE 2001; Faragher et al., 2004; Schaufeli, Bakker & Salanova, 2006).

TABLE 9.1 The main sources of workplace pressure (Faragher et al., 2004)

Main sources of workplace pressure	Ideal conditions in these categories
Resources and communication	The availability of resources that allow workplace challenges to be met, visible and available leadership, and the provision of information that allows a reduction in ambiguity and uncertainty.
Control	Having influence on how, what and when things are done. This can be as simple as control over break times.
Work demands and work life balance	The ability to have a suitable balance between work and life with challenging but achievable demands.
Job security and change	Employees feel a sense that their jobs are secure and change is considered beneficial, purposeful and well-managed.
Work relationships	Work relationships are considered to be supportive and collaborative, but also developmentally stimulating.
Job conditions	The role is stimulating and embodies the opportunity for challenge, fair reward, a sense of competency, achievement, and autonomy.

Managers wishing to assess how each factor is impacting on their team can use a survey tool designed specifically for this purpose. Examples are tools based on the Stress Management Standards (HSE, 2001) or the ASSET model of psychological wellbeing in the workplace (Johnson, 2010). These have the advantage of evidence-based questions and organisational norms against which to benchmark your team. It is, however, important to be able to take stock on a regular basis. For this, a range of other sources provides valuable insights on an ongoing basis. Examples include the organisation's annual employee attitude/engagement survey, focus group discussions convened specifically for the purpose, team meetings, team away days, and various forms of management information that help to highlight relevant trends and issues. As explained later in this chapter, other assessments may be useful for evaluating individual or team attributes known to impact on the sources of workplace pressure, such as leadership style or personal resilience.

The task of managing team resilience can initially seem overwhelming. Assessing and "chunking" the problem into definable categories (Table 9.1) makes it more manageable, and practical steps can be taken to build resilience at the team level.

Where are the stress/burnout risks? In the long-established tradition of stress auditing (now often broadened to include broader wellbeing), team and organisational surveys tend to put the emphasis on risk assessment, and questionnaires are designed to measure the sources of workplace pressure directly. For example, the questionnaire based on the ASSET model invites employees to indicate their agreement with statements such as: "I am troubled that I work longer hours than I choose or want to" and "I am troubled that I am not involved in decisions affecting my job", as well as responding to questions about how enthusiastic, inspired, content, committed etc. they feel.

Depending on the questionnaire used, an analysis of the audit results usually provides a detailed and specific account of the positive factors "topping up" employee wellbeing, as well as the negative factors that are "draining" it and that risk creating damaging levels of stress. For example, the results may show that most team members feel involved and that their ideas are listened to. From this it could be concluded that control is being well managed and is having a positive influence on morale and motivation, and that the risk of this source of workplace pressure causing burnout is low within the team as a whole. Where control is found to be a risk area, managers need to consider what more can be done to take team members' views into account, give them a say in decisions affecting their work, delegate responsibility and avoid micro-management.

As implied by the name, "topping up" factors are those that add to the availability of both physical and psychological resources that facilitate wellbeing and assist in the management of pressure. In contrast, "draining" factors tend to reduce personal and team resources. These workplace factors basically refer to characteristics of the workplace that either create resources (generating support) or erode resources (generating stress). The amount of resource availability versus factors that erode resources is of well-known importance in the psychological literature on stress management. The Conservation of Resources Model (Hobfoll, 1989) suggests that sufficient resources need to be available in order for adaptation to stress to occur. If the impact of the factors draining resources outweighs the impact of the factors restoring them, then the ability to manage and adapt to stress is largely undermined.

A formal wellbeing audit may be seen as a risk assessment that helps to identify and pre-empt potential problems before they occur, as well as evaluating factors currently having a significant positive or negative impact on the team. However, as we have already discussed, the assessment can be based on other sources of information and risks should in any case be evaluated on a routine basis.

Where is the positive energy coming from? While the audit/survey approach has broadened out over the years, the main focus still tends to be on assessing and addressing risks. A different, but complementary, approach that has gained popularity in recent years involves applying findings from the field of positive psychology (Seligman & Csikszentmihalyi, 2000) to the workplace. The science of positive psychology can be summarised as the study of: the positive subjective experience of the past, present and future; positive individual characteristics (strengths and virtues); positive institutions and positive communities (Seligman, 2003). One of the core concepts of this approach is that of "flourishing", defined as "a state in which an individual feels positive emotion toward life and is functioning well psychologically and socially" (Keyes, 2003, p. 293).

This approach is welcomed by many as a way of shifting the emphasis of workplace interventions (including those aimed at improving wellbeing and engagement) from dealing with deficits and problems to building the "necessary conditions, resources and skills that will enable people to flourish and reach their full potential" (Hart, Cotton & Scollay, 2014, p. 281).

Those interested in applying positive psychology to the workplace often refer to the sources of workplace pressure, although not necessarily in the same terms. For example, Sprietzer *et al.* (2005) discuss the concept of thriving (experiencing a sense of vitality and learning) in the work context, emphasising its importance for individual development and health. Their model refers to organisational influences including discretion in decision-making (*control*), the sharing of information (*resources and communication*) and a climate of trust and respect (*work relationships*). Others have demonstrated how thriving and other positive psychology constructs such as happiness are related to lower levels of burnout and other outcomes with positive implications for individuals, teams and organisations (e.g. Porath *et al.*, 2012; Lyubomirsky *et al.*, (2005). As with the stress risk approach it is important routinely to take stock of factors influencing positivity in the team, but there are also survey tools designed specifically for the purpose. An example is the Happiness at Work Survey, which is based on a model of wellbeing developed for the UK Government Office of Science's "Foresight Programme" (2008).

Whatever approach managers use to take stock of, and manage, the workplace antecedents (*work relationships, control* etc.)[1] of positive subjective experiences, there are well-documented benefits of doing so that relate to team resilience in ways that go beyond individual wellbeing and performance. For example, the recently revised approach of Barbara Fredrickson (2013) delivers a persuasive list of benefits to be gained from working out how to increase the level of positive emotions experienced by team members. These benefits include better decision-making; improved "connectedness" with other people; greater concern for others and more helpful behaviour; a greater sense of "we" rather than "me" or "them" and "us"; increased open-mindedness and curiosity; enhanced creativity; better management of complexity; a more positive attitude towards ambiguity or uncertainty (Fredrickson, 2013).

Relating this list back to our model of the sources of workplace pressure, it can be seen that *work relationships* and *change (job security and change)* are strong themes in Fredrickson's list. This supports the feedback loop in our framework (Figure 9.2), where managing the sources of workplace pressure strengthens the team's capacity for responding in a resilient way, feeding in turn to increased capacity. For example, a manager may notice that being able to work from home once a week during office renovations has had a positive influence on morale and energy in the team. As a result, she may agree to keep this home-working arrangement on a permanent basis (work demands and work life balance). The positive subjective experiences that this action helps to sustain may then be expected to pay off in the form of, for example, improved collaboration (*work relationships*) and more confident management of change (*job security and change*).

In summary, whether we refer to them as the sources of workplace pressure or as the antecedents of flourishing, wellbeing, and engagement, factors such as resources and communication, work relationships, work demands, and work life balance need to be managed actively to preserve and strengthen team resilience.

What is the impact of your own style as a leader on team resilience? Perhaps unsurprisingly, leadership approaches have been shown to impact on the six ASSET sources of workplace pressure. When following up on employee stress/wellbeing surveys we noticed some time ago that the style and impact of the leadership group was a common theme in focus group discussions and action plans. This observation is consistent with the wider literature on leadership, psychological wellbeing and organisational outcomes (Robertson & Flint-Taylor, 2009). Indeed, few would argue with the notion that a leader's behaviour has a significant effect on how the team feels. Nevertheless, there is scope for understanding more about the specific connections between leaders' style and stress/wellbeing in their teams.

The effect of leader behaviour on individuals has been studied from various perspectives, including that of stress management (van Dierendonck et al., 2004), authoritarian or abusive leadership (Tepper, 2007) and leadership derailment (Burke, 2006). Poor-quality leadership has been linked with poor mental health outcomes, "whereas, high-quality leadership is related to both reduced incidences of these negative outcomes as well as increased wellbeing" (Barling & Carson, 2008 p. 2).

Taking personality as a good measure of an individual's "natural" leadership style, a recent line of investigation has been to study the relationship between leaders' personality on the one hand, and their teams' experience of workplace stressors (see Figure 9.3) on the other hand. In other words, does a leader's personality profile tell us anything about what we might expect to find if we measure levels of well-being in their team? More specifically, is there a predictable connection between certain personality traits in the leader and the team's experience of work relation-ships, workload, communication, control and the other sources of workplace pressure?

The foundation for this research was a solid body of work demonstrating clear connections between personality and work-related outcomes (Barrick, Mount & Judge, 2001). In particular, studies found that individuals' scores on the five personality dimensions (Neuroticism, Extraversion, Openness, Agreeableness, and Conscientiousness) measured by personality inventories such as the NEO Per-sonality Inventory-Revised (NEO PI-R) (Costa & McCrae, 1992) predicted the 360° feedback ratings that the same individuals receive on leadership competencies such as "Influencing and Communication", and "Involving and Supporting Others" (Flint-Taylor, Robertson & Gray, 1999; Barrick et al., 2001).

Well established as these findings are, it seemed quite a stretch to expect a leader's personality scores to predict the team's wellbeing survey results, especially as only a very small number of questions in the survey relate directly to the style or behaviour of the "boss". Nevertheless, the results so far have borne out this expectation. For example, leaders' high levels of achievement striving have been found to be linked to poor work-life balance scores for their teams (Robertson et al, 2014); as explained in more detail below, leaders' high levels of sympathy are linked to their teams being troubled that "other people at work are not pulling their weight"; leaders' high levels of confidence (specifically their sense of their own capability and resourcefulness) are linked to their teams being troubled that they are "not involved in decisions affecting my job" (Flint-Taylor, 2008).

It is important to emphasise that these results do not in any way suggest that qualities such as achievement striving, sympathy, or confidence are undesirable characteristics in a leader. Rather, they are character strengths that may become "too much of a good thing" if they are over-played, that is, if they are relied on too heavily regardless of the particular context or situation to which the leader is responding. In other words, the relationship between leader personality and team wellbeing is not a linear one. This insight connects directly to the leadership literature on over-using strengths (Kaiser & Hogan, 2011), as well as to the related concepts of career "de-railers" and the "dark side" of leadership (Harms, Spain & Hannah, 2011).

Taking sympathy as an example, the practical implication is that a team may benefit in various ways from having a sympathetic leader, but is at risk if the leader is inclined to be overly sympathetic. One of the main reasons for this is that leaders who have a very sympathetic nature often find it difficult to deal firmly and objectively with unconstructive behaviour or poor performance. Clearly, failing

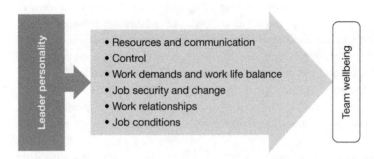

FIGURE 9.3 Leader personality impacts team wellbeing via the sources of workplace
pressure

to do so creates a whole range of problems that have a negative impact on work
relationships and other factors related to morale and wellbeing in the team.

Although personality is not completely fixed in adulthood, it is known to change
relatively little over time. So are leaders and their teams stuck with outcomes such
as those described above? Fortunately, our research suggests not. The relationship
between the personality of the leader and team wellbeing appears to be relatively
indirect, operating via the effect of the leader's personality on the main sources of
workplace pressure identified in the ASSET model (Table 9.1).

Managers can, therefore, improve the impact they have on wellbeing in the team,
by becoming more aware of the effect that their natural style is likely to have on
the six ASSET pressures (e.g., *work relationships*). Once these impacts are identified
managers need to adapt their behaviour accordingly. For example, a manager notices
a common theme in his upward feedback, to the effect that he needs to get better
at having difficult conversations. In the annual staff survey, his team's scores reflect
lower than average levels of trust and cooperation among team members (work
relationships). His coach suggests completing the NEO PI-R personality questionnaire, and draws his attention to a score that indicates he is inclined to be much
more sympathetic than other managers. They agree that sympathy is a useful character
strength in many situations, but appears to be putting him at risk of being too
understanding towards individuals in the team – especially those who are inclined
to be selfish or manipulative. Working with his coach, the manager gradually
improves his ability to flex his style by taking a more rational, objective approach,
for example when a team member tries to play on his sympathy. When the time
comes to work out and evaluate new shift patterns for the team, he finds it easier
to deal fairly with all members of the team (work relationships, work life balance,
change). This change is later reflected in the annual 360° feedback exercise.

For managers looking to take stock of their leadership style and its impact on
the sources of workplace pressure, it can be useful to include as one of the sources
of information a personality questionnaire such as the NEO PI-R (or the latest
version, the NEO Personality Inventory-3). Gathering feedback from the team

and others, in the form of a 360° or upward feedback exercise, can also add valuable insights.

In summary, when leaders become skilled at flexing their style "in the moment", they are less at risk of unintentionally adding to the stress in a situation by over-using their strengths. This in turn has the effect of strengthening the whole team's ability to remain positive and productive under pressure.

What is the impact of member personal resilience on team resilience? Helping people to strengthen their personal resilience plays a useful role in improving a team's ability to manage pressure and tackle challenges. In particular, specific resilience development techniques have been directly associated with improved morale, retention and performance in sales roles and other contexts. We have written about this in detail elsewhere (Cooper, Flint-Taylor & Pearn, 2013). In Table 9.2, we provide a brief overview of some of the most important thinking styles that impact individual-level resilience capacity identified by researchers. Often addressing unhelpful thinking styles is the target of individual resilience training programmes offered to organisations. An important aim for managers is to support the resilience of individual team members, since doing so can be expected to improve the way team members manage all the sources of workplace pressure, to the benefit of the team as a whole as well as themselves.

Resilience resources for individuals and teams

Based on a wide review of personal resilience research, we identified that the individual "protective factors" involved could be grouped into the four main clusters set out in Figure 9.4 and presented in the broader framework in Figure 9.2. We refer to these as *personal resilience resources*, to reflect our view that personal resilience is more like a capability that develops through the individual's interaction with their situation, than it is like a trait or set of personal qualities. Here we describe resilience resources at both the personal and team levels

(1) Confidence. Having a negative explanatory style, as described above, is just one way in which mind-set can undermine morale and performance. Given that the most helpful mind-set is realistic as well as positive, efforts to boost confidence need to include skill development as well as teaching people how to challenge and re-frame their assumptions and make the most of their strengths. At the team level, confidence depends on members feeling well informed about current events and future plans. They need to be consulted, listened to and involved in decisions. They also need guidance, feedback, and stretching opportunities to learn and develop.

(2) Purposefulness/living by goals and values. People draw strength from having a clear sense of what matters to them – what they really care about. Managers often come across the implications of this in the context of organisational change. At such times, it is common for people to feel that the organisation's values are

TABLE 9.2 Individual resilient thinking approaches

Thinking style	Description
A positive mind-set	A positive mind-set is essential to success. While it is important to be realistic about problems and risks, all too often individuals and teams are undermined by negative perspectives based on inaccurate assumptions. In this context, the solution is not about thinking positively, but actually thinking *accurately*. Many of us have bias, unrealistic and unhelpful ways of thinking about the world and other people. This impacts the way we feel. Sometimes this bias can be positive and sometimes it can be negative. That is, people can be overly optimistic about future outcomes and this represents a positive bias. At other times, people can be overly pessimistic about the future reflecting a negative bias. Both biases have the potential for negative consequences because behaviour, decision-making and problem-solving is not based on the best representation of reality.
Thinking errors	The assumptions mentioned above are sometimes known as "*thinking errors*" or "*thinking traps*", because they drive the way we see and respond to a situation but are not supported by the evidence. For example, someone who is prone to the error of "all-or-nothing thinking" might think "The competitor's products are cheaper, so there is absolutely no point in trying to sell ours." A more realistic, accurate thought might be "The competitor's products are cheaper, which makes things tough for me, but price isn't the only factor people care about." Someone who thinks in this way is more likely to make an effort, try different and creative approaches and achieve small wins to build on.
Re-framing	Developing a positive mind-set is a very personal endeavour, as everyone has to learn to challenge their own assumptions and find helpful, believable alternatives that work for them. There is a limit to what can be achieved by appealing to reason and expecting others to see things the way you do. Fortunately, however, the technique of recognising, challenging and correcting ("re-framing") thinking errors, is something that can be taught. This technique can be applied to inaccurate assumptions that undermine people's sense of purpose, confidence and adaptability in various ways.
Individual explanatory style	The re-framing technique can also help to develop a more positive explanatory style. Explanatory (or attributional) style (Gillham et al., 2001) refers to the way each of us typically thinks about our successes and failures. Some people, for example, see most of their successes as due to luck or circumstance, while others are good at recognising the contribution of their own skill and ability. Conversely, when it comes to failures or disappointments, some people are too hard on themselves rather than recognising the role of temporary or situational factors. Unsurprisingly, a positive explanatory style is particularly strongly associated with success in sales roles (Proudfoot et al., 2009). While explanatory style is a long-term, personality-related characteristic, it can be modified and improved through the right development intervention. Doing so has been demonstrated to improve morale, retention and financial performance.

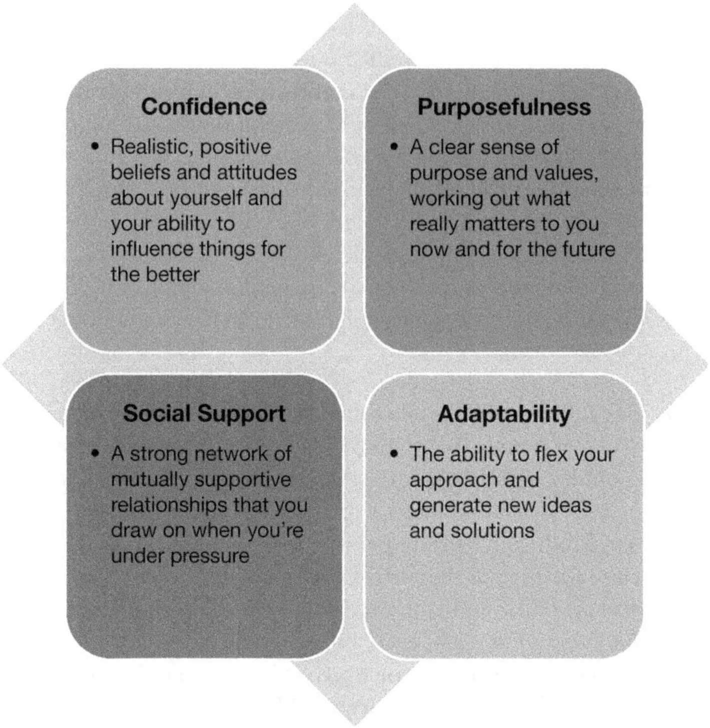

FIGURE 9.4 Four resilience resources

moving out of alignment with their own. To the extent that this is truly the case, it is important for people to be clear about it and then to make a decision about whether they are prepared to work within the organisation's expectations or whether the differences are too great.

All too often, however, the differences are perceived as greater than they actually are. This may be a result of how change is communicated and/or how the messages are received – another case where re-framing may be helpful. Someone might, for example, believe that what a manager means by being more commercially focused is incompatible with putting patient needs first, or that following up proactively to close a sale is incompatible with a relationship-building approach. Such "black and white" assumptions are common and natural, but very unhelpful in responding to the challenge of a changing organisational and market environment.

At the team level, clear objectives and a shared sense of purpose strengthen the team's morale and motivation. Achieving this involves ensuring that goals are clear and realistic, work is interesting and meaningful, and demands are reasonable. It is important to adjust the pace of work to suit different styles and capabilities, and to ensure that people have sufficient responsibility and accountability. The issue of purpose is addressed extensively in Chapter 2.

(3) Adaptability. Adaptability involves being able to flex your approach and generate new ideas and solutions. The personal characteristics of general intelligence and openness to experience have both been shown to be predictors of adaptability. Knowledge, experience and learned skills (e.g. problem-solving) also play a major part, as does looking after your physical and pyschological health.

At the team level, the team as a whole needs to be ready to adapt in a flexible and efficient way to both planned and unexpected developments. This involves being organised and well equipped, with good plans in place for anticipated requirements. It also means being psychologically nimble and collaborative enough to abandon existing plans and procedures when necessary, developing new solutions and approaches quickly and creatively. Diversity in the team has an important role to play here.

(4) Social support. This element of personal resilience relates to building and maintaining a strong network of supportive relationships both at work and outside it, and actively drawing on this in difficult times. A person's network does not need to be extensive – we are not talking about superficial connections of the social media or cocktail party kind. More to the point is the importance of keeping in touch with family, close friends and supportive colleagues, even – or especially – when you feel you have no time and work demands seem all-consuming.

At the team level, this does not mean everything should be done by consensus, but any conflict needs to be managed constructively. It is important that colleagues trust each other and that differences are respected. Managers are encouraged to address selfish, lazy or manipulative behaviour promptly as these behaviours are understood to be disruptive to team cohesiveness, but also be an unnecessary drain on team resources.

What actions can be taken to strengthen team resilience?

There is no doubt that levels of complexity, change, uncertainty and other pressures are generally on the increase in today's work environment. While there is always going to be something draining the team, the good news is that like personal resilience team resilience can be improved. Teams can be strengthened, rather than worn down, by working through tough challenges together, as long as they are well-equipped to do so.

As we have made clear, building a resilient team is not simply a matter of selecting team members for their resilience. In fact, attempting to do so could weaken the team by decreasing its diversity. Nor is it a case of simply investing in developing everyone's personal resilience, although of course that can play a part. The most important focus for managers is creating the right climate and conditions where teams can thrive in the first place.

Managing stress and pressure. When the focus is on equipping the team to manage pressure, it can be helpful for managers to "chunk" the way they think about the climate and conditions in the team by reviewing each of the sources of workplace pressure regularly and on an informal basis. How are things right now in relation to resources and communication etc.? Do people feel they have the information and equipment they need to do their work? Is the workload manageable? Is there another organisational change coming down the track before the team has had a chance to implement the last one? Can you help to "top up" levels of wellbeing in the team by facilitating the resolution of niggling interpersonal tensions? Is there a general sense that people are paid fairly for the work they do – would greater transparency help in this regard? Are you unintentionally undermining personal resilience by allowing people to stay in their comfort zone; what can you do to build confidence by providing stretching opportunities backed up by support?

Supporting flourishing and positivity. As the section on positive energy makes clear, building resilience goes beyond managing the stress risks faced by the team. Attention also needs to be paid to boosting levels of positivity. Easier said than done of course, but the trick is to consider what more can be done to increase the number of positive emotions the members of the team experience over the course of the day. What is it that energises and inspires the team, challenging them in a positive way? How can humour and a sense of fun help to lift the mood, how can positive interactions be encouraged to create feelings of goodwill, gratitude and happiness?

As explained earlier, increased positivity has a protective effect on the team by improving decision-making, creativity and the ability to deal with uncertainty and ambiguity. Collaboration both within and across teams will be strengthened, with people being more likely to help colleagues achieve their objectives, cover their work in their absence, and generally work together towards shared goals.

Communication and support from managers. Although the aim is to boost levels of morale, motivation and wellbeing in the team as a whole, it is important for managers to take account of the fact that pressure means different things to different people. What seems like an achievable sales target for one may feel out of reach for another. An individual's ability to cope with pressure is also affected by events in their lives outside work, which their manager may know nothing about. Empathy, open communication and the building of trust are all critical managerial skills that help in "fine-tuning" the management of pressure to take account of the subjective experience of individual team members.

Empowering the team. Stress is often triggered when individuals feel they have little power to influence decisions or events, especially when this relates to how they approach their own tasks, manage their time, or protect their career interests. This goes to the heart of why it is so important for managers to share information, consult people on decisions and involve them in solving problems. Broader benefits at the team level include better collaboration, quicker resolution of issues, enhanced innovation and retention of valued team members in times of change. In many ways, empowering the team to have an appropriate influence on plans, decisions and problem solving is the most fundamental building block of team resilience.

Final thoughts

Above all, the message of this chapter is that team resilience is not a vague or intangible concept of little practical relevance. Managers who take the trouble to understand and manage the factors that build team resilience will find that progress can be made in many small and everyday ways. As a result, managers and their teams will feel more confident and better equipped to deal with what the future holds in store.

KEY MESSAGES FROM THIS CHAPTER

- Team resilience is not simply the aggregated personal resilience of individual team members. Team resilience is, in part, about a team culture or norms that embody team behaviours, which in turn support the resilience of the team. Leadership style and how the team is managed are central to team resilience.
- Strengthening team resilience is complex and involves many elements including assessing and managing core pressures and resources; developing a level of insight into how one's own leadership style impacts team resilience, and supporting team members in protecting and building their personal resilience.
- It can be hard to know where to start with assessing and managing the sources of workplace pressure, but this task can be aided by using frameworks like the ASSET model that "chunk" workplace pressures into key categories.
- Managing team resilience is an on-going process that involves frequent appraisal of the key pressures and an assessment of the availability of required resources to address those pressures.
- Increasing positive emotions within the team can go a long way to building the capacity for team resilience.
- Empathy, open communication, and the building of trust are all critical managerial skills that help in "fine-tuning" the management of pressure to take account of the subjective experience of individual team members and the group dynamics of the team as a whole.
- Allowing the team influence over their job and work characteristics is a fundamental building block of resilience.

Note

1   There is a strong overlap between the sources of workplace pressure and the constructs that positive psychologists often refer to as the "antecedents" of flourishing, wellbeing or engagement

References

Alliger, G. M., Cerasoli, C. P., Tannenbaum, S. I. & Vessey, W. B. (2015). Team resilience: How teams flourish under pressure. *Organizational Dynamics, 44*, 176–184.

Barling, J. & Carson, J. (2008). The impact of management style on mental well-being at work. *State-of-science review, SR-C3 Foresight Mental Capital and Well-Being Project*. London: Government Office for Science.

Barrick, M. R., Mount, M. K. & Judge, T. A. (2001). Personality and performance at the beginning of the new millennium: what do we know and where do we go next? *International Journal of Selection and Assessment, 9*, 9–30.

Blatt, R. (2009). Resilience in entrepreneurial teams: developing the capacity to pull through. *Frontiers of Entrepreneurship Research, 29*, 11.

Burke, R. J. (2006). Why leaders fail: Exploring the dark side. In R. J. Burke & C. L. Cooper (eds), *Inspiring leaders* (237–246). Oxford: Routledge.

Cooper, C. L., Flint-Taylor, J. & Pearn, M. (2013). *Building resilience for success: A resource for managers and organizations*. Basingstoke: Palgrave Macmillan.

Costa, P. T. & McCrae, R. R. (1992). *Revised NEO personality inventory and NEO Five-Factor inventory professional manual*. Psychological Assessment Resources Inc.

Edson, M. C. (2012). A complex adaptive systems view of resilience in a project team. *Systems Research and Behavioral Science, 29*, 499–516.

Faragher, E. B., Cooper, C. L. & Cartwright, S. (2004). A shortened stress evaluation tool (ASSET). *Stress and Health, 20*, 189–201.

Flint-Taylor, J. (2008). Too much of a good thing? Leadership strengths as risks to well-being and performance in the team. *Proceedings of the British Psychological Society Division of Occupational Psychology Annual Conference*, January 2008.

Flint-Taylor, J. & Cooper, C. (2014) 'Well-being in organisations'. In T. Hämäläinen, and J. Michaelson (eEds), *Well-being and beyond – Broadening the public and policy discourse*, New Horizons in Management series. Cheltenham; Edward Elgar. Pp. 244–269.

Flint-Taylor, J., Robertson, I. T. & Gray, J. (1999). The Five-Factor Model of personality: levels of measurement and the prediction of managerial performance and attitudes. *Proceedings of the British Psychological Society Division of Occupational Psychology Annual Conference*, January 1999.

Foresight Mental Capital and Wellbeing Project (2008). *Final project report*. London: The Government Office for Science.

Fredrickson, B. L. (2013). Updated thinking on positivity ratios. *American Psychologist, 68*, 814–822.

Gillham, J. E., Shatté, A. J., Reivich, K. J. & Seligman, M. E. P. (2001). Optimism, pessimism, and explanatory style. In Chang, E. C. (ed.). *Optimism & pessimism: Implications for theory, research, and practice*. Washington, DC: American Psychological Association, 53–75.

Harms, P. D., Spain, S. M. & Hannah, S. T. (2011). Leader development and the dark side of personality. *The Leadership Quarterly, 22*, 495–509.

Hart, P. M., Cotton, P. & Scollay, C. E. (2014). Flourishing at work: improving wellbeing and engagement. In Burke, R. J., Page, K. M. & Cooper, C. L. (eEds). *Flourishing in life, work and careers: Individual wellbeing and career experiences*. Cheltenham, Edward Elgar, 281–314.

Harter, J. K., Schmidt, F. L. & Keyes, C. L. M. (2003). Well-being in the workplace and its relationship to business outcomes. In Keyes, C. L. M., Haidt, J. & Seligman, M. (eEds), *Flourishing, positive psychology and the life well-lived*. Washington DC: American Psychological Society, 205–224.

Hobfoll, S. E. (1989) Conservation of resources. A new attempt at conceptualizing stress. *American Psychologist, 44*, 513–524.

HSE (2001). *Tackling work-related stress: a managers' guide to improving and maintaining employee health and well-being*. Sudbury: HSE Books.

Johnson, S. (2010). Organizational screening: the ASSET model. In S. Cartwright and C. L. Cooper (eds), *Oxford handbook on organizational well-being*. Oxford: Oxford University Press.

Kaiser, R. B. & Hogan, J. (2011). Personality, leader behavior, and overdoing it. *Consulting Psychology Journal: Practice and Research, 63*, 219–242.

Kaplan, S., LaPort, K. & Waller, M. J. (2013). The role of positive affectivity in team effectiveness during crises. *Journal of Organizational Behavior, 34*, 473–491.

Keyes, C. L. M. (2003) Complete mental health: An agenda for the 21st century. In C. L. M. Keyes & J. Haidt, *Flourishing: Positive psychology and the life well-lived*. Washington: American Psychological Association.

Luthans, F., Avolio, B. J., Avey, J. B. & Norman, S. M. (2007). Positive psychological capital: Measurement and relationship with performance and satisfaction. *Personnel Psychology, 60*, 541–572.

Lyubomirsky, S., King, L. & Diener, E. (2005). The benefits of frequent positive affect: Does happiness lead to success? *Psychological Bulletin*, 131, 803–855.

Macleod, D. & Clarke. N. (2009). *Engaging for success: Enhancing performance through employee engagement*. London: Department for Business, Innovation and Skills.

Meneghel, I., Salanova, M. & Martínez, I. M. (2016). Feeling good makes us stronger: How team resilience mediates the effect of positive emotions on team performance. *Journal of Happiness Studies, 17*, 239–255.

Morgan, P. C. B., Fletcher, D. & Sarkar, M. (2013). Defining and characterizing team resilience in elite sport. *Psychology of Sport and Exercise, 14*, 549–559.

Paton, D. (2003). Stress in disaster response: A risk management approach. *Disaster Prevention and Management: An International Journal, 12*, 203–209.

Peterson, C. & Seligman, M. E. P. (2004). *Character strengths and virtues*. Oxford University Press, New York.

Piccolo, R. F. & Colquitt, J. A. (2006). Transformational leadership and behaviors: The mediating role of core job characteristics. *Academy of Management Journal, 49*, 327–340.

Porath, C. G., Spreitzer, C. G. & Garnett, F. G. (2012). Thriving at work: Toward its measurement, construct validation, and theoretical refinement. *Journal of Organizational Behavior, 33*, 250–257.

Proudfoot, J. G., Corr, P. J., Guest, D. E. & Dunn, G. (2009). Cognitive-behavioural training to change attributional style improves employee well-being, job satisfaction, productivity, and turnover. *Personality and Individual Difference, 46*, 147–153.

Reich, J. W., Zautra, A. J. & Hall, J. S. (eds). (2010). *Handbook of adult resilience*. New York: The Guildford Press.

Robertson, I. & Cooper, C. (2011). *Well-Being: Productivity and happiness at work*. Basingstoke: Palgrave Macmillan.

Robertson I. T. & Flint-Taylor, J. (2009). Leadership, psychological well-being and organisational outcomes. In S. Cartwright and C. L. Cooper (eds), *Oxford handbook on organisational well-being*. Oxford: Oxford University Press.

Robertson, I., Healey, M. P., Hodgkinson, G. P., Flint-Taylor, J. & Jones, F. (2014). Leader personality and employees' experience of workplace stressors. *Journal of Organizational Effectiveness: People and Performance, 1*, 281–295.

Schaufeli, W. B., Bakker, A. B. & Salanova, M. (2006). The measurement of work engagement with a short questionnaire: A cross-national study. *Educational and Psychological Measurement, 66*, 701–716.

Seligman, M. E. P. (2003). The past and future of positive psychology. In C. L. M. Keyes, C. L. M. & J. Haidt, *Flourishing: Positive psychology and the life well-lived.* Washington: American Psychological Association.

Seligman, M. E. P. & Csikszentmihalyi, M. (2000). Positive Psychology: An Introduction. *American Psychologist, 55,* 5–14.

Somers, S. (2009). Measuring resilience potential: An adaptive strategy for organizational crisis planning. *Journal of Contingencies and Crisis Management, 17,* 12–23.

Sprietzer, G. M., Sutcliffe, K., Dutton, J., Sonenschein, S. & Grant, A. M. (2005). A socially-embedded model of thriving at work. *Organization Science, 16,* 537–549.

Tepper, B. J. (2007). Abusive supervision in work organizations: Review, synthesis and research agenda. *Journal of Management, 33,* 261–289.

Turner, J. C. (1991). *Social influence.* Belmont, CA: Thomson Brooks/Cole Publishing Co.

van Dierendonck, D., Haynes, C., Borrill, C. & Stride, C. B. (2004). Leadership behavior and subordinate well-being. *Journal of Occupational Health Psychology, 9,* 165–175.

West, B. J., Patera, J. L. & Carsten, M. K. (2009). Team level positivity: Investigating positive psychological capacities and team level outcomes. *Management Department Faculty Publications (Paper 21).* Lincoln: University of Nebraska.

Yarker, J., Donaldson-Feilder, E., Lewis, R. & Flaxman, P. E. (2008). *Management competencies for preventing and reducing stress at work: Identifying and developing the management behaviours necessary to implement the HSE Management Standard: Phase 2.* London: HSE Books.

10

BUILDING TEAM AND ORGANISATIONAL IDENTIFICATION TO PROMOTE LEADERSHIP, CITIZENSHIP AND RESILIENCE

Dr. Niklas K. Steffens and
Professor S. Alexander Haslam

Acknowledgement

Work on this chapter was supported by a grant from the Australian Research Council (FL110100199).

Workforces in the twenty-first century are becoming increasingly global and flexible. The pressure on workers to perform is growing, and, with this, so too are the demands on their wellbeing. In this context, the health and wellbeing of employees are a significant organisational resource that have profound implications for both their motivation and their capacity to contribute to organisational functioning. Yet recognising this poses challenges for organisations (a) to better understand the factors that shape the wellbeing and productivity of employees, and subsequently (b) to develop sustainable strategies and practices that serve to promote employees' wellbeing and, with this, their willingness to exert energy on behalf of those organisations.

To address these issues, in the present chapter, we outline a social identity approach to leadership and health in organisational contexts. This approach centres on understanding people's self-concept at work and, in particular, the sense of self that they share with others in their team and organisation (i.e., the sense of "we" and "us" that informs their *social* identity). More specifically, we outline the factors that contribute to people's social identification in the workplace (with a team, an organisation etc.), as well as the consequences of this for their wellbeing and citizenship. Finally, we demonstrate that leaders play a pivotal role in building employees' identification and, as a result, have an important influence on whether employees are vitalised and engaged or burnt out and disengaged.

The approach we present is unique in allowing us to see issues of leadership, health, and citizenship in terms of an integrated framework. It suggests that leaders who successfully manage shared identity are not only more effective as leaders (i.e., having a greater capacity to influence others), but also better able to ensure the vitality of employees and ultimately of the organisation as a whole. Throughout the chapter we refer to leaders rather than managers (even though a leader may have formal management responsibility for other people) because, as Bennis (2009) points out, these two roles are not interchangeable. Whereas a manager can be seen as someone who occupies a formal management position and relies on power and control that is ascribed to them on the basis of that role, a leader can be seen as someone who inspires others and influences how they think and feel and thus what they *want* to do. Certainly, many managers aspire to do this, and many succeed. Nevertheless, there are many leaders who are not managers, and, more importantly, there are many managers who are not leaders.

Identification with groups at work: what does it mean to identify with a team or organisation?

In a range of contexts, we think about and see ourselves (as well as other people) as unique individuals. In these contexts, we reflect on what makes each individual "distinctive" and "special" and we compare ourselves with other individuals on an array of dimensions – from how we look to what we do. By way of example, Rachel, as a member of her marketing team, can focus on what distinguishes her from Sharon (e.g., believing that "I always respond to emails in a timely fashion, Sharon does not"), from Mark (e.g., believing that "I am always fair and friendly with colleagues no matter how tricky the situation, whereas Mark gets caught up in the heat of an argument"), and from various other colleagues. As Turner (1982) noted, this sense of self furnishes people with a sense of personal identity.

Yet in many contexts – including the workplace – we see the world through a very different lens. In these contexts, we reflect on ourselves and other people as part of a *group* – as "we" and "us". This group may be a formal group (e.g., a team, a department, or an organisation) or an informal one (the old-timers in an organisation, the feminists or the people inhabiting the same part of a building). When we see ourselves as a member of a collective, we are not attuned so much to what makes us unique as individuals, but rather to what makes "us" – the team, department, or organisation – unique and special. Here, we compare the group we belong to (our *ingroup*) with other outgroups and strive for a sense that this ingroup is important, distinct, and enduring. Along these lines, Rachel may focus on what distinguishes Sharon, Mark, herself, and others who are part of the marketing team from those who are part of the human resources team (e.g., believing that "they do a 9-to-5 job, but we work long hours when we have to get a project completed") and from those who are part of the accounting team (e.g., believing that "they add up numbers, but we do the creative work that keeps the organisation running"). Tajfel (1978) referred to this group-based sense of self as a person's social identity.

This distinction between personal and social identities is a central feature of the social identity approach (Haslam, 2004) – an approach that integrates insights from two theories: social identity theory (Ashforth & Mael, 1989; Tajfel & Turner, 1979) and self-categorisation theory (Turner *et al.*, 1994). The approach asserts, and has shown, that once people identify with, or self-categorise as a member of, a collective ("us"), then this qualitatively transforms their subsequent thoughts, feelings, and behaviour (including, as we will discuss in more detail below, their health and citizenship).

So what exactly do we mean when we say "I identify with group X or Y"? Social identification can be defined as the psychological sense of being part of a group including the "emotional and value significance" that a person experiences as a result of his or her group membership (Tajfel, 1972, p. 292). This is reflected in the way a person thinks about their group, their sense of belonging to the group, and what the group means to them.

This experience also has an emotional component that is reflected in the value that a person experiences as a result of being a member of the group, as well as a behavioural component that shapes their actions as a member of the group. By way of example, Rachel may see herself, together with Sharon and Mark, as "us members of the Marketing team" but she may also feel good about being part of that team and also act in ways that advance the team's interests and goals (e.g., thinking creatively about running marketing campaigns that promote the team's goals and promote its interests). In this way, group identification is a key process that drives behaviour that serves to support and further group interests.

When we identify with a group our behaviour also tends to be consistent with what it means to be a group member. That is, what we do and the way we do it is oriented towards the particular shared norms, values, and goals that define the group as a distinct entity – that is, its social identity content. Along these lines, two people who are members of two different teams may identify equally strongly with their respective groups, but the particular norms and goals that characterise each team will lead each person to engage in very different behaviours. For example, the shared identity of the human resources team may comprise particular norms about communication (e.g., writing brief emails, providing clear instructions) and professional conduct (e.g., dressing formally, adhering strictly to rules and practices) that Rachel is likely to follow herself because she identifies highly as a member of the team. These norms may be particular about her team as well as very different from those of the marketing team.

The importance of team and organisational identification for wellbeing and citizenship: why does identification matter?

By now it should be apparent that identification and the content of group identities play an important role in the way employees think and feel about their team and organisation and the way they behave within them. In line with this point, research has shown that the psychological sense of being part of a group is the basis for a range of fundamental forms of group and organisational behaviour (Ashforth, Harrison & Corley, 2008; Haslam, Postmes & Ellemers, 2003; Turner, 1991;

van Dick, 2004). These range from processes of motivation and leadership (Ellemers, de Gilder & Haslam, 2004; Haslam, Reicher & Platow, 2011; Platow, Haslam, Reicher & Steffens, 2015; Steffens *et al.*, 2014) to those of communication and cooperation (Blader & Tyler, 2009; Tyler & Blader, 2003). Moreover, research informed by the social identity approach has shown that social identification has important consequences for people's resilience as reflected in their health and wellbeing (Cruwys *et al.*, 2014; Jetten, Haslam & Haslam, 2012; Haslam *et al.*, 2009; Steffens, Haslan, Schuh, Jeffen & van Dick, 2016). In this regard, researchers have argued that meaningful and fulfilling group life that allows people to feel at home in – and to identify with – their group provides the basis for several health-promoting experiences. These include a sense of belonging, a sense of direction and purpose and the experience of social support (Haslam *et al.*, 2005; Levine *et al*, 2005; Walsh *et al.*, 2015). Yet, is there any evidence that identification with groups at work has any substantive bearing on people's stress and wellbeing in the workplace?

Addressing this question, van Dick and Wagner (2002; Study 2) conducted a field study with teachers that assessed their identification with both their team (and their profession) as well as the frequency with which they experienced physical health symptoms (having a headache, back pain, heart problems, etc.). The researchers found that to the extent that teachers had incorporated their team (as well as their profession as teachers) into their sense of who they are, they experienced fewer physical health symptoms. This evidence suggests that social identification with a team may serve as a health-protective factor. Similarly, other research conducted in schools by Bizumic *et al.* (2009) found that teachers' identification with their school was negatively related to their levels of depression. This suggests that identification is related not only to physical, but also to psychological (or mental) health at work. Interestingly too, the researchers found similar patterns of results among pupils, but in their case identification with the school was not only protective of health but also associated with their behaviour in class – such that the more they identified with the school, the less likely they were to engage in disruptive behaviour.

Further evidence for the relevance of identification for health comes from research by Wegge *et al.* (2006) who conducted a field study in a number of call centres in Germany. Call centre employees are recognised as performing a client- or customer-focused labour that is characterised as involving strong regulation of emotions in the interests of satisfying other people's needs. This has been des-cribed as a form of "emotional labour" (Brotheridge & Grandey, 2002) that poses a particular challenge to people's health. Yet while the nature of such work may be generally stressful and demanding, it is also apparent that people vary in their experience of this work and that it has variable impact on their wellbeing. Indeed, in Wegge and colleagues' research it was clear that employees' identification with the organisation was important in shaping their orientation to work in so far as it was negatively associated with the extent to which they reported being burnt out – feeling exhausted and cynical, and lacking any sense of accomplishment at work.

In addition, and speaking to the notion that organisational identification can be an important work-relevant resource, high organisational identification in call centre employees also predicted greater organisational citizenship behaviour. That is, employees who identified more strongly with the organisation demonstrated a greater willingness to exert effort on its behalf and to go beyond what was formally required of them (e.g., in duty statements, or contractual specifications of roles and responsibilities). In summary, evidence indicates (a) that health is associated with organisational identification defined both at the level of the team and at the level of the organisation as a whole, and (b) that these forms of identification predict both physical and psychological health as well as positive organisational behaviours.[1]

A key question that arises from the research discussed above is whether identification with groups at work is merely a by-product of good health (e.g., a correlate or a consequence of health) or whether identification is in fact a *cause* of better health and wellbeing in the workplace. A key point to note here is that the research we have discussed up to this point only measured (rather than manipulated) identification and so this makes it impossible to answer this question. Yet this is a practically important issue to resolve because if it is the case that identification leads to better health and wellbeing, then this paves the way for workplace interventions that can enhance people's health in the workplace (and beyond) by strengthening employees' organisational identifications.

To address this question, Häusser et al. (2012) conducted an experiment in which they manipulated participants' social identification. This involved putting half of the participants in groups that strengthened their sense of personal identity (e.g., by getting them to wear unique t-shirts and to write down characteristics that made them unique and different from other individuals in their group), and putting the remaining half in groups that strengthened their social identity (e.g., by wearing the same team t-shirts, by writing down characteristics that they shared with other fellow group members). Afterwards, participants performed a stressful task – the Trier Social Stress Test task – that involved having a job interview and giving a formal, video-taped presentation to a selection committee in which they needed to convince the committee that they were the best candidate for the job. Following this task, physiological measures of stress (levels of cortisol in participants' saliva) were found to be significantly lower among those whose social identity had been reinforced than among those whose personal identity had been emphasised. This research provides evidence both that there are ways in which social identification can be enhanced and that this is causally related to lower stress (for further evidence, see Frisch et al., 2014; Haslam & Reicher, 2006).

One might well ask, though, how representative these studies are of the large body of research that has investigated issues of identification and health. What picture emerges when all the available evidence is put together? To answer these questions and provide a comprehensive quantitative review of work in the area, Steffens, et al. (2016) conducted a meta-analysis that examined the reliability and strength of the relationship between social identification and health in organisational contexts. A meta-analysis involves a systematic review of studies involving similar variables. Using statistical methods, results from multiple studies are then combined and compared to find points of agreement and disagreement and to reveal the overall pattern across multiple individual studies. In this case, the meta-analysis was based on 58 studies involving more than 19,000 employees across the globe and assessed the relationship between measures of team or organisational identification and various measures of health – ranging from stress, burnout, and physical symptoms to engagement at work and general health.

A number of key findings emerged from this meta-analysis that are relevant to the current discussion. First, there appeared to be a weak to moderate association between employees' identification with their team or organisation and their health in the workplace. Second, it did not seem to matter if an employee identified with their organisation or team, as the association with better health was positive in both cases and similarly strong. Third, across the studies, identification was related (a) to both psychological and physical health, (b) to both positive and negative indicators of health (e.g., general health and burnout) and (c) these relationships were apparent in studies using both correlational and longitudinal or experimental designs – the latter being particularly important in providing evidence of causal relationships. In sum, a large body of evidence shows that social identification in organisational contexts is an important health-promoting organisational resource.

Yet social identification is a broad organisational resource that is associated not only with health and wellbeing, but also with other key organisational behaviours such as performance and organisational citizenship. Indeed, another meta-analysis showed that people's identification with their team or organisation is positively related to their general extra-role (or citizenship) behaviour (i.e., helping the team or the organisation; Riketta & van Dick, 2005). These relationships have also been substantiated in a meta-analytic review by Lee, Park, and Koo (2015) of an even larger body of evidence. This found that the extent to which people identify with their organisation is a significant basis for both their "in-role" behaviour (or job performance) and their "extra-role" (or citizenship) behaviour. Overall, then, to the extent that employees feel connected to a group at work they tend to feel good about themselves and their work and to be engaged with both their colleagues and their job.

Assessing identification: how to know how strong an identity is?

Employees' identification with a team or an organisation may be integral to resilience in the workplace, but how can we *assess* the extent to which people identify with a given group? To address this question, researchers have developed a range of tools to measure social identification. Most typically, assessments involve questionnaires in which people indicate their level of agreement with statements relating to their identification with a given group (e.g., "I identify with [Group X]"). Table 10.1 summarises some of the most widely used and reliable social identification measures. As well as being cost- and time-efficient to administer, in well over 100 studies these have also proved to be highly reliable and to have utility as predictors of key group and organisational outcomes (for reviews, see Ashforth *et al.*, 2008; Postmes, Haslam & Jans, 2013). They have the additional benefit of being easy to adapt for use in different contexts and with an array of groups (e.g., a team, a department, an organisation).

TABLE 10.1 A sample of reliable key social identification scales suitable for use in organisations.

Authors	Scale	Number of Items	Item Wording
Doosje, Ellemers, & Spears (1995)	Group Identification Scale	4	I identify with other [members of the group]. I see myself as a member of [the group]. I am glad to be a member of [the group]. I feel strong ties with other [members of the group].
Mael & Ashforth (1992)	Organisational Identification Scale	6	When someone criticises [the group], it feels like a personal insult. I am very interested in what others think about [the group]. When I talk about [the group], I usually say 'we' rather than 'they'. [The group's] successes are my successes. When someone praises [the group], it feels like personal compliment. If a story in the media criticised [the group], I would feel embarrassed.
Postmes, Haslam, & Jans (2013)	Four-Item Social Identification (FISI) Scale	4	I identify with [the group]. I feel committed to [the group]. I am glad to be a member of [the group]. Being a member of [the group] is an important part of how I see myself.
Postmes, Haslam, & Jans (2013)	Single-Item Social Identification (SISI) Scale	1	I identify with [the group].

Note. The framing of the items can be adapted by replacing [the group] with the particular group (e.g., my team, my organisation, explicit name of group). 7-point (or 5-point) Likert scales are common scales that can be used with anchors ranging from 1 *(not at all)* to 7 *(completely)* or from 1 *(strongly disagree)* to 7 *(strongly agree)*.

In addition to standard rating scales, researchers have also developed graphical scales to assess social identification (Bergami & Bagozzi, 2000; Schubert & Otten, 2002). An example is presented in Figure 10.1. In this, respondents indicate experienced alignment or overlap (in norms, values, beliefs, goals) between themselves and their group (e.g., their team or organisation) with reference to pairs of circles that have varying degrees of overlap. At one extreme a complete lack of overlap indicates that they are set apart from this group (i.e., indicating a very low level of social identification); at the other extreme total overlap indicates that they and their group are isomorphic (i.e., indicating a very high level of social identification). Graphical scales such as this are highly reliable and extremely easy to complete. They are also particularly useful in situations where participants are asked to indicate their identification with multiple entities because they allow for a visual comparison of responses.

Finally, it is important to note that asking employees to complete a measure of identification (of the above form) makes it necessary to specify a particular group with which they indicate their identification (typically a formally identified workgroup, department, or organisation). In other words, this involves researchers and practitioners making assumptions – and ultimately a decision – about the group that is the specific focus of (potential) social identification. For instance, researchers and practitioners may design a workplace survey in which they decide to assess respondents' identification with the department that they are part of (rather than with their organisation or their specific team within the department). They may find that people seem rather disengaged and do not identify with their group (department) and they may make particular recommendations on that basis. Yet had they assessed people's identification with their particular sub-group within the department they may have reached a very different conclusion (i.e., that people are highly engaged and identified), and this would have led them to make very different recommendations. In many contexts, these assumptions about which groups are a basis for such identification are likely to map onto employees' own psychological representations and experiences of their groups at work. Nevertheless, in some contexts they do not.

To address this issue and ensure that the work-related groups that are the focus of identification assessment are those that are subjectively meaningful for employees, it can therefore be useful to pre-empt such assessment with an attempt to first discover exactly which group(s) matter most for employees as they go about their day-to-day work. As noted above, rather than being a formal workgroup (e.g., a marketing department), this may be one that is less formally defined (e.g., a group of junior consultants, "old-timers", a project team). For this purpose, researchers interested in Actualising Social and Personal Identity Resources (ASPIRe; Haslam, Eggins & Reynolds, 2003) have developed an "organisational identity mapping" process (for a detailed description and application, see Cruwys et al., 2016; Peters et al., 2014) that can be used to identify (a) the various groups that employees see themselves as belonging to and that they perceive as being important to their daily work as well as (b) the various other groups that they and their group deal with that they are not members of. Rather than having to rely on formal organograms

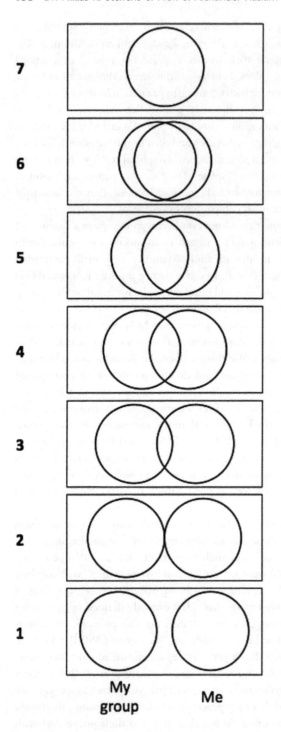

FIGURE 10.1 A graphical social identification scale.

that may not reflect psychological reality, this mapping process allows users to gain a better understanding of the psychologically meaningful groups that define employees' subjective organisational landscapes. This in turn can inform interventions that seek to develop or mobilise social identifications at work with a view to enhancing organisational functioning (e.g., by improving leadership, communication, or organisational strategy; Haslam *et al.*, 2003; Haslam *et al.*, 2017).

Building identification: what strategies can foster a strong sense of identity in the workplace?

The million-dollar question that emerges from the preceding discussion is thus "How can one encourage people to identify with a given group?" Tackling this issue has been a key concern for organisational researchers and their efforts have provided insights into a range of strategies and interventions that can help to build a shared sense of "us" within a particular group of employees. In what follows, we discuss some of those that appear to be most effective.

Empowering groups in the workplace. Work has shown that office design can have important ramifications for people's experience of their work and ultimately their ability to form a bond with their colleagues in the workplace. For instance, in two intervention studies Knight and Haslam (2010) assigned participants randomly to work in either (a) a lean office (that did not contain any decoration), (b) an enriched office (that contained potted plants and wall pictures placed by the experimenters), (c) an empowered office (where potted plants and wall pictures were provided and could be arranged by participants as they liked), or (d) a disempowered condition (where, as in the empowered condition, participants first arranged potted plants and pictures according to their taste before the experimenter then rearranged the decoration). Results indicated that when participants worked in an enriched or empowered (rather than in a lean or disempowered) environment, this led not only to greater organisational identification but also to enhanced wellbeing. This suggests that strategies and interventions that provide groups with autonomy and decision power are likely to be conducive to members' identification with their group.

Further evidence of the role that group empowerment plays in building identification is provided by an intervention study that Knight, Haslam, and Haslam (2010) conducted in a series of care homes. Here the researchers found that when residents were able to make decisions about the design and decoration of newly renovated spaces they came to share a stronger sense of social identification than was the case when there was no decision input (because decisions were made for them). Moreover, greater decision input was associated with increased social interaction and wellbeing, compared to conditions in which there was no such input. Such work suggests that bringing people with similar interests together and allowing them to explore and articulate their shared concerns can be a powerful way of encouraging forms of interaction that turn a collection of individuals into a psychologically meaningful group (i.e., one whose members perceive themselves as sharing social identity; see also Jans, Postmes & van der Zee, 2011; Postmes, Haslam & Swaab, 2005).

Developing a strategic plan that identifies shared challenges and goals. Bringing people together to explore and discuss group-related challenges and goals is another way to build a sense of group identification. In particular, previous research has shown that people's identification with groups at work can be fostered by engaging in processes specified in the ASPIRe model (Haslam *et al.*, 2003). These build upon the mapping process discussed above by (a) bringing members of the groups that are identified through this process together to discuss their group's challenges and goals and then (b) developing strategies to overcome the challenges and achieve the goals – a process that is completed first by each group on its own and then by all the groups together. The model has been applied successfully (in full or in part) to address key organisational challenges in diverse contexts ranging from managing the merging of academic departments (Peters *et al.*, 2014) to negotiation (Batalha & Reynolds, 2012) and the management of health care in military units (Peters *et al.*, 2013). The latter research showed clearly that working through the ASPIRe process can increase participants' identification with both their own team and the organisation as a whole.

Leadership to create, advance, represent, and embed shared identity. The previously discussed interventions suggest that the path to strong identities (as well as greater wellbeing and citizenship) in the workplace generally requires group member participation and engagement. Sometimes this will occur naturally, but often it will not. As a result, leaders have an important role to play in this process. Illustrative of this point, Haslam and colleagues (2015) adapted and extended the ASPIRe model to develop a leadership development program — the 5R program — that trains leaders to work with members of the teams for which they have responsibility and takes them through the various stages of the ASPIRe process. In the first instance, this involves workshops in which leaders are trained in leadership theory and introduced to the practical tools and processes specified in the ASPIRe model. This is then followed by the practical task of working with the groups that they are tasked with leading – first to identify shared challenges and goals and then to define pathways to collective progress. Findings from an initial test of 5R indicated that, among other things, the programme served to facilitate leaders' identification with their team, to increase the perceived clarity of shared goals, and to enhance their confidence to engage in (identity) leadership.

Additional evidence of the critical role that leaders play in facilitating employees' connections with groups at work comes from a longitudinal study with organisational newcomers conducted by Smith *et al.* (2012). This showed that new employees ultimately came to identify more strongly with their team and their organisation to the extent that they felt socially validated by team members and their leaders – such that they felt more confident both about their place in the team and about the forms of workplace behaviour that were appropriate. Moreover, this increased identification also fed into those new employees' desire to stay with (rather than leave) the organisation (see also Smith *et al.*, 2013).

This leads us to the more general proposition that leadership can be seen as a process of *social identity management*, and that it is by promoting a special shared sense of "us" that leaders are able to influence and mobilise followers (Haslam *et al.*, 2011; Hogg, van Knippenberg & Rast, 2012; van Dick & Kerschreiter, 2016; van Knippenberg, 2011). Put simply, rather than dealing with employees as individuals this involves dealing with employees as group members – as part of a team or organisation that has a set of common goals, values, and norms. As shown graphically in Figure 10.2, this process can be broken down into four separate dimensions that involve leaders (a) creating a sense of shared group membership (Huettermann, Doering & Boerner, 2014; Reicher & Hopkins, 2001; Reicher, Haslam & Hopkins, 2005; Steffens & Haslam, 2013) and then (b) representing what it means to be a member of the group (Platow & van Knippenberg, 2001; Steffens, Haslam & Reicher, 2014a). Beyond this, it also involves leaders (c) being seen to advance the shared interests of a group (Haslam & Platow, 2001; Steffens *et al.*, 2013; Steffens, Mols, Haslam & Okimoto, 2016), and (d) working to embed a shared sense of "us" through the development of structures and practices that allow group members to live out their group membership (Haslam *et al.*, 2011; 2017). To assess the degree to which leaders succeed in these various elements of identity leadership, Steffens and colleagues (2014b) recently developed the Identity Leadership Inventory (ILI). This tool can be adapted to the particular group in question (team, department, organisation) and has been shown to have construct, discriminant, and criterion validity. The full 15-item ILI including its four-item short form is presented in Table 10.2.

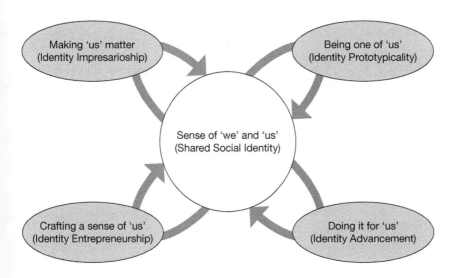

FIGURE 10.2 A four-dimensional model of identity leadership.

TABLE 10.2 The Identity Leadership Inventory (ILI): a reliable four-dimensional scale of identity leadership suitable for use in organisations.

Authors	Dimension	Number of Items	Item Wording
Steffens, Haslam Reicher, Platow, Fransen et al. (2014)	Identity Prototypicality	4	This leader embodies what [the group] stands for. This leader is representative of members of [the group]. ★This leader is a model member of [the group]. This leader exemplifies what it means to be a member of [the group].
	Identity Advancement	4	This leader promotes the interests of members of [the group]. ★This leader acts as a champion for [the group]. This leader stands up for [the group]. When this leader acts, he or she has [the group's] interests at heart.
	Identity Entrepreneurship	4	This leader makes people feel as if they are part of the same group. ★This leader creates a sense of cohesion within [the group]. This leader develops an understanding of what it means to be a member of [the group]. This leader shapes members' perceptions of [the group's] values and ideals.
	Identity Impresarioship	3	This leader devises activities that bring [the group] together. This leader arranges events that help [the group] function effectively. ★This leader creates structures that are useful for [group members].

Note. For a shorter four-item measure of identity leadership, one can use the Identity Leadership Inventory-Short Form (ILI-SF) that consists of the four items marked with ★.

The framing of the items can be adapted by replacing [the group] with the particular group (e.g., my team, my organisation, explicit name of group) and by replacing [this leader] with the particular leader in question (e.g., my team leader, the CEO of my organisation, explicit name of leader). 7-point (or 5-point) Likert scales are common scales that can be used with anchors ranging from 1 *(not at all)* to 7 *(completely)* or from 1 *(strongly disagree)* to 7 *(strongly agree)*.

Evidence also suggests that the extent to which a leader engages in identity leadership will be predictive of the degree to which the group members for whom he or she has responsibility will identify with their group. Moreover, in line with the previously discussed links between employees' organisational identification and their health and citizenship at work, there is evidence that leaders who create and advance a shared identity among employees will also curb employees' burnout while also enhancing their work engagement (Steffens *et al.*, 2014c).

Final thoughts

In the present chapter, we outlined an approach that identifies employees' group-based social connections with others as a basis for resilience and vitality in the workplace. This approach contends that a significant part of employees' engagement at work originates from the sense of "we" and "us" that they share with fellow members of their team and with members of their organisation as a whole. Yet employees' identification with groups at work is not set in stone and employees vary in the degree to which they internalise potentially relevant shared group memberships. This alerts us to the fact that leaders play a pivotal role in cultivating and promoting people's social connections in the workplace and that there are a variety of strategies that they can employ in order to do this more effectively. Yet, by the same token, it follows that leaders who fail to engage with employees as group members and who prove incapable of fostering a sense of "us" that is shared by those they lead are unlikely to meet with much success. The reason for this is that they will find it hard to foster engagement and resilience among employees. Indeed, at an even more fundamental level they will find it hard to have a positive influence on what those employees think, feel and do. In short, in the absence of shared identity, they will find it hard to demonstrate any form of leadership.

KEY MESSAGES FROM THIS CHAPTER

- Social identification has important consequences for employee resilience as reflected in their health, wellbeing, and organisational citizenship.
- Leaders play a pivotal role in fostering team or organisational identification.
- Leaders can enhance social identification among employees by empowering groups (e.g., giving them control over aspects of the work environment) and helping employees to develop strategies to deal with shared challenges and achieve collective goals.

Note

1   It is important to note that social identification can also have detrimental effects on people's
    health and wellbeing in at least two different ways. First, it can be harmful to the extent
    that the norms and ideals that are characteristic of a group promote behaviours that are
    health-debilitating (e.g., abusing other members, sabotaging the work of other members,
    working very long hours). Second, it can be harmful to the extent that the norms and
    values of different groups (team, organisation) that a person identifies with are in conflict
    with each other, as this can create role conflict and compromise goal achievement.

References

Ashforth, B. E. & Mael, F. (1989). Social identity theory and the organization. *Academy of Management Review, 14*, 20–39.

Ashforth, B. E., Harrison, S. H. & Corley, K. G. (2008). Identification in organizations: An examination of four fundamental questions. *Journal of Management, 34*, 325–374.

Batalha, L. & Reynolds, K. J. (2012). ASPIRing to mitigate climate change: Superordinate identity in global climate negotiations. *Political Psychology, 33*, 743–760.

Bennis, B. (2009). *On becoming a leader (4th edn)*. New York: Basic Books.

Bergami, M. & Bagozzi, R. P. (2000). Self-categorization, affective commitment and group self-esteem as distinct aspects of social identity in the organization. *British Journal of Social Psychology, 39*, 555–577.

Blader, S. L. & Tyler, T. R. (2009). Testing and extending the group engagement model: Linkages between social identity, procedural justice, economic outcomes, and extrarole behavior. *Journal of Applied Psychology, 94*, 445–464.

Bizumic, B., Reynolds, K. J., Turner, J. C., Bromhead, D. & Subasic, E. (2009). The role of the group in individual functioning: School identification and the psychological well-being of staff and students. *Applied Psychology, 58*, 171–192.

Brotheridge, C. M. & Grandey, A. A. (2002). Emotional labour and burnout: Comparing two perspectives of "people work". *Journal of Vocational Behavior, 60*, 17–39.

Cruwys, T., Haslam, S. A., Dingle, G. A., Haslam, C. & Jetten, J. (2014). Depression and social identity: An integrative review. *Personality and Social Psychology Review, 18*, 215–238.

Cruwys, T., Steffens, N. K., Haslam, S. A., Haslam, C., Jetten, J. & Dinle, G. A. (2016). Social Identity Mapping (SIM): A procedure for visual representation and assessment of subjective multiple group memberships. *British Journal of Social Psychology, 55*, 613–642.

Doosje, B., Ellemers, N. & Spears, R. (1995). Perceived intragroup variability as a function of group status and identification. *Journal of Experimental Social Psychology, 31*, 410–436.

Ellemers, N., de Gilder, D. & Haslam, S. A. (2004). Motivating individuals and groups at work: A social identity perspective on leadership and group performance. *Academy of Management Review, 29*, 459–478.

Frisch, J. U., Häusser, J. A., van Dick, R. & Mojzisch, A. (2014). Making support work: The interplay between social support and social identity. *Journal of Experimental Social Psychology, 55*, 154–161.

Haslam, S. A. (2004). *Psychology in organizations: The Social Identity Approach* (2nd edn). London: Sage.

Haslam, S. A., Eggins, R. A. & Reynolds, K. J. (2003). The ASPIRe model: Actualizing social and personal identity resources to enhance organizational outcomes. *Journal of Occupational and Organizational Psychology, 76*, 83–113.

Haslam, S. A., Jetten, J., Postmes, T. & Haslam, C. (2009). Social identity, health and well-being: An emerging agenda for applied psychology. *Applied Psychology: An International Review, 58*, 1–23.

Haslam, S. A., O'Brien, A., Jetten, J., Vormedal, K. & Penna, S. (2005). Taking the strain: Social identity, social support, and the experience of stress. *British Journal of Social Psychology, 44*, 355–370.

Haslam, S. A. & Platow, M. J. (2001). The link between leadership and followership: How affirming social identity translates vision into action. *Personality and Social Psychology Bulletin, 27*(11), 1469–1479.

Haslam, S. A., Postmes, T. & Ellemers, N. (2003). More than a metaphor: Organizational identity makes organizational life possible. *British Journal of Management, 14*, 357–369.

Haslam, S. A. & Reicher, S. (2006). Stressing the group: Social identity and the unfolding dynamics of responses to stress. *Journal of Applied Psychology, 91*, 1037–1052.

Haslam, S. A., Reicher, S. D. & Platow, M. J. (2011). *The New Psychology of Leadership: Identity, Influence and Power*. London & New York: Psychology Press.

Haslam, S. A., Steffens, N. K., Peters, K., Boyce, R. A., Mallett, C. J. & Fransen, K. (2017). A social identity approach to leadership development: The 5R program. Journal of Personnel Psychology. Advance online publication. doi:10.1027/1866-5888/a000176.

Häusser, J. A., Kattenstroth, M., van Dick, R. & Mojzisch, A. (2012). "We" are not stressed: Social identity in groups buffers neuroendocrine stress reactions. *Journal of Experimental Social Psychology, 48*, 973–977.

Hogg, M. A., van Knippenberg, D. & Rast III, D. E. (2012). The social identity theory of leadership: Theoretical origins, research findings, and conceptual developments. *European Review of Social Psychology, 23*, 258–304.

Huettermann, H., Doering, S. & Boerner, S. (2014). Leadership and team identification: Exploring the followers' perspective. *The Leadership Quarterly, 25*, 413–432.

Jans, L., Postmes, T. & van der Zee, K. I. (2011). The induction of shared identity: The positive role of individual distinctiveness for groups. *Personality and Social Psychology Bulletin, 37*, 1130–1141.

Jetten, J., Haslam, C. & Haslam, S. A. (eds) (2012). *The Social Cure: Identity, Health and Well-Being*. New York, NY: Psychology Press.

Knight, C. & Haslam, S. A. (2010). The relative merits of lean, enriched, and empowered offices: An experimental examination of the impact of workspace management strategies on well-being and productivity. *Journal of Experimental Psychology: Applied, 16*, 158–172.

Knight, C., Haslam, S. A. & Haslam, C. (2010). In home or at home? How collective decision making in a new care facility enhances social interaction and wellbeing among older adults. *Ageing and Society, 30*, 1393–1418.

Lee, E. S., Park, T. Y. & Koo, B. (2015). Identifying organizational identification as a basis for attitudes and behaviors: A meta-analytic review. *Psychological Bulletin, 141*, 1049–1080.

Levine, M., Prosser, A., Evans, D. & Reicher, S. D. (2005). Identity and emergency intervention: How social group membership and inclusiveness of group boundaries shape helping behavior. *Personality and Social Psychology Bulletin, 31*, 443–453.

Mael, F. & Ashforth, B. E. (1992). Alumni and their alma mater: A partial test of the reformulated model of organizational identification. *Journal of Organizational Behavior, 13*, 103–123.

Peters, K., Haslam, S. A., Ryan, M. K. & Fonseca, M. (2013). Working with subgroup identities to build organizational identification and support for organizational strategy: A test of the ASPIRe model. *Group and Organization Management, 38*, 128–144.

Peters, K., Haslam, S. A., Ryan, M. K. & Steffens, N. K. (2014). To lead, ASPIRe: Building organic organizational identity. In S. Otten, K. van der Zee & M. Brewer (eds.), *Towards inclusive organizations: Determinants of successful diversity management at work*. (pp. 87–107). Hove, UK: Psychology Press.

Platow, M. J. & van Knippenberg, D. (2001). A social identity analysis of leadership endorsement: The effects of leader ingroup prototypicality and distributive intergroup fairness. *Personality and Social Psychology Bulletin, 27,* 1508–1519.

Platow, M. J., Haslam, S. A., Reicher, S. D. & Steffens, N. K. (2015). There is no leadership if no one follows: Why leadership is necessarily a group process. *International Coaching Psychology Review, 10,* 20–37.

Postmes, T., Haslam, S. A. & Jans, L. (2013). A single-item measure of social identification: Reliability, validity, and utility. *British Journal of Social Psychology, 52,* 597–617.

Postmes, T., Haslam, S. A. & Swaab, R. I. (2005). Social influence in small groups: An interactive model of social identity formation. *European Review of Social Psychology, 16,* 1–42.

Reicher, S. D., Haslam, S. A. & Hopkins, N. (2005). Social identity and the dynamics of leadership: Leaders and followers as collaborative agents in the transformation of social reality. *The Leadership Quarterly, 16,* 547–568.

Reicher, S. D. & Hopkins, N. (2001). *Self and Nation: Categorization, Contestation, and Mobilisation.* London: Sage.

Riketta, M. & van Dick, R. (2005). Foci of attachment in organizations: A meta-analytic comparison of the strength and correlates of workgroup versus organizational identification and commitment. *Journal of Vocational Behavior, 67,* 490–510.

Schubert, T. W. & Otten, S. (2002). Overlap of self, ingroup, and outgroup: Pictorial measures of self-categorization. *Self and Identity, 1,* 353–376.

Smith, L. G., Amiot, C. E., Callan, V. J., Terry, D. J. & Smith, J. R. (2012). Getting new staff to stay: The mediating role of organizational identification. *British Journal of Management, 23,* 45–64.

Smith, L. G., Amiot, C. E., Smith, J. R., Callan, V. J. & Terry, D. J. (2013). The social validation and coping model of organizational identity development: A longitudinal test. *Journal of Management, 39,* 1952–1978.

Steffens, N. K. & Haslam, S. A. (2013). Power through 'us': Leaders' use of we-referencing language predicts election victory. *PLoS ONE, 8,* e77952.

Steffens, N. K., Haslam, S. A., Schuh, S. C., Jetten, J. & van Dick, R. (2016). A meta-analytic review of social identification and health in organizational contexts. *Personality and Social Psychology Review,* doi: 10.1177/1088868316656701

Steffens, N. K., Haslam, S. A., Kerschreiter, R., Schuh, S. C. & van Dick, R. (2014c). Leaders enhance group members' work engagement and reduce their burnout by crafting social identity. *Zeitschrift fuer Personalforschung (German Journal of Research in Human Resource Management), 28,* 173–194.

Steffens, N. K., Haslam, S. A., Kessler, T. & Ryan, M. K. (2013). Leader performance and prototypicality: Their inter-relationship and impact on leaders' identity entrepreneurship. *European Journal of Social Psychology, 43,* 606–613.

Steffens, N. K., Haslam, S. A. & Reicher, S. D. (2014a). Up close and personal: Evidence that shared social identity is a basis for the 'special' relationship that binds followers to leaders. *The Leadership Quarterly, 25,* 296–313.

Steffens, N. K., Haslam, S. A., Reicher, S. D., Platow, M. J., Fransen, K., Yang, J., Jetten, J., Ryan, M. K., Peters, K. & Boen, F. (2014b). Leadership as social identity management: Introducing the Identity Leadership Inventory (ILI) to assess and validate a four-dimensional model. *The Leadership Quarterly, 25,* 1004–1025.

Steffens, N. K., Mols, F., Haslam, S. A. & Okimoto, T. (2016). True to what WE stand for: Championing collective interests as a path to authentic leadership. *The Leadership Quarterly, 27,* 726–744.

Tajfel, H. (1972). La catégorisation sociale (English trans.) In S. Moscovici (ed.), *Introduction a la psychologie sociale* (Vol. 1, pp. 272–302). Paris: Larousse.

Tajfel, H. (1978). Instrumentality, identity and social comparisons. In H. Tajfel (ed.), *Social identity and intergroup relations* (pp. 483–507). Cambridge: Cambridge University Press.

Tajfel, H. & Turner, J. C. (1979). An integrative theory of intergroup conflict. In W. G. Austin & S. Worchel (eds.), *The social psychology of intergroup relations* (pp. 33–47). Monterey, CA: Brooks/Cole.

Turner, J. C. (1982). Towards a redefinition of the social group. In H. Tajfel (ed.), *Social Identity and Intergroup Relations* (pp. 15–40). Cambridge: Cambridge University Press.

Turner, J. C. (1991). *Social influence*. Milton Keynes: Open University Press.

Turner, J. C., Hogg, M. A., Oakes, P. J., Reicher, S. D. & Wetherell, M. S. (1987). *Rediscovering the Social Group: A Self-Categorization Theory*. Cambridge, MA: Basil Blackwell.

Tyler, T. R. & Blader, S. L. (2003). The group engagement model: Procedural justice, social identity, and cooperative behavior. *Personality and Social Psychology Review*, 7, 349–361.

van Dick, R. (2004). My job is my castle: Identification in organizational contexts. *International Review of Industrial and Organizational Psychology*, 19, 171–204.

van Dick, R. & Kerschreiter, R. (2016). The social identity approach to leadership: An overview and some ideas on cross-cultural generalizability. *Frontiers of Business Research in China*, 10, 363–384.

van Dick, R. & Wagner, U. (2002). Social identification among school teachers: Dimensions, foci, and correlates. *European Journal of Work and Organizational Psychology*, 11, 129–149.

van Knippenberg, D. (2011). Embodying who we are: Leader group prototypicality and leadership effectiveness. *The Leadership Quarterly*, 22, 1078–1091.

Wegge, J., van Dick, R., Fisher, G. K., Wecking, C. & Moltzen, K. (2006). Work motivation, organisational identification, and well-being in call centre work. *Work & Stress*, 20, 60–83.

Walsh, R. S., Muldoon, O. T., Gallagher, S. & Fortune, D. G. (2015). Affiliative and "self-as-doer" identities: Relationships between social identity, social support, and emotional status among survivors of acquired brain injury (ABI). *Neuropsychological Rehabilitation*, 25, 555–573.

PART 5

Promoting resilient thinking and behaviour

11

HOW ORGANISATIONS AND LEADERS CAN BUILD RESILIENCE

Lessons from high-risk occupations

Dr. Amy B. Adler and CPT Dr. Kristin N. Saboe

By now you will have a fairly good understanding of resilience and that it is an important characteristic that includes being able to withstand stress and bounce back from adversity. Arguably, nowhere is the need for this characteristic more evident than in occupations that place extreme stressors on employees. Occupations that encompass the work of first-responders, like the police and fire-fighters, and the military routinely and repeatedly require individuals to perform in extreme and sometimes unpredictable conditions.[2] Individuals working in these high-risk settings have to perform even when faced with exposure to potential danger to themselves and others, or to potentially traumatising experiences.

In this chapter, we will describe how high-risk occupational settings, such as the military, attempt to maintain and develop the resilience of their workforce. We will touch on several aspects that are important for the promotion of resilience including policy, assessment, training and organisational culture, and we will describe their relevance to all organisational settings.

The impact of potentially traumatic experiences occuring in the workplace

These potentially traumatic experiences can impact employees in terms of mental health, physical health, their relationships and their performance. Numerous studies have documented the link between experiencing traumatic events and greater risk of post-traumatic stress disorder (PTSD), a diagnosis that includes four symptom dimensions: intrusion symptoms, avoidance, negative alterations in cognition and mood, and alterations in arousal and reactivity (American Psychiatric Association, 2013).

Studies estimate that 13 per cent of police officers may have PTSD (Robinson, Sigman & Wilson, 1997), and 17 per cent of firefighters (Bryant & Harvey, 1995).

In a more recent study of rescue and recovery workers at the World Trade Center site, approximately 12 per cent had PTSD two to three years after the terrorist attacks (Perrin et al., 2007). By integrating results of several studies with service members returning from combat in Iraq and Afghanistan, Kok and colleagues (2012) reported there was a 6 per cent PTSD prevalence rate for all deployed personnel, and a 13 per cent rate for those in infantry units (units more directly at risk for encountering threat). Other mental health outcomes include anxiety, depression and alcohol problems (Thomas et al., 2010). Another problem associated with these kinds of experiences is an increased risk for anger and aggression (Adler et al., 2011; Rona et al., 2015; Thomas et al., 2010). Anger and aggression are associated with disruptions to both the employee's work and personal relationships. Therefore, high-risk workplaces can take a toll on marriages (Riviere et al., 2012) and on being able to function at work (Herrell et al., 2014).

Physical health is also affected. These physical symptoms include back pain, joint pain and stomach complaints and can be found in both the short term – as in the example of soldiers who have been home from combat for a couple of months (Hoge et al., 2007) and long term, meaning even decades later. In a study of Vietnam veterans 20 years later, for example, Boscarino (1997) found increased risk of circulatory, digestive, musculoskeletal and other medical conditions associated with exposure to combat stress.

Resilient individuals may be less likely to experience these reactions or may recover more quickly, but it is important to acknowledge that everyone has a point at which their resilience may falter. This is especially the case in high-risk occupations where the normal stressors of work and life can be compounded by potentially traumatic experiences. Thus, employees in high-risk settings may experience significant difficulties sustaining their resilience. To meet the unique demands of high-risk occupational settings policy, assessment, culture and training must come together to support the employee's resilience. The practices of high-risk occupational settings are transferable to all organisations wishing to support the resilience of their employees.

Policy, assessment, culture and training functioning together to support the resilience of employees in high-risk occupations

Policies are the formal mechanisms that organisations use to create goals, standards and expectations. Without these, managers will not necessarily be able to recognise whether or how a particular programme should be implemented or whether it is a priority of the organisational leadership. Policies in support of organisational actions that foster resilience are at the foundation of a resilience-oriented organisation.

There are numerous examples of how policies can play a role in promoting resilience. In the US military, for example, after years of managing two wars simultaneously, a "dwell time" policy was instituted. "Dwell time" was the official requirement to allow personnel returning from a combat deployment to remain at their home unit for a particular period of time before being eligible to deploy again. The purpose of this was to allow personnel a chance to recover adequately and support their resilience in the face of subsequent deployments (Bliese *et al.*, 2011). The UK's harmony guidelines are the equivalent and research has demonstrated that when deployment schedules are consistent with these guidelines, UK military personnel have better mental health (Rona *et al.*, 2014).

If and when mental health training is rolled out is another example of an organisational policy that promotes resilience. In the US Army, for example, a policy requiring post-deployment mental health training was issued, enabling a standardised approach to mental health training. The decision to roll-out this training was fueled by two factors: first, a study demonstrating the efficacy of the training had just been completed (Adler *et al.*, 2009); Second, researchers had just returned from conducting an anonymous assessment of soldiers deployed to Iraq. This assessment not only provided the leadership with a snapshot of the mental health problems in the force, but also suggested that the training be rolled out as a potential counter measure. The training, called *Battlemind*, went on to be instituted across the Army. The example demonstrates how policies can emerge from a well-timed identification of a need, demonstration of a validated intervention and a recommendation to senior leaders (Hoge *et al.*, 2011). We will return to the topic of training after discussing the importance of assessment.

The importance of assessing workforce wellbeing and resilience

In high-risk occupations, assessment is an important tool for being able to understand the resilience of individuals, teams and even the organisation as a whole and the adverse effects of stressor exposures. Ideally, routine assessment of personnel working in high-risk settings allows for the detection of early signs of distress and allows for the timely intervention at the individual or group level.

Importantly, assessment is critical to determining who is in need of intervention. Assessments designed to identify those in need of additional support can be described as a kind of mental health 'check-up'. The benefits of this type of assessment are that the individual being assessed gets personalised attention and an individualised plan can be developed to help support them.

Routine and robust assessment of organisation and employee wellbeing are a great way to inform policy and identify the impacts of policy changes on employee wellbeing. The example highlighted in Box 11.1 demonstrates how regular assessment and research can alert the organisational leadership to a problem and how a policy can be established to address the problem. While the organisation's

BOX 11.1 CHARACTERISING MENTAL HEALTH PROBLEMS FOLLOWING COMBAT

A prototypical example of how assessments are informative is rooted in the U.S. Army's experience with psychological screening. In particular, this case study highlights the importance of giving assessment *timing* careful consideration when it comes to screening for mental health issues for those in high-risk occupations. In 2004, researchers from the Walter Reed Army Institute of Research surveyed soldiers returning from a year of combat in Iraq. The survey was part of a mental health screening designed to identify at-risk soldiers who were in need of follow-up care. The survey was conducted in the week following their return from deployment and was not anonymous because the goal was to identify at-risk soldiers.

Results from the screening found that rates of mental health problems were significantly lower in the unit being screened than those that had been reported in other surveys conducted with comparable troops of soldiers (Hoge et al., 2004; Thomas et al., 2010). These other surveys were anonymous and typically conducted after the soldiers had been home from combat for about 3 months. The question emerged as to why the screened group had such uncharacteristically low rates. There were two possible but competing explanations: (1) the timing of the survey was earlier than during other studies; and (2) the surveys were not anonymous whereas the survey in the symptomatic units was anonymous.

So the team went back and surveyed the units again several months later, linked up the survey responses with the soldiers' responses from the first week and looked at the patterns. While anonymity was associated with a small increase in symptom reporting, the results were startling when it came to comparing how soldiers reported symptoms over time: 3 to 5 times as many soldiers reported symptoms of mental illness several months later compared to the initial screen (Bliese et al., 2007). While the data could not determine for certain why the increase in symptoms occurred, the likely explanation is that individuals may not have noticed their symptoms until garrison life resumed and then they had ample opportunity to notice that they were not adjusting as smoothly as they thought they would.

Results were provided to senior leaders in the U.S. Army and within weeks, the Department of Defense issued a new requirement to screen service members returning from a combat deployment not just at reintegration immediately following their return home from deployment, but also between 3 and 6 months after returning home (Bliese, Adler, & Castro, 2011).

This example demonstrates several critical points about characterising challenges from which all organisations, not just the military, can learn. First, the Army was able to identify a potential issue early because there was an active research programme that provides real-time assessments of employee experience. This active research programme ensured that employee well-being was being assessed in order to proactively identify potential threats to well-being and resilience. Second, leadership was willing to translate lessons learned into action. In this example, senior U.S. Army leaders were receptive to feedback regarding the wellbeing of their employees, and they responded with a change in policy to ensure that employee health would be supported. This evidence-based policy provided a specific approach for potentially improving mental health outreach for employees coping with extreme work demands and also sent a message to the Army as a whole that employee health was an organisational priority.

problems were not solved, this example still illustrates how research, assessment and policy can function together.

What to consider when assessing wellbeing and resilience

Frequent measurement. In the case of individual assessment after a potentially traumatic exposure, frequency of assessment should be considered since symptoms may be problematic and may take time to resolve (Bisson, Brayne, Ochberg & Every, 2007). It may also be useful to consider that some individuals may experience difficulties in functioning in the short run, or may experience a worsening of symptoms over time. Others may have few if any reactions to the traumatic event or may have an initial reaction and recover quickly.

Making comparisons. Assessments may be for the purpose of getting an overall report card of how the organisation or team is going as a whole in terms of wellbeing. If the goal is to get a snapshot of the group, then the assessment needs to be conducted with teams throughout the organisation. Assessment of multiple teams allows policymakers to get a sense of team resilience relative to one another. Similarly, if assessments occur at the organisational level it is important to have comparisons to other organisations within a particular sector. For example, if paramedics working at the Springfield Hospital on average report the experience of high stress, but paramedics working in other equivalent hospitals indicate lower stress levels, that might be an indication that there is something about a particular hospital that would be worth addressing further, rather than concluding that the stress level is due exclusively to the occupation.

Timing of assessments. The timing of assessments also needs to be considered, as identified in the above case example. If employees are about to embark on a potentially difficult or high-risk mission, then an organisation may wish to measure initial wellbeing (prior to exposure) and gather a follow-up assessment post-exposure. This approach functions most clearly in organisations where the exposures are defined in time (e.g., pre and post military deployment). For organisations where there are on-going exposures (e.g., fire fighters) it is more appropriate to assess employees on commencement and then routinely thereafter.

Addressing reporting bias. A major challenge for assessments is reporting biases. Individuals can be motivated to over or under report their experience of mental health issues for several reasons. In some work-place settings, a predominant issue is underreporting. For example, there might be a mistrust about how information gathered via assessment will be used, how records are kept, or who will be able to see the information provided. The good news is that these problems can be reduced if the organisation is upfront about these issues and provides safeguards to protect the privacy of employees. The use of psychologists for conducting assessments is recommended to manage these important challenges. Psychologists are trained in the administration of mental health assessment and in the management and security of sensitive mental health information. Psychologists are trained to communicate the safeguards relating to assessment information and explain the various ways that employee confidentiality is protected.

The importance of an organisational culture that supports resilience

A culture that promotes organisational resilience ensures that the mental health and wellbeing of employees is everyone's responsibility, not just the responsibility of health care providers. However, if mental health and wellbeing is everyone's role this means that managers and employees at all levels need to be provided with the appropriate training to initially identify mental health problems in themselves and others. Moreover, people need to know what steps to take when potential issues are identified. Strategies to achieve this are outlined in more detail in Chapter 5.

Making wellbeing everyone's responsibility has one very critical benefit. Employees in high-risk occupations are typically good at functioning under stress given that they have passed initial rigorous screening and training. Thus, they may end up concealing early warning signs of problems (with or without a formal assessment). There are a handful of individuals, however, who may notice nuanced changes: family members, colleagues and supervisors. Each of these key informants needs to know what to look for and empowered to take the steps to provide proactive support. For example, the US Air Force has developed a guide to leaders about how to identify signs of distress in subordinates and including symptom checklists called "*Leader's Guide for Managing Personnel in Distress*" (2007) (Shubert *et al.*, 2008). In order to sustain a culture that promotes resilience in employees, the individuals, family members, colleagues and supervisors need to work together and to see themselves as responsible for supporting one another. Organisations can enable these critical players by training their employees and leaders on the indicators of stress reactions, physical and psychological issues, and resources available to assist those in need.

An additional path is to integrate this responsibility into the actual formal responsibilities of managers. Just as managers are formally required to undertake project management in the service of particular deliverables, they can also be required to support the resilience of their team members by undertaking required training, responding to early warning signs that may indicate a mental health problem in staff (e.g., decline in performance) and ensuring that appropriate strategies and policies are in place to support team wellbeing. Including employee wellbeing as a formalised part of the managerial role also means that the wellbeing of staff is a factor considered when making other decisions (e.g., staffing needs, project timelines, resource availability).

A second issue relating to culture is the language used when discussing mental health and the way leadership approaches mental health. Language and approach can set the tone for how employees experience, react and recover from their unique job challenges. For instance, seeking help from a mental health professional for psychological trauma is ideally akin to seeking help from a physician for a torn ligament from an occupational accident. Creating a culture that views mental health problems as an occupational hazard as opposed to a sign of individual weakness or inadequate performance increases feelings that employees are supported and understood by their organisation. This topic is addressed in detail in Chapter 5.

The role of leaders in promoting a resilient culture is also critical. Leaders at all levels can serve as a role-model for resilience and modelling resilient behaviour. Whether the leader chooses to embrace the concept of resilience or dismiss it, the occupational culture will reflect the leader's perspective.

While considerable research has focused on relatively global leadership styles such as transactional and transformational leadership (Bass, 1985), a growing field of research is examining not just styles of leadership, but also specific types of leader behaviours that promote resilience and wellbeing for the unique demands of high stress occupations. These studies have demonstrated that even controlling for global leadership skills, the addition of very specific health-promoting leadership behaviours are linked with better outcomes for the employees (Adler et al., 2014).

There are several sets of leader behaviours that are being explored. In studies being conducted with the US Army, specific leader behaviours have been associated with better resilience. Studies with US soldiers on combat and non-combat deployments have found that leadership behaviours that promote sleep are associated with better outcomes such as sleep quality and morale (Gunia et al., 2015). These behaviours are not complex nor evidence that the successful leaders were experts in the scientific literature on sleep; rather these behaviours included things as simple as: asking service members about their sleep habits, encouraging personnel to get adequate sleep particularly before important missions that require long hours, and emphasising adequate sleep as an important planning factor. The exciting finding here is that these kinds of behaviours are doable and within the scope of what leaders can achieve, making these behaviours relatively easy targets for training.

In similar research, we examined the extent to which leaders followed US Army doctrine in managing the psychological stress of their soldiers during military operations and whether behaviours consistent with this doctrine resulted in benefits to team members. This doctrine, called Combat Operational Stress Control, provides information on strategies to address stress associated with deployment, and identifies leader behaviours that can promote mental health and resilience under stressful combat-related conditions (Adler *et al.*, 2014). We asked soldiers to rate their leaders on a range of these behaviours, such as: "Encourages soldiers to seek help for stress-related problems," "Demonstrates concern for how families are dealing with stress," "Intervenes when a soldier displays stress reactions such as anxiety, depression or other behavioural health problems". We found that when soldiers reported that their leaders engaged in these kinds of behaviours, soldiers reported better mental health. This relationship was evident even after accounting for differences in the global leadership skills of their leaders, the degree to which they had experienced stressful combat-related events, and their military rank. Again, these results are intriguing because the findings suggest that there is additional benefit to be gained when leaders demonstrate specific behaviours focused on promoting health in their teams.

Cumulatively, these behaviours create a culture that values relationships and effective coping for stressful and demanding occupations. There is also evidence to suggest not only do these specific behaviours displayed by leaders assist individual wellbeing, but they also promote group-level cohesiveness, performance, and perceptions of readiness (Saboe, Anderson & Sipos, 2015).

Training resilience: some strategies used in high-risk occupations

High-risk occupations also promote resilience through training. Just as an organisation might train an individual to perform the specific tasks required of a job, training coping strategies supports resilience where there is an expectation of exposure to potentially traumatic or difficult events.

In this chapter, when we refer to training, we mean a range of topics, including job-related training, psycho-education, mental health training and mental skills training. These concepts are inter-related and reinforce one another. We want to clarify up front, however, that from our perspective it is essential that the organisation ensure the training is effective. There are many training options available, and it is essential to distinguish between good-sounding ideas that are not evidence-based and effective ideas validated by research. Chapter 14 includes a review of the current evidence supporting resilience training and what to consider when selecting training for your organisation (see also vanHove *et al.*, 2015, for a meta-analysis of resilience training in work settings).

We will briefly review some of the training strategies used in high-risk occupational settings that have demonstrated a level of effectiveness in building resilience. We focus on a few main concepts: cognitive-behavioural education, imagery, attention control, mindfulness and social fitness. Each of these concepts overlap and can be integrated into one larger training programme.

Cognitive-behavioural education. Most resilience training programmes are based in cognitive-behavioural therapy. The fundamental concept in this therapy is how individuals think about their experiences influences how they respond emotionally and behaviourally. For example, if we get cut-off in line at the petrol pump, how we interpret that behaviour matters. If we think, "that person is trying to take advantage of me and is a jerk", then we may feel angry and physiologically hyper-aroused (e.g., increase in heart rate and breathing rate). However, if we think that person may have a reasonable explanation (maybe the person had a bad day, maybe they did not see us, maybe things are a bit more stressful for them than for us right now because they have young kids in the car with them), then we may feel vaguely irritated, but mostly patient and calm. In turn, these emotions (anger or patience) are likely to result in different behaviour. The angry individual may confront the driver, honking loudly and escalate the situation; the patient individual may use the time to listen to the radio, be relieved that this is the worst inconvenience of the day, and stay relaxed.

The fundamental concept here is that how we think about events is critical, and this processing entails several key points. First, people have a confirmation bias. If they expect to see negative outcomes, they will interpret the world in such a way that confirms what they expected to see. To people with a negative confirmation bias, getting cut-off at the petrol pump would reinforce their understanding of the world as a hostile and unfair place. Without this confirmation bias, the episode may be ignored.

Second, people may have stable patterns of interpreting events and these patterns may be generally unhelpful because they do not promote flexible thinking. Some individuals tend to interpret *others* as the cause of most problems and rarely look for how they may have contributed to an incident. This kind of pattern tends to reinforce feelings of anger and outrage. Other individuals may look at *themselves* as the cause of most problems, and these individuals may end up feeling guilty and depressed. Learning about the way we typically think about the negative and even positive events can be useful in identifying and challenging these patterns.

Our research team conducted an evaluation of how useful these skills were; 88 US Soldiers were taught these cognitive-behavioural concepts and then went through a rigorous training scenario in which they were "captured" by "opposing forces" and endured difficult conditions over the course of several days. Afterwards, the majority of these soldiers reported that they had used their new resilience skills to help them endure. In particular, they reported using skills that provided specific steps for problem-solving and putting things into perspective. As one soldier noted, "*Resilience training has helped me be more optimistic in life, especially through difficult training . . .*" This training, based on the Penn Resiliency Program and adopted by the US Army, helps build the competency of optimism (addressed in detail in Chapters 2 and 4), an essential characteristic of resilience (Reivich, Seligman & McBride, 2011).

The field of sport psychology, has adopted many of the fundamentals of cognitive behavioural education and used them to help individuals enhance their performance. The techniques taught in sport psychology to promote performance optimisation also involve classic skills such as goal setting, imagery and attention control.

Imagery. Imagery involves imagining a scenario and playing it out in your mind using all sorts of sensory cues – not just visual ones. The best imagery scenarios incorporate imagined sounds, smells and touch. It is also important that the imagery includes imagining a positive outcome to help prevent a self-defeating mindset.

The following case example describes the use of imagery in combination with relaxation in resilience training developed for Swedish police officers in recruit training.

Attention control. Attention control is regulating your focus and attention despite distractions. We have all had moments where our minds are racing and all we need to do is focus on the task at hand. Attention control optimises our performance by teaching us to not focus on the "noise" in our environment – the distractions – such as nonrelevant thoughts. Instead, attention control trains individuals to tunnel attention to the specific activity that will achieve the desired and present goal. For example, if firefighters need to focus on clearing a building but are instead distracted by thoughts about flashing lights or blaring alarms, they will unlikely be as effective. Distraction comes naturally to us because our powerful minds are constantly scanning our environment to maintain a level of awareness. This is great if our job is to stay alive in the jungle, and we need to scan for predators, but if we are trying to focus on a complex task it is not necessarily a good use of our attention or cognitive energy. For employees in high-risk occupations, attention control is a critical skill for performing their job, reacting appropriately to the unexpected, and maintaining resilience.

Mindfulness. Another way to keep the mind on track is through mindfulness, or focused attention on the present moment without judgement or mental elaboration.

BOX 11.2 POLICE RECRUITS RECEIVE IMAGERY TRAINING

Bengt Arnetz, a professor at Wayne State University in Detroit, Michigan, worked with 75 police officers in Sweden in their final term at the police academy (Arnetz et al., 2013). First, Arnetz and colleagues asked cadets to complete a baseline survey and then they randomly assigned half the cadets to receive preventive imagery training and the other half to receive training as usual. The cadets in the preventive imagery training condition received 10 sessions, 90 minutes each. Preventive imagery training meant guiding participants through a description of real-world scenarios using potentially stressful on-the-job examples while participants practiced relaxation techniques. Scenarios included dealing face-to-face with a suspect holding a gun and encountering a multi-vehicle accident with severely injured people. The high-stress scenarios were based on what experienced officers had said new police officers were likely to encounter in their first year of policing.

As part of these preventive imagery training sessions, trainers discussed adaptive coping strategies and the cadets practiced using their relaxation techniques to help manage their physiological responses to the scenarios; cadets also mentally rehearsed following police tactics. This combination of mental skills allowed for the recruits to become more familiar with potentially stressful events at work and to practice managing their reactions to these events.

Three weeks before graduating, and after the preventive imagery training was completed, the cadets were surveyed again. Results showed that those in the preventive imagery training reported better mental health, fewer stomach complaints and better sleep. But what about after they had been in the real world for a year? Did the training still help them?

Eighteen months later, after a year of policing, the police officers in the study completed another questionnaire, and the results were clear. Police officers who had received the training in imagery were still doing better. Their mental health had continued to be better, they had fewer stomach complaints and their sleep was better than before they had been trained whereas the year of policing was taking a toll on the police officers in the training as usual condition. These police officers were reporting worse mental health, more stomach complaints, and their sleep was worse. There were also indications that levels of prolactin, a biomarker of physiological stress, were better in the cadets who went through the imagery training than those in the control condition.

Then Arnetz and his colleagues went one step further (Arnetz et al., 2009). They invited 25 of the original participants to come back a year after the training to take part in a critical incident simulation. In all, 18 participants returned, and this included officers from both study conditions. The participants went through a live and highly credible simulation of responding to a robbery. Was there any difference in how the two groups responded? Police officers who had gone through the imagery training had better mood and less heart rate reactivity than the police officers who had not gone through the training. And there was a difference in performance, too. An expert observing from the rooftop rated the police officers on a range of dimensions, including tactics, communication and self-control. The expert did not know which police officers had gone through the imagery training. Based on this objective evaluation, the police officers in the imagery training condition performed better than their untrained counterparts.

While the research did not show improvements in all physiological markers, the number of participants was small, and the training condition may have benefitted from a kind of placebo effect since the training as usual condition did not receive any special attention, these studies are still important. They are important because they demonstrate that it is possible for mental skills training to result in improved mental health in employees entering high-risk professions, and that these benefits may have physiological and performance implications.

Training individuals in mindfulness, or other types of meditation, has been shown to boost mental health outcomes (Goyal et al., 2014) and build mental skills such as working memory and attention (Jha et al., 2010). Working memory and attention, skills associated with mindfulness, are linked to an increased ability to engage in reason, judgement and emotion regulation. While most of the research on mindfulness has been conducted with clinical populations, there is emerging evidence that mindfulness can also promote job performance, wellbeing and mental acuity (Allen & Kiburz, 2012; Brown & Ryan, 2003; Dane & Brummel, 2013; Weinstein, Brown & Ryan, 2009).

So do you have to be a meditation guru to receive a benefit from mindfulness? Research shows that while even a little practice in mindfulness can yield measureable effects, individuals do not need to sign up for a vacation in a cave to be one with their thoughts. In a series of implementation studies, Amishi Jha, a professor of neuroscience at the University of Miami, and her team have found that soldiers who are trained in mindfulness have improved working memory and attention even during the high-stress phase of preparing to leave for a military deployment. During the pre-deployment phase, soldiers who practiced mindfulness were able to maintain neurocognitive functioning, while soldiers who did not, experienced a drop in concentration and attention (Jha et al., 2015). In other words, the deploying soldiers were resilient to the stressors normally experienced during pre-deployment thanks to mindfulness.

Social resilience. Up until now, this chapter has emphasised individual skills associated with resilience. Resilience is not just an individual skill and the topic of *social* resilience deserves special mention. John Cacioppo, a professor of Cognitive and Social Neuroscience at the University of Chicago, defines social resilience as the "capacity to foster, engage in, and sustain positive relationships, and to endure, recover from, and grow as a result of life stressors and social isolation (p. 44)" (Cacioppo, Reis & Zautra, 2011). In high-risk occupations, a small team typically takes on even greater importance because individuals are dependent on one another for their wellbeing and even survival. Thus, ensuring that individuals are able to recognise the importance of their social network, establish practices that enhance their social network, and know how to look out for one another is an important part of social resilience. Social resilience is also an essential method for combating isolation and loneliness. While there are many threats to resilience and psychological health in general, being socially isolated and lonely are two unique threats that scientists have recently identified as particularly harmful.

Cacioppo and others have documented the physiological correlates of loneliness, including its link to elevated stress hormones (Adam *et al.*, 2006), elevated blood pressure (Hawkley *et al.*, 2006), and cardiovascular disease (Caspi *et al.*, 2006). Furthermore, Cacioppo and colleagues have documented examples of how loneliness can be contagious. In a social network, when one individual begins to feel lonely, other individuals near to them in the network are at heightened risk for loneliness as well. Thus, it is to the group's advantage to treat loneliness and social isolation as a threat to the whole and not just as an indivi-dual concern.

Cacioppo has pioneered a resilience-training programme designed to enhance social fitness with Army units (Cacioppo *et al.*, 2015). In this study, platoons were randomly assigned to receive training in social fitness or a comparison training (Afghan cultural awareness). Results based on surveys that were conducted following a week of training found that soldiers in the social fitness condition, when compared to the comparison training group, reported greater improvements in social cognition that included increases in skills like empathy, perspective taking and hardiness, and reduced loneliness. Interestingly, it was not simply that soldiers in the social fitness condition were generally happier about everything. While they reported increased social connection with their work teams, they *did not* report that their relationships beyond the work setting were enhanced. This suggests that the training had a specific effect on work relationships. If you would like to read more about how the social group can benefit resilience, Chapter 10 deals with this topic in considerable detail.

The role of leadership in resilience training. Managers are in a unique position to reinforce the lessons engendered in resilience training. Our team has conducted surveys with a US Army brigade and found that the more team leaders are seen by their subordinates as invested in the training (ensuring time to schedule the training, participating in the training and referring to the training content during the duty day), the more soldiers perceive resilience training to be valuable and the better the unit's climate.

Senior leaders play an important role in ensuring that resilience-promoting programmes are formally established. By placing this information in policy and regulations, senior leaders can institutionalise the behaviours and expectations that can help individuals bounce back and cope with adverse situations. In this way, policy can reward resilience and encourage skill development.

What managers can do: lessons from high-risk occupations

In this chapter, we have highlighted the role of policy, assessment, training and leadership in developing an approach to promoting resilience within high-risk occupations. We now highlight what managers might consider if they are responsible for developing a resilience programme in their organisation.

Policy

- *Ensure policies and doctrines are consistent.* Establish policies regarding programme implementation, assessment and programme evaluation to ensure that the organisation's initiatives are correctly aligned.
- *Be aware of clear protocols for supporting employees.* Ensure that you are aware of the organisation's procedures for supporting employees. If there are none, then raise this as an organisational priority and ensure appropriate support procedures exist.

Assessment

- *Conduct a needs assessment.* What are the current indicators of resilience or resilience problems? What are the risk factors? What should be targeted? Who should be targeted?
- *Determine assessments that can be used to track employee and team resilience.* What ongoing, periodic assessments can be used or developed to track changes over time and identify potential difficulties for early intervention?

Culture

- *Develop a common language.* Be sure that assessment initiatives, training programmes, and organisational values and policy are in alignment and use common terminology that reinforces one another.

- *Make the resilience and mental health of employees everyone's responsibility.* Consider how to skill-up managers and employees to identify potential warning signs, risk factors and the organisation's procedure for supporting employees.

Training

- *Examine resilience programmes already in place.* Are these programmes addressing the organisation's needs? What is the evidence that these programmes are effective? Are the programmes being implemented correctly and to acceptable standards?
- *Determine the resilience training that needs to be implemented.* What skills should this training target? How can the training be optimally effective? Should training be targeted for certain at-risk individuals or be universal to leverage group support and communication?
- *Integrate resilience training and other skills into existing occupational initiatives.* Identify opportunities to build on the training such as through recruit training, during professional education and schooling, and prior to or following key occupational incidents. For example, if there is a tough, realistic training event, ensure that employees are primed to use resilience skills during these training tasks. Many high-risk occupations engage in post-incident reviews with the team, and these reviews can integrate resilience skills in processing the occupational incident.
- *Identify the role that leaders play in training implementation and how they can reinforce training objectives.* How can leaders optimise the impact of training? How can leaders be prepared to make the most out of training and demonstrate resilience-specific behaviours?
- *Ensure high-quality training.* Implement effective training tested within the specific occupation, conduct programme evaluations, refresh the training at regular intervals and conduct quality control checks on the training to reduce drift.

Final thoughts

Resilience is essential in high-risk occupations. While demanding and realistic training is critical to building a resilient workforce, there are many other components that can reinforce and sustain resilience. Integrating efforts from policy and training into work culture and through leadership can build a compassionate and strong occupational environment that sustains the team, enabling committed professionals to accomplish their work and support one another.

KEY MESSAGES FROM THIS CHAPTER

- Organisations that do a good job at maintaining employee resilience are proactive in assessment, training and policy development to support resilience.
- Assessments that examine wellbeing are an important tool for determining the impact of stressors on resilience, identification of problems with employee resilience and how employees may benefit from resilience training.
- Organisations need to make employee resilience everyone's responsibility via an organisational culture that supports mental health. This means providing managers and employees at all levels with the tools to recognise potential warning signs and to respond appropriately. It can also mean making the mental health of employees a formalised part of the managerial role.
- Resilience training for employees needs to be carefully selected based on what the occupational risks are and associated training needs. Resilience training should be evaluated to ensure that it is effective in the context of the organisation.

Notes

1 The views expressed in this chapter are those of the authors and do not reflect the official position of the Walter Reed Army Institute of Research, the U.S. Army, or Department of Defense.
2 Most of the examples in this chapter come from the military however many of these examples have parallels in other high-risk occupations like the police, fire fighting, and other first responders.

References

Adam, E. K., Hawkley, L. C., Kudielka, B. M. & Cacioppo, J. T. (2006). Day-to-day dynamics of experience- cortisol associations in a population-based sample of older adults. *Proceedings of the National Academy of Sciences of the United States of America, 103,* 17058–17063.

Adler, A. B., Bliese, P. D., McGurk, D., Hoge, C. W. & Castro, C. A. (2009). Battlemind debriefing and battlemind training as early interventions with soldiers returning from Iraq: Randomization by platoon. *Journal of Consulting and Clinical Psychology, 77,* 928–940.

Adler, A. B., Britt, T. W., Castro, C. A., McGurk, D. & Bliese, P. D. (2011). Effect of transition home from combat on risk-taking and health-related behaviors. *Journal of Traumatic Stress, 24,* 381–389.

Adler, A. B. & Castro, C. A. (2013). An occupational mental health model for the military. *Military Behavioral Health, 1,* 41–45.

Adler, A. B., Saboe, K. N., Anderson, J., Sipos, M. L. & Thomas, J. L. (2014). Behavioral health leadership: New directions in occupational mental health. *Current Psychiatry Reports, 16*, 484–491.

Allen, T. D. & Kiburz, K. A. (2012). Trait mindfulness and work-family balance among working parents: The mediating effects of vitality and sleep quality. *Journal of Vocational Behavior, 80*, 372–379.

American Psychiatric Association (2013) *Diagnostic and statistical manual of mental disorders* (5th edn). Washington, DC: Author.

Arnetz, B. B., Arble, E., Backman, L., Lynch, A. & Lublin, A. (2013). Assessment of a prevention program for work-related stress among urban police officers. *International Archives of Occupational and Environmental Health, 86*, 79–88.

Arnetz, B. B., Nevedal, D. C., Lumley, M. A., Backman, L. & Lublin, A. (2009). Trauma resilience training for police: Psychophysiological and performance effects. *Journal of Police and Criminal Psychology, 24*, 1–9.

Bass, B. M. (1985). *Leadership and performance beyond expectation.* New York: Free Press.

Bisson, J. I., Brayne, M., Ochberg, F. M. & Everly, G. S. (2007). Early psychosocial intervention following traumatic events. *American Journal of Psychiatry, 164*, 1016–1019.

Bliese, P. B., Adler, A. B. & Castro, C. A. (2011). Research-based preventive mental health care strategies in the military. In A. B. Adler, P. B. Bliese & C. A. Castro (eds), *Deployment Psychology: Evidence-Based Strategies to Promote Mental Health in the Military* (pp. 103–124). Washington, DC: American Psychological Association.

Bliese, P. D., Wright, K. M, Adler, A. B., Thomas, J. L. & Hoge, C. W. (2007). Timing of post-combat mental health assessments. *Psychological Services, 4*, 141–148.

Bliese, P. D., Thomas, J. L., McGurk, D., McBride, S. & Castro, C. A. (2011). Mental health advisory teams: A proactive examination of mental health during combat deployments. *International Review of Psychiatry, 23*, 127–134.

Boscarino, J. A. (1997). Diseases among men 20 years after exposure to severe stress: implications for clinical research and medical care. *Psychosomatic Medicine, 59*, 605–614.

Brown, K. W. & Ryan, R. M. (2003). The benefits of being present: Mindfulness and its role in psychological well-being. *Journal of Personality and Social Psychology, 84*, 822–848.

Bryant, R. A. & Harvey, A. G. (1995). Posttraumatic stress in volunteer firefighters. Predictors of distress. *Journal of Nervous & Mental Disease, 183*, 267–271.

Cacioppo, J. T., Adler, A. B., Lester, P. B., McGurk, D., Thomas, J. L., Chen, H. & Cacioppo, S. (2015). Building social resilience in soldiers: A double dissociative randomized controlled study. *Journal of Personality and Social Psychology, 109*, 90–105.

Cacioppo,J. T., Reis, H. T. & Zautra, A. J. (2011). Social resilience: The value of social fitness with an application to the military. *American Psychologist, 66*, 43–51.

Caspi, A., Harrington, H., Moffitt, T. E., Milne, B. J. & Poulton, R. (2006). Socially isolated children 20 years later: Risk of cardiovascular disease. *Archives of Pediatrics & Adolescent Medicine, 160*, 805–811.

Dane, E. & Brummel, B. J. (2013). Examining workplace mindfulness and its relations to job performance and turnover intentions. *Human Relations, 67*, 105–128.

Goyal, M., Singh, S., Sibinga, E. M. S., Gould, N. F., Rowland-Seymour, A., Sharma, R., Berger, Z., . . .Haythornthwaite, J. A. (2014). Meditation programs for psychological stress and well-being: a systematic review and meta-analysis. *JAMA Internal Medicine, 174*, 357–368.

Gunia, B. C., Sipos, M. L., LoPresti, M. L. & Adler, A. B. (2015). Sleep leadership in high-risk occupations: An investigation of soldiers on peacekeeping and combat missions. *Military Psychology, 27*, 197–211.

Hawkley, L. C., Masi, C. M., Berry, J. D. & Cacioppo, J. T. (2006). Loneliness is a unique predictor of age-related differences in systolic blood pressure. *Psychology and Aging, 21,* 152–164.

Herrell, R. K., Edens, E. N., Riviere, L. A., Thomas, J. L., Bliese, P. D. & Hoge, C. W. (2014). Assessing functional impairment in a working military population: The Walter Reed Functional Impairment Scale. *Psychological Services, 11,* 254–264.

Hoge, C. W., Adler, A. B., Wright, K. M., Bliese, P. D., Cox, A., McGurk, D., Milliken, C. & Castro, C. A. (2011). Walter Reed Army Institute of Research contributions during operations Iraqi freedom and enduring freedom: from research to public health policy. In C. E. Ritchie (ed.). *Combat and Operational Behavioral Health* (pp. 75–86). In M. K. Lenhart (Series ed.). *The Textbooks of Military Medicine.* Washington, DC: Department of the Army, Office of The Surgeon General, Borden Institute.

Hoge, C. W., Castro, C. A., Messer, S. C., McGurk, D., Cotting, D. I. & Koffman, R. L. (2004). Combat duty in Iraq and Afghanistan, mental health problems, and barriers to care. *New England Journal of Medicine, 351,* 13–22.

Hoge, C. W., Terhakopian, A., Castro, C. A., Messer, S. C. & Engel, C. C. (2007). Association of Posttraumatic Stress Disorder with somatic symptoms, health care visits, and absenteeism among Iraq was veterans. *American Journal of Psychiatry, 164,* 150–153.

Jha, A. P., Stanley, E. A., Kiyonaga, A., Wong, L. & Gelfand, L. (2010). Examining the protective effects of mindfulness training on working memory and affective experience. *Emotion, 10,* 54–64.

Jha, A. P., Morrison, A., Dainer-Best, J., Parker, S., Rostrup, N. & Stanley, E. (2015). Minds "At Attention": Mindfulness training curbs attentional lapses in military cohorts. *PLoS ONE, 10,* 1–19.

Kok, B. C., Herrell, R. K., Thomas, J. L. & Hoge, C. W. (2012). Posttraumatic stress disorder associated with combat service in iraq or afghanistan: reconciling prevalence differences between studies. *Journal of Nervous & Mental Disease, 200,* 444–450.

Perrin, M. A., DiGrande, L., Wheeler, K., Thorpe, L., Farfel, M. & Brackbill, R. (2007). Differences in PTSD prevalence and associated risk factors among World Trade Center disaster rescue and recovery workers. *The American Journal of Psychiatry, 164,* 1385–1394.

Reivich, K., Seligman, E. P. M. & McBride, S. A. (2011). Master resilience training in the U.S. Army. *American Psychologist, 66,* 25–34.

Riviere, L. A., Merrill, J. C., Thomas, J. L., Woilk, J. E. & Bliese, P. D. (2012). 2003–2009 Marital functioning trends among U.S. enlisted soldiers following combat deployments. *Military Medicine, 177,* 1169–1189.

Robinson, H. M., Sigman, M. R. & Wilson, J. P. (1997). Duty-related stressors and PTSD symptoms in suburban police officers. *Psychological Reports, 81,* 835–845.

Rona, R. J., Jones, M., Hull, L., MacManus, D., Fear, N. T. & Wessely, S. (2015). Anger in the UK Armed Forces: Strong association with mental health, childhood antisocial behavior, and combat role. *Journal of Nervous and Mental Disease, 203,* 15–22.

Rona, R. J., Jones, M., Keeling, M., Hull, L., Wessely, S. & Fear, N. T. (2014). Mental health consequences of overstretch in the UK Armed Forces, 2007–09: A population-based cohort study. *The Lancet Psychiatry, 1,* 531–538.

Saboe, K. N., Anderson, J. & Sipos, M. (2015, April). Multilevel assessment of how leader-behaviors promoting resilience improve unit performance. *Presented at Society for Industrial-Organizational Psychology* annual conference. Philadelphia, PN.

Shubert, J., Ritchie, E. C. (Col.), Everly Jr, G. S., Fiedler, N., Williams, M. B., Mitchell, C. S. & Langlieb, A. M. (2008). A missing element in disaster mental health: Behavioral health surveillance for first responders. *International Journal of Emergency Mental Health, 9,* 201–214.

Thomas, J. L., Wilk, J. E., Riviere, L. A., McGurk, D., Castro, C. A. & Hoge, C. W. (2010). Prevalence of mental health problems and functional impairment among active component and national guard soldiers 3 and 12 months following combat in Iraq. *Archives of General Psychiatry, 67,* 614–623.

vanHove, A. J., Herian, M. N., Perez, A. L. U., Harms, P. D. & Lester, P. B. (2015). Can resilience be developed at work? A meta-analytic review of resilience-building programme effectiveness. *Journal of Occupational and Organizational Psychology, 89,* 278–307.

Weinstein, N., Brown, K. W. & Ryan, R. M. (2009). A multi-method examination of the effects of mindfulness on stress attribution, coping, and emotional well-being. *Journal of Research in Personality, 43,* 374–385.

12

USING AUTONOMOUS MOTIVATION TO BUILD EMPLOYEE RESILIENCE

CPT Danny Boga[1]

When we think about what makes employees resilient perhaps the nature of their motivation towards work activities is not something that immediately comes to mind. The term motivation is used to describe the forces that provide an incentive for people to initiate and persist at some form of behaviour that will lead to desired outcomes or goals (Deci & Ryan, 2000). However, research in the area of motivation and wellbeing suggests that the reasons employees are motivated to perform job tasks may have important implications for their resilience. In this chapter, we focus on motivational processes that are key to encouraging an environment that is conducive with developing resilience and sustainable workplace performance. Moreover, we describe how managers can facilitate the "right" type of motivation to maintain and encourage employee resilience. According to one prominent theory of motivation, that will be introduced shortly, autonomous motivation is a desirable form of motivation. *Autonomous* motivation, put simply, is where behaviour is driven by self-regulated motives (e.g., personal goals, values, connection with others, interest or enjoyment). It is distinct from *controlled* forms of motivation that are directive in nature (e.g., reward, punishment, imposed rules, obligations or expectations).

The terms manager and leader may seem to be used interchangeably in this chapter, however they do imply different focuses. The manager is an appointed position that holds formalised authority. The manager's primary goal is to achieve performance outcomes through the direction of tasks and allocation of resources (e.g., time, equipment, people etc.). Whereas the primary goal of the leader is to influence others' behaviour (i.e., motivating people towards desired outcomes). An efficient manager might be able to achieve excellent results without any leadership ability as one does not necessarily need good leadership skills if they have the power to direct other peoples' actions. However, if people are not motivated or lack a sense of purpose, competence or team identity, it is unlikely they will respond well to workplace stressors as they arise. Staff resilience problems such as poor retention, workplace absences and minimum workplace effort are likely issues facing managers who do not develop their leadership skills in conjunction with their management skills.

Introducing the self-determination theory of motivation

Self-determination theory is a macro-theory of motivation that introduces the concepts of autonomous and controlled motivation as alternatives to the more commonly referenced 'intrinsic motivation' versus 'extrinsic motivation' (Deci & Ryan, 2000). *Intrinsic* motivation is behaviour that is driven by a personal sense of enjoyment or desire to perform an activity. Extrinsic approaches to motivation are commonly used in the workplace as rewards. Punishments are strong incentives to change behaviour and can provide quick results (consider common parenting approaches to raising children; Skinner, 1950). There are, however, some notable limitations to exclusively using rewards and punishments as a source of motivation. In particular, constant surveillance of employees is often necessary in order to reward desired behaviour or punish undesirable behaviour when it occurs. Failure to apply the anticipated incentives will often result in staff resentment or effort only being applied to a level required to obtain a reward or avoid a punishment.

Intrinsic motivation is often considered the alternative to extrinsic motivation. It is intuitive that people will invest more energy and effort into activities they enjoy. Enjoyable activities are also less likely to be perceived as taxing. However, outside of selecting people for jobs based on their interests, it is often beyond the scope of a manager's ability to make people enjoy specific job tasks. Self-determination theory assists us to think about motivation beyond what is or is not enjoyable and explores the potential for external influences on motivation that have very similar benefits to intrinsic motivation. This is a key consideration because, as noted above, a manager cannot make someone enjoy work tasks and thus can never truly make someone intrinsically motivated. However, self-determination theory provides some good alternatives to intrinsic motivation and suggests that by creating the right conditions managers can motivate employees in a way that allows the directed and sustained pursuit of organisational goals. Importantly, more recent thinking on the issue of motivation suggests that the type of motivation a person experiences may also play a critical role in resilience. Research has consistently demonstrated a strong link between intrinsic forms of motivation and a range of beneficial mental health outcomes (e.g., Hackman & Oldham, 1976; Kasser & Ryan, 1996; Nix *et al.*, 1999). Thus, understanding how to generate autonomous forms of motivation in employees is likely to not only promote performance, but resilience as well.

Autonomous and controlled motivation. Self-determination theory suggests that there are two overarching motivational types: controlled and autonomous motivation. These two overarching motivational categories describe the source of motivation; that is, whether the motivation for behaviour is from external or internal sources. These two broad motivational categories are illustrated in Figure 12.1. As the name implies, *controlled motivation* occurs when behaviours are undertaken due to external influences such as reward (e.g., money) or punishment (e.g., being let-go) or by socially prescribed values that are perceived to impact one's self-image. For example, an employee understands that being a confident public speaker is significant to the organisation and might practise public speaking in order to avoid embarrassment or gain recognition from others. Thus, controlled motivation is a source of influence outside the individual's direct control (e.g. praise or ridicule are still provided by others or the individual's assessment of what others might be thinking).

Autonomous motivation on the other hand, is when individuals engage in behaviour because they enjoy the activity (intrinsic motivation), or when they are influenced by personal values or goals that are important to one's sense of value. An employee may understand that being a confident public speaker is important to their sense of self-worth and therefore views opportunities to practise speaking skills as important or satisfying. Being a good public speaker becomes important to the individual whether or not it is considered inherently enjoyable. The behaviour people display when motivated in this manner is almost identical to that associated with purely intrinsic motivation or enjoyment. Autonomous motivation can even exceed performance results associated with purely intrinsic motivation. This is because people doing an activity purely for fun are not always interested in investing effort to improve their performance as more effort might not equate to greater enjoyment of the activity (e.g., "I enjoy what I do and don't want to change how I do it just to be more competitive").

Figure 12.1 illustrates the types of motivational regulation described in self-determination theory and the relationship between different motivational types, and how they influence behaviour. It should be noted that while moving from left to right through the model depicts increasing levels of internalised motivation, this is not a developmental continuum with stages of motivation that must be passed through. Instead, individuals may be simultaneously influenced by multiple motivational states, to differing degrees, for different tasks and situations. It is the strongest motivational influence that will have the strongest influence on observable behaviour. For example, an employee may receive a good salary or be offered a bonus to achieve a task (external regulation), while he/she may also see their work as important (identified regulation) and feel a sense of self-worth and achievement by acting in a way consistent with their identity as a competent professional (integrated regulation). All of these factors will drive the employees' behaviour; however, whichever influence is the strongest for the individual will likely have the greatest observable effect on how the person relates to why they are engaging in the activity or task. How controlled and autonomous motivation influence performance and resilience can be better understood by examining more closely the five sub-domains of motivation, which are: (1) external regulation, (2) introjected regulation, (3) identified regulation, (4) integrated regulation and (5) intrinsic motivation. The two

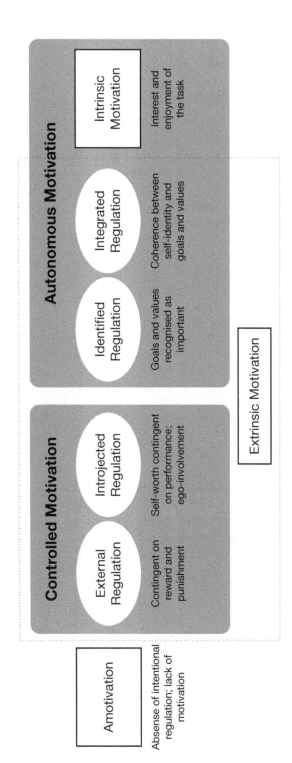

FIGURE 12.1 An illustration of motivational regulation within Self-Determination Theory

sub-domains of motivation, which make up controlled motivation are external regulation and introjected regulation and are described below.

The sub-domains of controlled motivation

External regulation. External regulation reflects the classic definition of extrinsic motivation where an individual's behaviour is instigated by external factors, such as attaining tangible rewards or avoiding punishment. While offering quick and notable changes to behaviour, external regulation has been linked to poor maintenance and transfer of behaviour once the external influences have been withdrawn. For example, a person might engage in professional development training in order to gain a pay increase/promotion or to meet/maintain trade requirements. In this case, they are likely only to seek professional development when required and engage only to a level allowing them to meet an acceptable or minimum standard. Remove the reward or punishment and the behaviour decays. There is little incentive to engage in behaviour outside of what has been mandated and actively monitored.

Introjected regulation. Introjected regulation is similar to external regulation, but instead of the reward or punishment coming from other people, the consequences are administered by individuals onto themselves (e.g., shame, guilt). However, the internalised reward or punishment is still a controlled type of motivation as it is based on the individual's assessment of what others think or a comparison to others achievements. Some common examples of this type of motivation are pride, or threats of guilt and shame. Using the professional development example, a person might engage in training to avoid feeling shame if he/she cannot meet a group standard, or he/she may seek the admiration of others for exceeding the standard. This type of motivation is still considered a form of both extrinsic and controlled motivation because although it is regulated within the individual it is socially derived and dependent on the feedback of others. Remove the perceived social scrutiny and feedback and once again the behaviour decays.

The sub-domains of autonomous motivation

The three sub-domains of motivation that make up autonomous motivation are identified regulation, integrated regulation and intrinsic motivation. Identified and integrated regulation has the most interest here as they are both simultaneously considered forms of extrinsic motivation and therefore can be influenced by external sources such as good leadership. However, these dimensions also reflect forms of autonomous motivation and therefore share the benefits of self-directed behaviours such as optimal performance and resilience.

Identified regulation. Identified regulation is when individuals recognise the value of a behaviour. This behaviour is more likely to occur without requiring constant external feedback. For example, an individual recognises the importance of professional development for their career or ability to meet job demands, so he/she will train without needing to be directed. He/she might do this in order to experience professional mastery and improved performance, but training is not engaged primarily for enjoyment. This means that the individual will at times find excuses not to seek or engage in professional development, but overall will routinely undertake training, so they can maintain a personally set standard.

Integrated regulation. Integrated regulation is the most internalised form of extrinsic motivation that is considered a fully autonomous type of motivation. It involves recognising the importance of behaviours as well as assimilating them into personal values. In short, the behaviour becomes part of the individual's identity. From observation, integrated regulation is almost indistinguishable from intrinsic motivation, but it is still considered extrinsic because the behaviours are done to attain particular outcomes rather than for their own inherent enjoyment. The value of these outcomes can be influenced by environmental factors and are thus still something a leader can affect. Considering the example of professional development, an individual may engage in training because having professional mastery is perceived to be part of their identity, but again they do not engage in training because it is inherently enjoyable. Behavioural responses of integrated regulation are so similar to intrinsically motivated individuals that many people will often say they do an activity for the enjoyment while still being strongly motivated by the external influences. For example, a person who considers being a highly knowledgeable and skilled professional as a valued part of their identity will often state they enjoy professional development opportunities. But if for some reason their level of competence was no longer effected by the amount or complexity of their training, most would likely change how they train or start to use their time for other activities. Thus the enjoyment is derived by the measurable gains and is therefore extrinsically influenced.

Intrinsic motivation. Intrinsic motivation is when a behaviour or task is engaged in because it is enjoyable for its own sake. It is strongly associated with self-regulated behaviour and individuals will seek opportunities to engage in intrinsically motivated activities; however, it is next to impossible for a leader to make someone enjoy a workplace task if it is not already considered enjoyable.

The link between autonomous motivation and resilience

Autonomous forms of motivation have been shown to be a reliable predictor of high performance, wellbeing over time, workplace satisfaction and retention (e.g., Gegenfurtner et al., 2009; Yelon et al., 2004). Autonomous motivation sets the conditions for an individual to perceive a situation as a challenge, rather than a hindrance, and thus provides a protective buffer to the negative effects of job strain, exhaustion and burnout (Hakanen, Bakker & Demerouti, 2005). An example of how stress and discomfort can be internalised as a valued challenge can be seen in people undertaking physical exercise. Physical exercise by its very nature puts the body under stress, discomfort and sometimes pain (ask any athlete about the joys of delayed onset muscle soreness); however, thousands of people still sacrifice time and money to join gyms or engage in physical training, while expressing different levels of enjoyment for the activities involved.

Evidence of the role autonomous motivation plays in resilience comes from studies investigating a well-known model of workplace stress: The Job Demands-Resources Model. This model defines job demands as any aspects of a job that require sustained physical or mental effort and are therefore associated with psychological costs (e.g., feeling exhausted). In contrast, job resources are aspects of a job that are functional in achieving workplace goals and promote personal development. Job resources are considered to reduce the costs of demands. Importantly, many of the identified job resources relate directly to psychological needs, which have been recognised in self-determination theory as likely to promote autonomous motivation. Studies examining the Job Demands-Resource model show that job demands are fairly consistently related to job strain, which is associated with reduced energy and increased health problems. In contrast, job resources relate to greater motivation (e.g., engagement and commitment; Bakker & Demerouti, 2007). Moreover, job-resources tend to buffer the negative effects of job-demands. Importantly, workers with high levels of motivation were found to report less job strain and workplace distress when confronted with high levels of workplace stress (Bakker et al., 2007; Demerouti et al., 2001). From this perspective, the conditions (or job resources) leading to higher autonomous motivation also buffer and diminish the negative effects of job strain therefore promoting resilience.

From a performance perspective, when employees are autonomously motivated towards organisationally desirable activities, the burden on managers is reduced as individuals self-regulate and monitor their own performance. Staff are more likely to self-correct errors (monitored against internalised standards) and often show a greater desire for skill mastery (e.g., Legault & Inzlicht, 2013). This results in not only higher workplace performance and worker resilience, but also has the additional effect of reducing workplace demands and associated job strain on managers who are required to monitor and performance manage staff. There is emerging evidence that autonomously motivated people are more likely to tolerate and persist with tasks even if they create physical and emotional discomfort, frustration and anxiety (e.g., Hodgins et al., 2010). Perhaps you have experienced such a situation yourself where a task requires significant mental or physical effort, and is inherently challenging, and yet you are willing to persist because the outcomes of the task are of great personal value. Such motivational factors are likely predictors of task and goal achievement as well as greater individual resilience.

Enhancing the conditions for autonomous forms of motivation

Self-determination theory not only identifies why autonomous motivation is beneficial for developing good mental health and sustainable performance, it also identifies what is required to foster autonomous motivation. Three universal psychological needs are considered to be required for the development and expression of autonomous motivation, as well as psychological health and wellbeing: (1) autonomy, (2) relatedness and (3) competence (Deci & Vansteenkiste, 2004). The importance of these needs is that by fulfilling them in the workplace autonomous motivation can be increased. In the following section, I describe each of these needs and then give you tips about managing staff in a way that increases their fulfilment.

(1) Autonomy. Autonomy is the human desire for self-governance. Specifically, autonomy concerns a need to behave in a way consistent with who we are. Autonomy should not be confused with related ideas of independence, separateness or individualism. An individual might work independently or without direct supervision, but still be bound by policy and procedure to such an extent that no self-governance can occur. It is one thing to be told what you need to do and another thing entirely to be told exactly how to do it. People who do not have their needs for autonomy met often feel trapped, frustrated or unappreciated. Micromanagement directly undermines the need for autonomy and is often seen to be a notable source of workplace stress.

(2) Relatedness. Relatedness (sometimes referred to as belongingness) is defined as the feeling that one is close and connected to significant others. It requires a sense of mutual respect, trust, support and engagement with others in order to be satisfied. A sense of purpose and having your contribution recognised and appreciated by others within a valued group/team is important for the satisfaction of this basic psychological need.

(3) Competence. Competence is the third basic psychological need and is defined as an individual's desire to feel effective in interacting with the environment. It pertains to one's ability to succeed at challenging tasks and to attain desired outcomes. It is fulfilled when individuals feel they are able to engage in challenging tasks in order to test and extend valued skills.

Fostering autonomous motivation in the workplace: what managers can do

Managers are able to do several things to enhance each of the psychological needs (autonomy, relatedness and competence) in order to allow autonomous motivation to flourish. In this next section, I address how managers can create the right conditions for these needs in the workplace.

The following suggestions are not intended to be a comprehensive "recipe" that is to be rigidly applied in all situations. Instead, these are some possible approaches to satisfying these three basic psychological needs and thus facilitate the development of autonomous motivation and resilience in others. With some lateral thinking a leader should be able to integrate the underlying intent of these suggestions and apply the principles in contextually appropriate ways. In addition, by role modelling flexible approaches to changing situations, leaders will also be displaying those skills and abilities, which are predictive of resilient individuals.

While by no means a comprehensive list, the following approaches are useful examples for how to encourage the development of autonomous motivation through the satisfaction of basic psychological needs. The following examples have been adapted from those proposed by Stone, Deci and Ryan (2009), and Steffens *et al.* (2014). While these suggestions have been grouped under headings of the individual basic psychological needs, many of the suggestions strongly influence all three needs concurrently.

Creating autonomy: getting the right balance

Micro-management, the enemy of autonomy. One of the most common management activities that directly reduces the experience of autonomy is 'micro-management'. Micro-management is often one of the leading reported causes of dissatisfaction and perceived stress in the workplace. Micro-management can occur as a consequence of several concerns or conditions such as time pressure, being held accountable for the mistakes of staff, and worry that the task will not be completed exactly as required. Consequently, managers may place additional restrictions and reporting requirements on staff or detailed dictation of how tasks are to be achieved. This often gives managers some peace of mind and a greater feeling of control. The irony is that micro-management is time consuming and likely to reduce autonomous motivation and therefore lead to poorer performance.

Managers who engage in micro-managing often do not see their close monitoring and specific directions to staff as micro-management. Often they view their close involvement as mentoring or developing staff. However, staff often perceive this as supervisor mistrust. More importantly, it also does little to develop employee competency (by reducing employees' need to think for themselves and consider potential consequences of what they do), thus reducing effective learning and independent ability to adapt to unforeseen problems.

As a general rule, if the task is routine or within the expected work role of the staff member then managers should allow as much autonomy as possible. In order to do this, it is important that a manager realises two things. First, he/she must acknowledge the connection between increased stress (e.g. time-pressure or accountability concerns) and the tendency to micro-manage. Second, he/she must realise that micro-management is unlikely to achieve faster or more satisfactory long-term outcomes because undermining employee autonomy also undermines performance. If the task is new, unique or requires specialist skills that staff lack, the manager needs to be clear about providing the guidance as *training* and not an ongoing form of task *management*. Thus, the supervision is now framed as part of professional development, rather than a form of monitoring. As with all training, the trainee needs to be given greater scope to demonstrate their mastery of the skills as they develop.

Asking employees about the satisfaction of autonomy. Sometimes giving employees too much freedom to choose can undermine the experience of autonomy as people can start to become distracted by decisions not previously considered. For example, a high school may not have a school uniform and therefore a student has the freedom to choose what they wear. However, the benefit of this autonomy might be negated by perceived social rules of how they should dress. Furthermore, parents, teachers and peers may all have different expectations, to the point that any choice made highlights potential repercussions that otherwise might not have been considered. In short, greater freedom can sometimes create feelings of less autonomy due to a greater need to align our "choices" with external expectations. Similarly, an open plan workplace with no assigned desk spaces leads to greater freedom of where to sit or who to sit near, but might reduce feelings of autonomy due to increased social expectations or drawing staff attention to their inability to set up their workspace as they might like.

Too much autonomy can also leave employees feeling as though they lack direction or a clear and valued place within the team or organisation (e.g. "they don't really care what I do"). This can reduce feelings of relatedness with others, or inhibit the development of valued workplace competencies across a range of skills (another important psychological need). This is particularly likely with less experienced staff who may desire a greater level of direction. So, how is the right balanced achieved? The right balance is about good judgement and is likely to be a negotiation with the individual employee. Most staff are able to report if the level of autonomy is right for them, or whether they require more or less direction (e.g., "do you feel comfortable with this level of autonomy, or would you like more direction?"). Identifying how staff perceive the level of autonomy and whether it meets their individual needs allows for autonomy to be satisfied without the downsides of too much freedom or too much/little guidance or direction.

Offer choices within structure, including the clarification of responsibilities. When the completion of a task is more important than how the task is to be achieved, managers can also offer a range of possible pathways to task completion or allow staff scope to develop their own approach within a specified framework. If clear structure and boundaries (along with clear guidelines of the leader/manager's intent) are provided, then staff will be more likely to engage in beneficial acts of initiative without crossing into problematic behaviour. This approach also encourages individuals to problem solve and reflect on their approaches to doing their job. This in turn also contributes to the satisfaction of the basic psychological need of competence. Relatedness is also developed through the sense that the organisation/leader has trust in workers' abilities.

The clarification of responsibilities and individual contributions is critical. This is true for both the satisfaction of autonomy as well as relatedness. A meaningful rationale should be provided for undertaking uninteresting tasks and staff's perspectives should be acknowledged, while at the same time clarifying their responsibilities and the utility or purpose of why the activity is meaningful to individuals, the team, and wider organisation. For example, a manager might reinforce why a mandatory audit is an opportunity for team members to identify areas for improvement or to address inefficiencies/problems within the team or organisation. While not an interesting activity, it is a chance for the team to demonstrate their professionalism in getting it done. This can be a difficult leadership challenge; however, a key leadership skill is to be able to reframe organisational tasks and align them with important team values.

Active listening including acknowledging others' perspectives. Encouraging autonomy (and also relatedness) often requires an individual to feel that their view point has been heard and acknowledged. This is often easy to achieve in a workplace setting through the use of active listening. This includes the explicit acknowledgment of an individual's perception of a problem. Leaders who use active and reflective listening and are effective at summarising points generally find that employees report more perceived workplace support (Stone *et al.*, 2009). It is through acknowledgement from immediate supervisors that employees often develop greater trust in the leader's support. Statements of affirmation are also identified as being critical to active listening as they acknowledge and confirm to the speaker that their message has been understood.

An effective leader should be able to provide affirmation without necessarily endorsing what is being communicated. Acknowledging the merits and reasons an employee has expressed an opinion will reinforce their feelings of being a valued part of the team. If the suggestions or perspectives of an employee are not viable or are unreasonable then the staff member(s) should be informed that their suggestions were considered (if only briefly) and some context provided as to why a decision was made. Ideally this would include how their contributions were integrated or helped inform the decision, or identify reasons or context for why their suggestions were not applied. While this level of feedback is not always viable or desired, acknowledging employees' contributions and suggestions generates feelings of being valued, competent and respected in their workplace. This is a good approach to generating employee loyalty to their team leader and a feeling of membership in their organisation.

Minimising coercive controls such as rewards and comparison with others. Using reward or punishment is often a well learnt and instinctive reaction for many people in authority. That is because there is strong psychological evidence to show it works (e.g., Skinner's Operant Conditioning Theory). However, rewards and punishment are also the poster child for controlled motivational approaches. Controlled motivation is resource intensive to sustain from a leadership perspective because the good behaviour will disappear if the behaviour cannot be observed or the reward/punishment is removed. Additionally, punishments often have the greatest effect on those individuals who already value the desired behaviours or outcomes. For less conscientious individuals, motivational changes are rarely sustained beyond the opportunity for reward. Punishment is an effective method of initiating behavioural change from what should not be done; however, punishments do not inherently teach someone what should be done. More often the behavioural change that occurs is only to a minimum standard to avoid further punishment. In some cases, punishment only leads to greater effort being invested in not being caught while continuing to engage in the undesired behaviour.

Competition schemes are often seen as great motivators; however, research suggests for the few winners who benefit there are more losers who are adversely affected (Stone *et al.*, 2009). This is not to say that appropriate compensation should not be provided for good work or that disciplinary action not be taken where appropriate. Similarly, it does not suggest competitive activities do not have positive effects on developing teamwork and shared purpose. However, when applied at the *individual* level it should not be the default method to encourage long-term motivation or resilience.

As a side note, research has observed a significant relationship between high value placed on money/reward and poor mental health and unethical workplace behaviour (e.g. Stone, Bryant & Wier, 2010), so encouraging performance primarily through financial rewards might not be a sound long-term organisational strategy if integrity and good mental health is a valued organisational goal.

Feeling a sense of relatedness

In Chapter 10, we discuss in more detail the way leaders can build team cohesion and identification. Thus, if you are particularly interested in these aspects of team building and how it relates to psychological resilience than it is suggested that you also give some attention to Chapter 10. However, here are some additional suggestions for how to increase individual-level relatedness.

Valuing the team and its duties. Militaries around the world have often conceptualised relatedness as Esprit de Corps or morale. In corporate environments it can be described as organisational climate. Relatedness also reflects important aspects such as task meaning and shared intent; that is, not only do people need to feel like a valued part of a team, but the purpose of the team or related activities need to have value as well. The need for relatedness can be undermined when an individual or team's contribution is not valued. One common way that team member relatedness is adversely affected is when a meaningful task is not given the resources to realistically achieve the objective to a desired standard (e.g., unrealistic time demands, lack of staff, under trained/equipped etc.). This leads team members to question how valuable the task actually is to the organisation and by extension the value of the team's contribution to the wider organisation.

The leader as part of the team. Being one of the team means the leader represents the unique qualities that define the team and embodies the core attributes of the team, which make it special and unique. The leader should aim to be a role-model and exemplary representation of what it means to be a member of that team. Double standards between leaders and team members are a commonly seen workplace example of not meeting the intent of being part of the team (e.g., the boss demands people to be punctual, but routinely arrives late to work or meetings). Leading by example is a good way to illustrate this identity prototypically. One does not have to be a greater subject matter expert than their team to lead by example. Rather, the leader should aim to embody the values they want others to demonstrate.

Crafting a sense of the team. Crafting a sense of the team involves making individuals feel they are part of the same team and increasing cohesion and a sense of inclusivity within the group. In order to achieve this, leaders need to make sustained efforts to clarify people's understanding of what the team stands for (and what it does not) by defining core values, norms and ideals. It has been found to be more effective to build a team identity from the bottom up; that is, move from sub-group identity (e.g. small team, section, department etc.) to superordinate identity (e.g., branch, company, franchise etc.); as opposed to moving from a superordinate identity to a subgroup identity. Specifically, this might involve providing a physical reality for the group by creating group-related material (e.g., team uniforms, printed stationery, brew-mugs etc.) or team/section based meetings regarding the direction of the team within the greater organisational context.

Militaries around the world have done this for centuries through the use of battalion standards (banners) and colours, Corps mottos, platoon names and logos, and clearly defined professional roles and responsibilities (e.g., the role of the infantry is learnt almost as a mantra within the Royal Australian Infantry, above the role of the Army as a whole). External, but relevant, social activities are another means of creating a sense of team identity. Sporting activities are often used within the military as a means of team identity building/bonding in a non-routine work environment. Within the military, sports reflect the organisational values of fitness, skill and teamwork. The relevance of social activities to team building is important. Activities should clearly reflect the pursuit of values embraced by the team.

Doing it for the team. A leader is required to stand up for, and defend, the team's interests (not personal interests or those of other groups). It also involves championing concerns and ambitions that are important to the team as a whole. Double standards and leaders pushing their own agenda for career advancement at the expense of the team are often cited as examples of violation of this principle (e.g., volunteering the team for extra tasks where the leader will get the majority of the benefits and recognition while the team does the majority of the work, or being seen to support other teams, departments or management above the team's needs).

Making the team matter. Leaders need to deliver concrete outcomes that give weight to the team's existence and allow team members to see their role and team membership as meaningful. Leaders can achieve this through the development and promotion of shared understanding, coordination and success. This relates to having the team deliver tangible outcomes, which are related to the team's identity and purpose. Overall, this represents making the team matter by raising the team profile not only to group members (e.g., "our section achieved the highest productivity/sales/performance rating within the company this month"), but also to people outside the team (e.g., advertising team achievements in a public forum, media, organisational publications or championing the team's achievements to upper management, the public and key stakeholders etc.).

To be effective, the profile projected should be aligned with values reflected by the team's core identity. Providing opportunities for the team to express these values and receive recognition for their efforts not only satisfies an individual's basic psychological need of relatedness, but it also encourages a closer and more supportive team identity. Tangible outcomes are generally work specific; however, they also can reflect valued social activities (e.g., sporting competitions, charity events, public interests).

Creating competence

The relationship between competence and autonomy. Competence is the third basic psychological need and is really about one's sense of control when interacting with their environment. Competency is fulfilled when individuals are able to engage in challenging and complex tasks in order to test and extend their knowledge, skills and abilities. However, like autonomy, it is important to get the balance right. If the need for competence is under satisfied then motivation would be negatively affected. A skilled employee is not likely to remain motivated if they are denied the opportunity to fully use their skills in a meaningful environment. So if an employee holds a self-identity as a competent and well-trained professional, being required to undertake tasks inconsistent with their core skills is not going to satisfy the basic need of competence. Conversely, if competence needs are exceeded an individual might feel set up to fail or overwhelmed, and they are unlikely to be motivated towards attempting tasks perceived as impossible. Moreover, as the individual's skills improve, more demanding work (congruent with training, mentorship and resources) must be provided in order to continue to meet the individual's competency needs.

The satisfaction of competence often relates closely with autonomy, particularly in high performance teams. As an individual's competence in an area increases he/she may require greater autonomy and challenge in order to satisfy their competency needs.

Ask open questions and invite participation in solving important problems. Some of the most common barriers to applying this principle are authoritative tendencies of establishing a premature conversational agenda, labelling, blaming or playing the "I'm the expert" role. While this is often done to establish personal authority and expert power (i.e., subject matter expertise) it does little to generate staff motivation. Staff who are not given the opportunity to provide input relevant to their level of experience are more likely to feel undervalued, under-utilised and generally more frustrated in their job.

Open questions allow for problems to be considered without a preferred leader driven solution influencing possible responses. This allows for staff to reason the problem through and apply a deeper level of analysis. Confrontation or blaming (e.g., "you screwed up") is likely to elicit responses such as quiet and resentful acknowledgment or angry or avoidant denial.

Genuine open questions (e.g., "what contributed to this error occurring?") encourages active participation and processing of the situation by staff, as well as gaining more information as to the employee's perception of the problem. This might sound like a waste of precious time, but keep in mind a quick fix now often requires greater monitoring and more frequent interventions over time. This approach is often in contrast to the traditional leader's desire to appear like the competent expert who can dictate solutions quickly and then get on with the job. For long-term loyalty, growth and satisfaction within a team, employees need to feel they are contributing and are a valued part of the team rather than a tool of the leader's greatness.

Provide sincere feedback that acknowledges initiative and factual, nonjudgmental observations about problems. For praise to be effective it needs to be sincere and specific. Praise that acknowledges mere compliance or base level performance tends to be perceived as controlling, while praise that acknowledges initiative is generally seen as supportive of people's competence and autonomy. For example, praising a staff member for performing an activity that is part of their routine job description can lead to the individual or other staff members to see the praise as insincere (e.g., "the boss is just trying to look like he/she is attentive" or "they never notice the real work that I do") or wonder why praise was given on that occasion (e.g., "what made that time special?" or "why are they only now realising that I always do that well?"). Whereas when the praise is for a specific action which provided a valued outcome or required an above average level of knowledge or skill then recognising the staff member's actions reinforces that the manager/team/organisation values the member's unique contribution, effort or personal qualities.

Equally, effective leaders may need to provide unwelcome feedback about workplace problems. The best approach for providing corrective feedback is by giving clear and concrete descriptions (i.e., just the facts), with neither judgement nor unnecessary confrontation. An effort should be made to hear and acknowledge the employee's perspective of what contributed to their performance and/or behaviour. This allows an opportunity for the employee to not only explore what contributed to the error but allows them to process and learn from the mistake.

The delivery of such feedback should avoid simultaneously demanding immediate improvement. The need for improvement is inherently implied in the provision of feedback, but when left unsaid it is often perceived as an opportunity for developing self-governed competence; whereas, when explicitly stated (e.g., "you better start getting this right from now on") the result is often perceived as controlling and generally promotes resentment. This often leads to the correct behaviour being conducted only when being observed or when there is a risk of being caught.

Of course, there are situations when immediate change and improvement needs to be demanded in cases of safety and outcome critical behaviour. In these cases, reward and punishment incentives are appropriate for immediate short-term gains; however, these should be followed-up with more autonomous approaches in order to encourage longer-lasting behavioural change and better mental health.

Develop talent and share knowledge. Mentoring and offering opportunities for staff to develop new skills as a means of personal and professional development promotes autonomous motivation. This occurs via both the development of competence as well as creating the conditions for more gratifying workplace applications of skills or increasing opportunities to collaborate with others. Competence is a constantly developing and demanding attribute. The more competence one develops the greater autonomy an individual will want in order to satisfy both the need for autonomy as well as continuing to grow further competence. A leader needs to be aware of their followers' competence levels as well as which areas staff feel are important both personally and professionally. Forecasting an achievable, sustainable, measurable and relevant plan to satisfy followers' competency needs requires time and ongoing monitoring. One method for satisfying the need for competency is by highlighting the meaning or reframing current tasks as opportunities to optimise performance or personal development in valued areas.

Raising awareness of the possibilities for learning and advancement opportunities can enhance subjective feelings of optimism, self-regulated motivation and overall wellbeing. However, the leader should be careful to promote learning or development possibilities as opportunities for self-directed engagement and growth rather than as rewards, which can be obtained if they deliver good performance. If seen as a reward the opportunity instead becomes a controlled form of motivation and would be unlikely to enhance motivation beyond what is required to obtain the desired reward. While this will have a short-term positive effect on performance, no motivationally associated mental health improvements would be likely. Or alternatively, once someone realises they are not competitive then the reward will no longer motivate them (e.g., a staff member realises that person 'X' is better and will obviously get the reward, so they no longer see the reward as a motivating influence). This is not to suggest that rewards given in acknowledgement of outstanding work are inappropriate. Rather it highlights that consideration needs to be given to the manner in which rewards are delivered so they are perceived as a reward for valued contributions rather than as a comparison to the efforts of others.

Some leaders are hesitant or unwilling to share knowledge or develop their staff members as they are concerned that it might weaken their position of power. This not only reduces the potential performance and workplace satisfaction of whole teams, but it is also likely to lead to high performance employees seeking other employment in order to satisfy their needs. This has obvious repercussions for retention, succession management and sustaining mentally resilient staff.

The satisfaction of needs is subjective

One final note on satisfying an individual's basic needs. The level for satisfying the need is subjective to the individual; that is, someone's perception of their own competence might not mirror their actual ability. When this occurs the individual's need for competence might have to be satisfied in other areas while efforts are made to align their actual ability with their beliefs (or vice versa). For example, an individual might have a self-perception that they are very good at a job and therefore feel that they should be given greater responsibilities. However, the person's actual performance might not be as good as they think, or they might not have the skills to meet higher demands. In this case, if nothing changes the individual may become bored or frustrated in their current role. To mitigate this issue the individual will either need to develop a more accurate self-assessment of their competence (which can be achieved through constructive feedback and performance management) or they can be given new challenges on other tasks in order to satisfy their competency needs while they continue to develop their other trade skills. Discrepancies in an individual's perceived and actual abilities often contribute to experiences of workplace frustration, reduced job satisfaction, motivation and even discipline problems.

Final thoughts

Autonomous motivation means that an individual engages with a task because they enjoy the activity or when the activity is in the service of, or consistent with, values or important goals. Apart from motivating particular behaviours and enhancing performance outcomes, in this chapter we have suggested that encouraging autonomous motivation toward workplace demands can enhance an employee's tolerance of such demands. Managers can attempt many strategies to enhance autonomous motivation broadly targeted at enhancing relatedness, autonomy and a sense of competency in their employees. These strategies are often cost neutral and only require a bit of creativity and motivation on the part of the manager. A small price to pay for engaged and resilient employees.

KEY MESSAGES FROM THIS CHAPTER

- While the primary focus of a manager's role is to sustain performance (which includes sustaining an effective workforce), when a manager increases autonomous motivation they are also enhancing the potential for staff resilience.
- The concept of autonomous motivation has an evidenced relationship with a range of organisationally beneficial outcomes such as staff engagement, self-regulated performance, resilience and overall mental health.
- An effective approach to building staff resilience via autonomous motivation is for leaders to become good at assessing the basic psychological needs of their followers (i.e. autonomy, relatedness and competence) and use various strategies to ensure these needs are satisfied.

Note

1   This chapter represents the research and perspective of the author and does not necessarily reflect the views of the Australian Defence Force or the Australian Army Psychology Corps.

References

Bakker, A. B. & Demerouti, E. (2007). The job demands-resources model: State of the Art. *Journal of Managerial Psychology, 22*, 309–328.

Bakker, A. B., Hakanen, J. J., Demerouti, E. & Xanthopoulou, D. (2007). Job resources boost work engagement, particularly when job demands are high. *Journal of Educational Psychology, 99*, 274–284.

Deci, E. L. & Ryan, R. M. (2000). The "what" and "why" of goal pursuits: Human needs and the self-determination of behaviour. *Psychological Inquiry, 11*, 227–268.

Deci, E. L. & Vansteenkiste, M. (2004). Self-determination theory and basic need satisfaction: Understanding human development in positive psychology. *Ricerche di Psichologia, 27*, 17–34.

Demerouti, E., Bakker, A. B., Nachreiner, F. & Schaufeli, W. B. (2001). The job demands-resources model of burnout. *Journal of Applied Psychology, 86*, 499–512.

Gagne, M. & Deci, E. (2005). Self-determination theory and work motivation. *Journal of Organizational Behaviour, 26*, 331–362.

Gegenfurtner, A., Festner, D., Gallenberger, W., Lehtinen, E. & Gruber, H. (2009). Predicting autonomous and controlled motivation to transfer training. *International Journal of Training and Development, 13*, 124–138.

Hakanen, J. J., Bakker, A. B. & Demerouti, E. (2005). How dentists cope with their job demands and stay engaged: the moderating role of job resources. *European Journal of Oral Sciences, 113*, 479–487.

Hackman, J. R. & Oldham, G. R. (1976). Motivation through the design of work: Test of a theory. *Organisational Behavior and Human Performance*, *16*, 250–279.

Hodgins, H. S., Weibust, K. S., Weinstein, N., Shiffman, S., Miller, A., Coombs, G. & Adair, K. C. (2010). The cost of self-protection: Threat response and performace as a function of autonomus and controlled motivations. *Personality and Social Psychology Bulletin*, *36*, 1101–1114.

Kasser, T. & Ryan, R. M. (1996). Further examining the American dream: Differential correlates of intrinsic and extrinsic goals. *Personality and Social Psychology Bulletin*, *22*, 280–287.

Legault, L. & Inzlicht, M. (2013). Self-determination, self-regulation, and the brain: Autonomy improves performance by enhancing neuroeffective responsiveness to self-regulation failure. *Journal of Personality and Social Psychology*, *105*, 123–138.

Nix, G. A., Ryan, R. M., Manly, J. B. & Deci, E. L. (1999). Revitalization through self-regulation: The effects of autonomous and controlled motivation on happiness and vitality. *Journal of experimental Social Psychology*, *35*, 266–284.

Skinner, B. F. (1950). Are theories of learning necessary? *Psychological Review*, *57*, 193–216.

Steffens, N. K., Haslam, S. A., Reicher, S. D., Platow, M. J., Fransen, K., Yang, J., Ryan, M. K., Jetten, J., Peters, K. & Boen, F. (2014). Leadership as social identify management: Introducing the identity leadership inventory (ILI) to assess and validate a four-dimensional model. *The Leadership Quarterly*, *25*, 1001–1024.

Stone, D. N., Bryant, S. M. & Wier, B. (2010) Why are financial incentive effects unreliable? An extension of self-determination theory. *Behavioral Research in Accounting*, *22*, 105–132.

Stone, D. N., Deci, E. L. & Ryan, R. M. (2009). Beyond talk: Creating autonomous motivation through self-determination theory. *Journal of General Management*, *34*, 75–91.

Yelon, S., Sheppard, L., Sleight, D. & Ford, J. K. (2004). Intention to Transfer: How do autonomous professionals become motivated to use new ideas. *Performance Improvement Quarterly*, *17*, 82–103.

13

DEVELOPING EMPLOYEES' SELF-EFFICACY THROUGH EXPERIENCE-BASED LEARNING

Dr. Bernd Carette

What do J. K. Rowling, The Beatles, Julie Andrews, Michael Jordan and Walt Disney have in common? Aside from the fact that all excel(led) in their chosen profession, they were all turned down before their breakthrough. It is a widespread belief that what made them rebound from these defeats and go on to greatness rather than throwing in the towel, was their confidence in their ability to succeed (Beck, 2008). The lay perception that the belief in one's ability to successfully execute a task is positively related to the ability to bounce back from difficulties and move forward, is supported by scientific research. This belief in one's ability is referred to by psychologists as self-efficacy and a vast body of research has pointed to positive effects of self-efficacy on individual employee performance and also on the performance of teams or groups of people (Stajkovic, Lee & Nyberg, 2009; Stajkovic & Luthans, 1998). Self-efficacy is particularly important in challenging situations that require resilient functioning. That is, according to the seminal research conducted by Albert Bandura (1997), people's self-efficacy beliefs influence how much effort they put forth in given endeavours and how long they will persevere in the face of obstacles and failures.

People's confidence in their ability to succeed in a certain situation is the product of (1) people's *general* self-efficacy across situations (Chen, Gully & Eden, 2001) and (2) people's *specific* self-efficacy beliefs related to the particular situation at hand (Gist & Mitchell, 1992). The importance of this latter situation-specific component indicates that self-efficacy is to some extent malleable and can change over time and with different situations. As people gain experience in a situation, their level of self-efficacy in that situation will evolve accordingly (Bandura, 1982). Put differently, people's self-efficacy beliefs are not entirely stable but can, to a certain extent, be learnt and encouraged. For example, when initially going to a new country it is normal to feel a bit lost and overwhelmed by the new environment, new food, and different functioning of the traffic or public transport. Often it feels exhausting to deal with such a new environment because routines that were typically done on automatic pilot at home need to be revised (e.g., catching a bus), which may cause feelings of insecurity and require a lot of attention. As each day passes, interacting with this new environment slowly becomes less exhausting and self-efficacy for navigating the new country improves.

The malleability of self-efficacy provides a window of opportunity for managers to enhance their employees' capacity for resilience. This chapter will describe situational determinants of self-efficacy and to distill strategies that can be used by managers to develop the self-efficacy of employees. The application of these strategies in the workplace will help improve employee resilience and allow them to perform effectively in the face of adversity.

A model of experience-based self-efficacy development

According to Bandura (1982), efficacy is instilled through experience. As such, the starting point of the model guiding this chapter is that the specific experiences one encounters, either personally or through observing others, have important effects on self-efficacy. Over the past decades, the link between experience and self-efficacy has been studied in various contexts involving almost 6,000 respondents. Using specialised statistical methods called meta-analysis, results from these multiple studies have been combined and compared with the hope of determining the overall message of this area of research. Meta-analytic findings indeed show that greater experience in a specific role was related to greater self-efficacy in that role (Judge et al., 2007). In this way, experience is predictive of feeling more efficacious in a particular task. For instance, entrepreneurs have more confidence in their ability to successfully perform entrepreneurial roles and tasks when they have higher levels of entrepreneurial experience (Zhao, Seibert & Hills, 2005). Similarly, in a study involving pre-service teachers it was found that as teachers gained practicum experience, their levels of teacher efficacy increased accordingly (Gurvitch & Metzler, 2009).

But how does experience increase self-efficacy? It is likely that the relationship between experience and self-efficacy emerges via two pathways. First, experience influences self-efficacy by allowing people to develop specific knowledge and skills related to the situation or task (e.g., Dragoni et al., 2011). Returning to our example about visiting a new country, as you make attempts to use public transport you begin to learn how the transport system works (e.g., where to buy bus tickets from, whether you need to validate your ticket). From successfully using the bus system you can make conclusions regarding behaviours that seem effective and are worthwhile imitating in the future. From failures you can infer lessons of actions that should be avoided in the future. Through developing such task-specific knowledge, people become more confident about their ability to be successful in the future.

The second pathway is about the way experience impacts emotions, and in particular the potential to feel overwhelmed. Experience provides people with precedents of successes and failures. The experience of success allows one to develop the expectation of success in a similar situation again. While the experience of failure means that one develops a realistic, and not an overly optimistic, estimate of the likelihood of attaining success, making it less likely that people would become emotionally overwhelmed when they fail. By gaining diverse experiences an adaptive sense of self-efficacy is developed, which eventually results in resilient functioning in the face of difficulties.

The model as displayed in Figure 13.1 illustrates these two pathways. In the initial box to the left is the starting point: *the occurrence of experiences.* These experiences can be both personal, but also can occur by observing others engage with challenges. The second set of boxes represent the two pathways described above: (1) increasing knowledge and skills, and (2) development of precedent for success and failure. The third box symbolises the development of self-efficacy that is thought to emerge via these pathways and the fourth box depicts the downstream impact on resilient functioning. In this context, self-efficacy is a personal resource that enhances the capacity for resilience and then when adversity is encountered there is a greater tendency for the actual demonstration of resilience. It is also important to note that the first four boxes are contained by a circle representing the organisa tional environment. This circle is intended to symbolise the effect that the organ-isational environment has on the translation of experience into self-efficacy via these pathways. In particular, leadership style and the opportunity for self-reflection are thought to influence whether or not self-efficacy emerges from the experiences within the workplace. This chapter will address in greater detail the role of both personal and others' experience, and critically the role of the organisational environment in which these experiences are gathered, for self-efficacy development.

Self-efficacy development through personal successes and failures

When we experience success at a particular task, or in a particular situation, typically these successes increase the expectation that we have the personal capability to achieve success again in that given situation. This link between experiencing success and self-efficacy has been considered in various contexts and at different levels of analysis. Kuo, Wu, and Lin (2013) found that perceived good performance on a computer-programming task (Visual Basic) at one point in time was related to an increase in that same person's level of confidence in their ability to learn how to programme at a later point. Similarly, positive feedback on a physical activity task (toss a tennis ball with one's non-dominant arm) has been found to enhance learners' self-efficacy beliefs at subsequent attempts of that same task (Saemi *et al.*, 2012). The significance of these findings is that previous success seems to translate to an expectation of greater personal capability on a similar task in the future.

Interestingly, the experience of past success does not only lead to the greater expectation of future success, it also results in *actual* success. Spurk and Abele (2014) followed university graduates from different German universities over nine years.

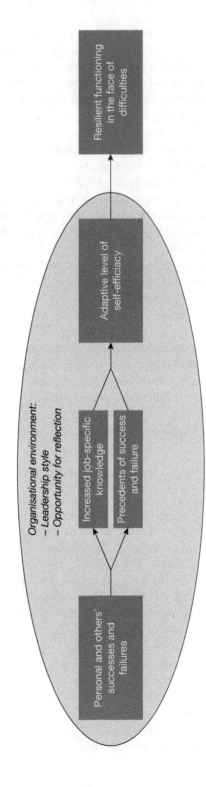

FIGURE 13.1 A model of experienced-based self-efficacy development

During this period, they were approached four times and were asked to complete questionnaires assessing their self-efficacy beliefs regarding occupational success, salary and personal perceptions of career success. In total, 608 people completed all four questionnaires. These researchers found a reciprocal relationship between career success (inferred from relative salary and the person's perception of career success) and an individual's belief in his/her capacity to successfully perform occupational tasks and demands. In other words, people's self-efficacy beliefs led to actual higher levels of career success AND higher success increased self-efficacy beliefs.

Together, these studies suggest that success experiences positively impact one's level of self-efficacy and in turn self-efficacy appears to yield the experience of more success. Yet, *only* experiencing success may also have a number of downsides. First, achieving high attainments involves dealing with challenges and setbacks. If people only experience success they may become overconfident. They come to expect quick results and may be quickly and easily discouraged by tasks they find challenging. This can result in outcomes like procrastination. A typically skilled and high performing employee may begin to procrastinate and become distracted by tasks they find easier to achieve. Furthermore, successes confirm prior expectancies and boost confidence in old routines, decreasing the inclination to invest additional psychological, financial and/or temporal resources in the task, while increasing complacency and risk aversion (Sitkin, 1992; Zakay, Ellis & Shevalsky, 2004). As such, too much success may breed failure through unrealistic expectations of success, limited perseverance when the going gets tough and limited investment in the development of new ways of dealing with the situation at hand, due to excessively high levels of self-efficacy.

As an anecdotal example, consider the crash of the space shuttle *Columbia*. On 1 February 2003, *Columbia* broke apart over Texas and Louisiana as it reentered Earth's atmosphere. None of the seven crew members survived. The crash was caused by a piece of foam insulation that broke off during launch. One of the major conclusions of the *Columbia Accident Investigation Board* – a NASA investigation team established to uncover the conditions that produced the tragedy and to draw lessons for the future – was that NASA's long history of success in the shuttle programme inflated NASA managers' confidence in their ability to manage the risks of human space flight, and as such contributed to the *Columbia* accident. Indeed, three months before the *Columbia* disaster, *Atlantis* was launched. A similar problem occurred as the one causing the disintegration of the *Columbia* space shuttle. Yet, in contrast to the *Columbia* orbiter, *Atlantis* returned to earth safely and the mission was considered a success. Limited discussion regarding the incident took place and there was no interference with the planned launch of *Columbia* three months later (example adopted from Madsen & Desai, 2010). You do not have to look far to find similar examples of catastrophic organisational failures that are the consequence of frequent successes leading to overconfidence and a failure to pay attention to the early warning signs of crisis. Such exaggerated self-efficacy is maladaptive and is likely to eventually yield negative outcomes.

An adaptive sense of self-efficacy is characterised by a balance between optimism and realism towards one's ability to attain success. In order to create an adaptive sense of self-efficacy careful consideration is required, as is a balancing act between challenge and success. A job situation or assignment that is challenging typically creates a perceived demand (although the magnitude of perceived demand may differ between individuals). This perceived demand negatively impacts one's level of confidence in the task (Bledow, 2013). Receiving positive feedback and experiencing success in the early days of getting acquainted with the new situation, is essential to develop positive self-efficacy beliefs. Experiencing failure could lead to disengagement. As self-efficacy increases over time, demand perceptions decrease. In order to avoid reaching a state at which self-efficacy is overly high causing overconfidence in one's abilities, an employee should receive new challenging assignments. A new challenging situation will temporarily decrease self-efficacy and increase demand perceptions, enhancing the motivation to step outside the comfort zone of established routines in order to get a better understanding of the situation at hand (Carette & Anseel, 2012). As such, a temporary decrease in self-efficacy through being regularly challenged should lead to the development of new knowledge and skills, which is instrumental for long-term self-efficacy development and resilient functioning (Carette, Anseel & Lievens, 2013). This process is illustrated in Figure 13.2. The staircase symbolises people's experience; the stairs in the staircase are challenges people face or have already faced. If one wants to reach a higher stair, it increases demand on the employee. Thus, there is still the potential for success with each new challenge, but at the same time failure may occur if the demand is not met with the necessary motivation and skill attainment. This increased demand causes a temporary decrease in self-efficacy. However, when one has already obtained a level of self-efficacy through experience (one has already climbed a number of steps), such a temporary decrease in self-efficacy may not lead to disengagement, but rather trigger exploration behaviour in order to find an alternative way of dealing with the situation at hand. As such, at intermediate levels of self-efficacy, failure may enhance innovative work behaviour and entrepreneurial achievement, which may be one of the explanations of Julie Andrews', J. K. Rowling's, The Beatles', Michael Jordan's and Walt Disney's success (for a more elaborate discussion, see Frese & Keith, 2015).

In sum, when it comes to the relationship between personal experience and self-efficacy, one often relies on Bandura's (1982, p. 126) conclusion that "successes heighten perceived self-efficacy; repeated failures lower it". Yet, the relationship is more complex than commonly thought. The research reviewed above shows that when facing a new task or situation, successes are vital. As one gains more experience with the task, a mix between successes and failures is most productive in terms of developing an adaptive sense of self-efficacy. That is also why the complete quote of Bandura reads: "Successes heighten perceived self-efficacy; repeated failures lower it, *especially if failures occur early in the course of events*" (1982, p. 126).

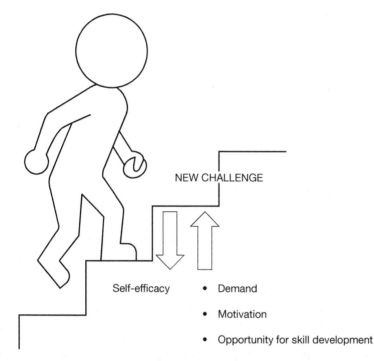

FIGURE 13.2 Achievable challenges serve to temporarily reduce self-efficacy, but increase demand, motivation and the opportunity for skill development

Self-efficacy development through vicarious experience

The children's book "*The Little Engine that Could*" tells the story of a long train that must be pulled over a high mountain. Larger engines are asked to pull the train but they refuse. A small engine agrees to try and succeeds. While he was pulling the train over the mountain he constantly repeated his motto: "I think I can". This story, or an adapted version, is popular in elementary school. The message it conveys is that although things can seem very tough at first sight, when one has confidence in his/her capabilities (i.e., has high self-efficacy), success is more likely. The idea is that through telling these stories to children, they will adopt the self-efficacious attitude of the little engine next time they face a challenge themselves. Indeed, video-modeling interventions, in which a child watches videotapes of positive examples, has been found to be a powerful teaching device (Delano, 2007).

The idea that people can develop their behaviour and their levels of self-efficacy not only through personal experience, but also through observing and modeling the experiences of others (i.e., vicarious experience), is not only widespread in educational settings but also in organisations. Common practices such as bench-marking (Collins, 2001), demonstration based-learning (Grossman *et al.*, 2013) and behavioural modeling (Taylor *et al.*, 2005) all build on the observation that people can draw valuable lessons from observing others. The theoretical underpinnings of vicarious learning lie in Bandura's (1977) social learning theory. Social learning theory outlines four processes through which observational learning takes place: attention, retention, reproduction and motivation. First, learners need to pay attention to the modeled behaviours in order to transfer the observed stimuli to short-term memory (e.g., watching someone make chocolate soufflé). Second, learners need to link the learned material with existing knowledge so it can be retrieved from long-term memory whenever necessary. This means linking the new learning to something already known (e.g., like a chocolate omelette that is lighter and airier). Third, the learner has to reproduce the actions he has observed and memorised. Finally, the learner will be most likely to apply the learned behaviour when it is motivated, for instance through social reinforcement (e.g., praise and requests for more chocolate soufflé). Vicarious learning is not limited to social learning on the individual level; it also plays an important role for learning at the organisational level. Organisational learning literature has shown that organisations replicate routines, strategies and designs of other successful organisations (e.g., Burns & Wholey, 1993; Ingram & Baum, 1997; Sitkin, 1992).

When observing the behaviour of others (either individuals or organisations), people can choose to focus their attention on successful or on unsuccessful others. In this regard, the children's story of "*The Little Engine that Could*" (Piper, 1930) is far more popular than the story of "*The Little Engine that Could Not*" (Kirkland, 2014). Similarly, employees tend to turn far more frequently to others' best practices rather than others' worst practices (Bandura, 1977). You have probably done this yourself. When thinking about how to best achieve a task or get that next promotion, your attention was probably drawn to those people who were successful at achieving that desirable outcome. Chances are this is also the case for the employees that you manage. Your employees are likely to be focusing their attention on successful examples, and ignoring unsuccessful examples, which means they are not getting the full benefit from observing others.

Learning about others' successes enhances self-efficacy in two ways. First, through observing others' successes and identifying the causes of success, people gain valuable knowledge about effective actions and behaviour, which they can apply themselves and build upon (Gino *et al.*, 2010). Gains in personal knowledge attained through indirect experience can make people more confident about their ability of reaching success. Second, the awareness that others have preceded in successfully dealing with the challenging situation one is facing, may lead to a more optimistic estimate of the likelihood of being successful.

Notwithstanding the learning potential inherent to other people's successes, other people's failures may also provide meaningful lessons. Yet, according to Denrell (2003), failure is under sampled in today's organisations, meaning that people observe the practices of top managers, but they may not observe the practices of those individuals who fail to be promoted. A one-sided focus on others' successes at the expense of their failures falls short of fully utilising the learning potential inherent to other people's experiences. Indeed, a growing body of studies point to the importance of others' failure as a fundamental source of learning across a variety of contexts (e.g., the railroad industry, Baum & Dahlin, 2007; firestations, Joung, Hesketh & Neal, 2006; hospitals, Diwas, Staats & Gino, 2013; the financial industry, Kim & Miner, 2007; and the aerospace industry, Madsen & Desai, 2010).

In one experiment, researchers were able to compare the learning effects of reading about others' failures versus successes (Bledow et al., 2016). In this experiment, one group of people was randomly assigned to reading about managerial failures. The other group read about managerial successes. In both groups the same knowledge about effective managerial practices was conveyed; they differ in whether this knowledge was embedded in a success or failure story. For instance, in one of the scenarios used in the study, a leader narrates about a project team she was responsible for that developed a new product. People who were assigned to the success-stories group read that the team was successful and that one of the reasons for the success of the team was that the leader composed a heterogeneous team. Conversely, people in the failure-stories group read that the team failed due to the fact that the leader did not ensure heterogeneity of skills among team members. The experimenters were interested in whether the two groups would perform differently when solving a managerial case study after reading these stories. The results show that people elaborate the content of failure stories more actively. That is, people who read failure stories remembered more lessons from these stories than people who read success stories. As a consequence, the knowledge gained from failure stories was more applied on a transfer task. This effect was particularly pronounced for people who view failures as valuable learning opportunities. Hence, in addition to one's own experiences, others' experiences also provide an effective source of self-efficacy development. Although people may be naturally inclined to focus their attention on others' successes, the scientific research reviewed above shows that a consideration of both others' successes and failures is most likely to yield adaptive levels of self-efficacy. As noted by Kim and Miner (2007, p. 687), failure and near-failure of others can serve as "wake-up calls, encouraging survivors to search for new actions or to devise new business models or routines".

So, when are success stories most adaptive and when should one be provided with more failure examples? When people lack confidence in their abilities, success stories may serve as inspirational examples and can build a learners' confidence in their abilities, in particular when they see similarities between themselves and a role model. Success stories may also be particularly effective for increasing people's confidence in the successful application of concrete behavioural routines. For instance, Gino and colleagues (2010) found that observing people who are successful at an origami exercise had a more positive impact on learners' performance as compared to observing people who were unsuccessful. For tasks that require more than merely imitating behaviour routines, failure stories may be particularly effective. Examples could be strategic choices managers have to make or dealing with difficult customers, employees or co-workers. When confronted with such challenges, failure stories that stimulate elaboration may help learners to develop the knowledge and heuristics to deal with such managerial challenges. Failure stories may also be particularly effective when learners are overly confident in their abilities and lack the motivation to think things through before making a decision because they underestimate its difficulty. For instance, related to the example above about team composition in the context of product development, people may underestimate the importance of making a well-informed decision regarding who to include in the team. Under those circumstances, failure stories could serve as wake up calls and draw learners' attention to the importance and difficulty of the subject.

As a manager it is key to develop a climate in which people feel safe and dare to share not only their wins, but also their losses. This can be achieved in a top down manner, with top management taking a constructive rather than an avoidant orientation toward errors. That is, top management should lead by example, by openly communicating about errors made in the organisation, and by encouraging others to do the same. BMW, as one example, explicitly mentioned in their mission statement that employees should not look for the guilty party in an error situation, but solve the problem instead by openly discussing it within the team (example adopted from van Dyck et al., 2005). Organisations can also provide a platform for employees to share failure experiences. This practice of sharing failure stories is common in the area of entrepreneurship, where entrepreneurs gather on a regular basis to share their entrepreneurial failures with one another (for an example, see http://fuckupnights.com).

The role of the organisational environment for self-efficacy development

The above discussion highlights how self-efficacy can be developed through personal and vicarious success and failure experiences. However, these experiences are not gained in a vacuum, but in an organisational environment. As alluded to earlier, the organisational context can have an important role in facilitating the transition of experiences into self-efficacy. In this next section, I explore two particularly important organisational facilitators of self-efficacy development through experience-based learning: *leadership style* and *opportunity to reflect*.

FACILITATOR 1: leadership style

In the above sections, I highlighted the role management can play in the development of a psychologically safe climate in which people feel comfortable sharing their failures with others. Leadership style may also directly influence self-efficacy of their team members. A substantive amount of research has looked at the relationship between transformational leadership style and subordinates' levels of self-efficacy. Transformational leadership has been defined as influencing subordinates by "broadening and elevating followers' goals and providing them with confidence to perform beyond the expectations specified in the implicit or explicit exchange agreement" (Dvir et al., 2002, p. 735), and is characterised by charisma, inspirational motivation, intellectual stimulation and individualised consideration (Bass & Avolio, 1994). Transformational leaders are proactive in thinking and generating new ideas, which may influence employees' confidence in their ability through observational learning from such leaders. Furthermore, transformational leaders can persuade employees that they too can be successful. Finally, transformational leaders may take a more open attitude towards errors and failures. As a result, research has repeatedly shown a positive relationship between transformational leadership and self-efficacy (e.g., Gong, Huang & Farh, 2009; Walumbwa & Hartnell, 2011).

Richard Branson, founder of the Virgin Group, is considered a textbook example of a transformational leader. He is able to inspire his followers through his creativity, vision and demonstrated trust. His leadership style is best described in the answer he gave to an interviewer about what he thought were Virgin's success factors: *"I'm absolutely certain that it's a question of the kind of people you have, and the way you motivate them. If you can motivate your people, use their creative potential, you can get through bad times and you can enjoy the good times together. If you fail to motivate your people, your company is doomed [. . .] We like to reward our key performers for their creative contribution [. . .] We don't have formal board meetings, committees, etc. If someone has an idea, they can pick up the phone and talk to me. I can vote "done, let's do it." Or better still, they can just go ahead and do it. They know that they are not going to get a mouthful from me if they make a mistake. Rules and regulations are not our forte"* (de Vries, 1999; p. 9–10)

Sharing power with subordinates is an important feature of transformational leadership. Transformational leadership is therefore closely related to empowering leadership. Srivastava, Bartol, and Locke (2006) demonstrated that leadership behaviours that allow subordinates to take part in decision-making and problem solving increase the self-efficacy beliefs of team members. Empowering leader behaviour is characterised by leading by example, participative decision-making, coaching and informing (Arnold et al., 2000). Each one of these behaviours can lead to opportunities for the subordinate to expand their knowledge, learn from each other and acquire new skills, thereby raising their efficacy.

Showing concern is a final example of empowering leadership behaviour. It refers to support by a leader in the form of trust, concern for subordinates' well-being, and willingness to help. Remember that failure experiences lead to the development of adaptive self-efficacy beliefs, but at the same time may be overwhelming for the person going through the experience. A leader who shows concern and provides support may therefore facilitate the relationship between experience and self-efficacy development, ultimately leading to improved team performance (Srivastava et al., 2006).

BOX 13.1 LEARNING TO EMPOWER EMPLOYEES

Let's explore the issue of empowerment in a case where the ability of leadership to empower employees became a large part of enhancing employee resilience. The context was a team of nurses working in a hospital. These nurses were responsible for the care of oncology patients in a very busy hospital ward. Management was concerned that the nurses were becoming burnt-out and this was evident in the cynical attitude many of the nurses were developing toward their work and the organisation. While working with patients with cancer is obviously emotionally challenging it became clear that the core stressor for these nurses was not the patients, but rather their feeling of low control over decisions that affected their team. When speaking with management, it appeared that managers did a really good job of seeking employee opinions about decisions or problems. However, when decisions were made there was no discussion about how decisions were arrived at, or what consideration had been given to staff suggestions. Moreover, staff suggestions were very rarely implemented. The result of this was that staff felt a very sincere lack of efficacy and control over their work. A lack of control is considered to be a stress 'super-factor' (Cooper, Flint-Taylor, & Pearn, 2013). Feeling little power over decisions or events that affect us is one of the main causes of pressure turning into stress. While management had requested their suggestions, there was still a feeling that their suggestions were not being taken seriously.

From the perspective of management, they believed that they were communicating with their staff effectively because they were: (1) seeking staff opinion and (2) informing staff of the decision that had been arrived at. However, there were a few key aspects missing that needed to be addressed:

(1) There was little feedback to staff about what suggestions had been received and how these suggestions were being considered.
(2) There was no feedback about how decisions were being made.
(3) There was no clear framework or strategy regarding how or when upward (to management) and downward (from management) communication was to occur.
(4) Management generally had not taken on very many suggestions from staff and were often concerned about the effectiveness of these suggestions.

These aspects left staff feeling like they had little control and pretty cynical about any attempts from management to gather their suggestions.

Implementing empowering leadership behaviours

In order to address the challenges of this situation it seemed important to increase staff empowerment over decisions that effected their work. This, at least in part, required addressing the above four problems. In order to turnthis situation around the following strategies were suggested and implemented.

(1) Getting staff involved in the development of a communication framework. It was recommended that the nursing staff be empowered with the role of developing a framework for greater upward and downward communication between staff and management. This would involve a more standardised feedback process for staff to pass information to managers, but also for staff to receive information about the decision-making process from managers. This addressed two issues. First, the fact that there was no existing communication strategy. Second, it was the first of many problem solving roles staff were going to be asked to be involved with.

(2) The introduction of quality projects. The second strategy for empowering staff was the introduction of 'quality projects'. This is where staff were encouraged to identify workplace practices that needed improvement and to develop strategies for improvement that they would share at meetings and later implement. Time was to be formally allocated to the conduct of quality projects and the quality projects were to be formally recognised as part of the workroles of staff. Importantly, quality projects provide experiences that are challenging allowing the opportunity for skill development.

(3) Piloting staff-driven solutions. To address the managerial concern that staff-driven solutions were ineffective it was recommended that managers allow staff-driven solutions to be piloted. The pilot could be for a limited time period or in a limited number of staff. Then staff would have the ability to discuss the pros and cons of the solution. This achieved several outcomes. First, staff started to get some sense of ownership over decision-making. Second, their ideas were being tested and evaluated by themselves and their peers. In this way, there is the opportunity to see to what degree the strategies were effective. Finally, if the solution is a complete 'bust' the detrimental impact on practice is minimised.

(4) The content of downward communication. Finally, it was important to address the issue of transparency in terms of how decisions were made, not just what decisions were made. Managers were asked to provide staff with feedback about what suggestions have been received and why a particular decision has been made (i.e., reasons behind decision-making). This would occur within the communication framework.

FACILITATOR 2: opportunity to reflect

A fundamental accelerator of experience-based learning is reflection on the experience. According to Ashford and DeRue (2012), systematic reflection on experiences is a necessary precondition for learning to take place. Systematic reflection is a learning procedure during which learners comprehensively analyse their behaviour and evaluate the contribution of its components to performance outcomes. In order for people to draw conclusions from their experience regarding the likelihood of being successful in the future, they need to create a sense of awareness of the experience – what the outcome was and how they contributed to that outcome. To facilitate this comprehensive processing of experiential data, After-Event Review (AER) sessions can be implemented. AERs give learners (individuals, teams or larger organisational units) an opportunity to systematic-ally analyse the various actions that they selected to perform or not to perform in carrying out a particular task or responding to a particular event, to determine which of them was wrong or not necessary, which was missing, which needed to be corrected and which needed to be reinforced. To that end, AERs require individuals or teams to engage in three activities: self-explanation, data verification and feedback (Ellis *et al.*, 2014). AERs have been successfully applied in various settings, including hospitals, the military, and aviation industry. Below, the different steps are illustrated in a case example of a leadership development programme at a government institution.

Transitioning leaders had monthly one-on-one AER meetings with an internal coach of the organisation. During those meetings leaders were asked to think about and actively reflect on a noteworthy experience that had taken place during recent weeks. First, during the process of *self-explanation* learners were asked to analyse their own behaviour and advance explanations for the resulting success or failure. Self-explanation is prompted by questions such as: "*How did you contribute to the performance observed in the experience?*" For instance, when reflecting on a performance appraisal interview, transitioning leaders were asked to think about (1) how the conversation partner reacted to the feedback and (2) how the way in which the feedback was given (verbal and non-verbal behaviour) may have caused that particular reaction. By attributing the causes for the outcome observed in an experience to oneself, people take more responsibility for their behaviour. Subsequently, during the process of *data verification* learners were confronted with a different perception of the same data. In the light of the above example, data verification would be triggered by questions such as: "*Consider how you could have given feedback differently and in what ways would the reaction of the employee have been different if that approach was chosen?*" Data verification enables to sidestep potential biases, including confirmation bias, whereby information that contradicts assumptions is overlooked, and hindsight bias, whereby outcomes strongly affect how past experience is viewed. Finally, *feedback* was generated by the leader him/herself during the systematic reflection process. When systematically reflecting, the learner is responsible for the analysis of his/her performance data and for generating reasons why things went right or wrong. Possible prompts are "*What worked during the performance appraisal interview and what did not work*", "*What has been learned from this experience*", and "*How will you behave in the future when giving feedback to someone?*"

Reflection on experience can foster self-efficacy beliefs through the positive impact it has on the number and the quality of lessons one draws from the experience (Ellis & Davidi, 2005). Also, reflecting on how things could have been worse when failing or could have been even better when succeeding, may help to put things in perspective in order to create an adaptive sense of self-efficacy. On a team level, reflection enhances similarity of team members' task representations (van Ginkel & van Knippenberg, 2009), which increases psychological safety within the team. Such feelings of safety enhance people's inclination to share successes and failures with one another.

Final thoughts

This chapter addresses the development of employees' self-efficacy beliefs, which is inextricably linked to the ongoing experience of resilience. As we have learnt, developing self-efficacy is achieved principally via personal or vicarious experiences, but it can be a delicate balancing act between experiences of success and failure. Taken together, work in this area suggests that success experiences should emerge early in the learning process, but in order to avoid complacency we must also provide increasing challenges. Based on our best understanding of self-efficacy this seems to be the right formula for efficacy building experiences. It is suggested that managers can play a critical role in the development of the self-efficacy of their staff and by doing this have positive impacts on the wellbeing of staff. However, developing the self-efficacy of staff requires thought and a level of commitment on behalf on the managers. In order to help managers with this task, I have provided two core strategies for supporting self-efficacy in staff. The first is enabling employees to feel empowered in their work by taking on their ideas, sharing power, providing decision-making autonomy and demonstrating concern when an employee's performance falls short. A second suggestion is the importance of providing time to reflect on the cause of both success and failures; a tool understood to accelerate the learning process and enhance self-efficacy.

KEY MESSAGES FROM THIS CHAPTER

- Today, there is general consensus that self-efficacy is, at least to some extent, dynamic, indicating that it can be developed.
- Investments in self-efficacy are likely to have downstream effects on employee resilience.
- Personal and vicarious experiences of success and failure contribute in a positive way to the development of an adaptive sense of self-efficacy.

- Leaders can play an active role in the development of self-efficacy in their employees by creating an environment in which employees learn from these experiences and share both their successes and failures with one another.
- Leaders can also facilitate the development of self-efficacy via a transformational and/or empowering leadership style and by providing employees with an opportunity to reflect.

References

Arnold, J. A., Arad, S., Rhoades, J. A. & Drasgow, F. (2000). The empowering leadership questionnaire: The construction and validation of a new scale for measuring leader behaviors. *Journal of Organizational Behavior, 21,* 249–269.

Ashford, S. J. & DeRue, D. S. (2012). Developing as a leader: The power of mindful engagement. *Organizational Dynamics, 41,* 146–154.

Bandura, A. (1977). *Social learning theory.* Englewood Cliffs, NJ: Prentice-Hall.

Bandura, A. (1982). Self-efficacy mechanism in human agency. *American Psychologist, 37,* 122–147.

Bandura, A. (1997). *Self-Efficacy: The Exercise of Control.* New York: Freeman.

Bass, B. M. & Avolio, B. J. (1994). *Transformational leadership: Improving organizational effectiveness.* Thousand Oaks, CA: Sage.

Baum, J. A. C. & Dahlin, K. B. (2007). Aspiration performance and railroads' patterns of learning from train wrecks and crashes. *Organization Science, 18,* 368–385.

Beck, M. (2008, April 28). If at first you don't succeed, you're in excellent company. *Wall Street Journal,* p. D1.

Bledow, R. (2013). Demand-perception and self-motivation as opponent processes: A response to Bandura and Vancouver. *Journal of Management, 39,* 14–26.

Bledow, R., Carette, B., Kuehnel, J. & Pittig, D. (2016). Learning from others' failures: The effectiveness of failure-stories for managerial learning. *Academy of Management Learning & Education,* amle-2014.

Burns, L. R. & Wholey, D. R. (1993). Adoption and abandonment of matrix management programs: Effects of organizational characteristics and interorganizational networks. *Academy of Management Journal, 36,* 106–138.

Carette, B. & Anseel, F. (2012). Epistemic motivation is what gets the learner started. *Industrial and Organizational Psychology-Perspectives on Science and Practice, 5,* 306–309.

Carette, B., Anseel, F. & Lievens, F. (2013). Does career timing of challenging job assignments influence the relationship with in-role job performance? *Journal of Vocational Behavior, 83,* 61–67.

Chen, G., Gully, S. M. & Eden, D. (2001). Validation of a new general self-efficacy scale. *Organizational Research Methods, 4,* 62–83.

Collins, J. C. (2001). *Good to Great: Why Some Companies Make the Leap. . . and Others Don't:* Random House.

Cooper, C., Flint-Taylor, J. & Pearn, M. (2013). *Building Resilience for Success: A Resource for Managers and Organizations.* London, UK Palgrave Macmillan.

Delano, M. E. (2007). Video modeling interventions for individuals with autism. *Remedial and Special Education, 28,* 33–42.

Denrell, J. (2003). Vicarious learning, undersampling of failure, and the myths of management. *Organization Science, 14*, 227–243.

de Vries, M. F. K. (1999). Charisma in action: The transformational abilities of Virgin's Richard Branson and ABB's Percy Barnevik. *Organizational Dynamics, 26*, 7–21.

Diwas, K. C., Staats, B. R. & Gino, F. (2013). Learning from my success and from others' failure: Evidence from minimally invasive cardiac surgery. *Management Science, 59*, 2435–2449.

Dragoni, L., Oh, I. S., Vankatwyk, P. & Tesluk, P. E. (2011). Developing executive leaders: The relative contribution of cognitive ability, personality, and the accumulation of work experience in predicting strategic thinking competency. *Personnel Psychology, 64*, 829–864.

Dvir, T., Eden, D., Avolio, B. J. & Shamir, B. (2002). Impact of transformational leadership on follower development and performance: A field experiment. *Academy of Management Journal, 45*, 735–744.

Ellis, S., Carette, B., Anseel, F. & Lievens, F. (2014). Systematic reflection: Implications for learning from failures and successes. *Current Directions in Psychological Science, 23*, 67–72.

Ellis, S. & Davidi, I. (2005). After-event reviews: Drawing lessons from successful and failed experience. *Journal of Applied Psychology, 90*, 857–871.

Frese, M. & Keith, N. (2015). Action errors, error management, and learning in organizations. *Annual Review of Psychology, 66*, 661–687.

Gino, F., Argote, L., Miron-Spektor, E. & Todorova, G. (2010). First, get your feet wet: The effects of learning from direct and indirect experience on team creativity. *Organizational Behavior and Human Decision Processes, 111*, 102–115.

Gist, M. E. & Mitchell, T. R. (1992). Self-efficacy: A theoretical analysis of its determinants and malleability. *Academy of Management Review, 17*, 183–211.

Gong, Y., Huang, J. C. & Farh, J. L. (2009). Employee learning orientation, transformational leadership, and employee creativity: The mediating role of employee creative self-efficacy. *Academy of Management Journal, 52*, 765–778.

Grossman, R., Salas, E., Pavlas, D. & Rosen, M. A. (2013). Using instructional features to enhance demonstration-based training in management education. *Academy of Management Learning & Education, 12*, 219–243.

Gurvitch, R. & Metzler, M. W. (2009). The effects of laboratory-based and field-based practicum experience on pre-service teachers' self-efficacy. *Teaching and Teacher Education, 25*, 437–443.

Ingram, P. & Baum, J. A. C. (1997). Opportunity and constraint: Organizations' learning from the operating and competitive experience of industries. *Strategic Management Journal, 18*, 75–98.

Joung, W., Hesketh, B. & Neal, A. (2006). Using "war stories" to train for adaptive performance: Is it better to learn from error or success? *Applied Psychology-an International Review-Psychologie Appliquee-Revue Internationale, 55*, 282–302.

Judge, T. A., Jackson, C. L., Shaw, J. C., Scott, B. A. & Rich, B. L. (2007). Self-efficacy and work-related performance: The integral role of individual differences. *Journal of Applied Psychology, 92*, 107–127.

Kim, J.Y. J. & Miner, A. S. (2007). Vicarious learning from the failures and near-failures of others: Evidence from the U.S. commercial banking industry. *Academy of Management Journal, 50*, 687–714.

Kirkland, K. (2014). *The little engine that could not: a triumph of grace.* Grapevine, TX: Frog Street Press.

Kuo, F. Y., Wu, W. H. & Lin, C. S. (2013). An investigation of self-regulatory mechanisms in learning to program visual basic. *Journal of Educational Computing Research, 49*, 225–247.

Madsen, P. M. & Desai, V. (2010). Failing to learn? The effects of failure and success on organizational learning in the global orbital launch vehicle industry. *The Academy of Management Journal, 53*, 451–476.

Piper, W. (1930). *The little engine that could.* New York, NY: Platt & Munk Publishers.

Saemi, E., Porter, J. M., Ghotbi-Varzaneh, A., Zarghami, M. & Maleki, F. (2012). Knowledge of results after relatively good trials enhances self-efficacy and motor learning. *Psychology of Sport and Exercise, 13*, 378–382.

Sitkin, S. B. (1992). Learning through failure: The strategy of small losses. *Research in Organizational Behavior, 14*, 231–266.

Spurk, D. & Abele, A. E. (2014). Synchronous and time-lagged effects between occupational self-efficacy and objective and subjective career success: Findings from a four-wave and 9-year longitudinal study. *Journal of Vocational Behavior, 84*, 119–132.

Srivastava, A., Bartol, K. M. & Locke, E. A. (2006). Empowering leadership in management teams: Effects on knowledge sharing, efficacy, and performance. *Academy of Management Journal, 49*, 1239–1251.

Stajkovic, A. D., Lee, D. & Nyberg, A. J. (2009). Collective efficacy, group potency, and group performance: Meta-analyses of their relationships, and test of a mediation model. *Journal of Applied Psychology, 94*, 814–828.

Stajkovic, A. D. & Luthans, F. (1998). Self-efficacy and work-related performance: A meta-analysis. *Psychological Bulletin, 124*, 240–261.

Taylor, P. J., Russ-Eft, D. F. & Chan, D. W. L. (2005). A meta-analytic review of behavior modeling training. *Journal of Applied Psychology, 90*, 692–709.

van Dyck, C., Frese, M., Baer, M. & Sonnentag, S. (2005). Organizational error management culture and its impact on performance: A two-study replication. *Journal of Applied Psychology, 90*, 1228–1240.

van Ginkel, W. P. & van Knippenberg, D. (2009). Knowledge about the distribution of information and group decision making: When and why does it work? *Organizational Behavior and Human Decision Processes, 108*, 218–229.

Walumbwa, F. O. & Hartnell, C. A. (2011). Understanding transformational leadership-employee performance links: The role of relational identification and self-efficacy. *Journal of Occupational and Organizational Psychology, 84*, 153–172.

Zakay, D., Ellis, S. & Shevalsky, M. (2004). Outcome value and early warning indications as determinants of willingness to learn from experience. *Experimental Psychology, 51*, 150–157.

Zhao, H., Seibert, S. E. & Hills, G. E. (2005). The mediating role of self-efficacy in the development of entrepreneurial intentions. *Journal of Applied Psychology, 90*, 1265–1272.

14

HOW RESILIENCE TRAINING CAN ENHANCE WELLBEING AND PERFORMANCE

Dr. Mustafa Sarkar and Dr. David Fletcher

Can we change an employee's level of resilience?

Before considering the role of resilience training in your organisation, it is first worth giving some thought as to whether resilience is really amenable to change at all. As pointed out in the introduction of this book, considerable research evidence now suggests that resilience, at least in part, changes over the course of someone's life and is responsive to a person's experiences. Definitions of resilience are now beginning to reflect this understanding (see: Fletcher & Sarkar, 2012, p. 675, 2013, p. 16), encapsulating the idea that resilience has both aspects that are more fixed or stable (e.g., relating to one's personality) and aspects that can be changed as a consequence of interacting with one's environment (cf. Egeland, Carlson & Sroufe, 1993) and this can include well designed resilience training. Collectively, the research on psychological resilience suggests that resilience is largely a malleable phenomenon, and as such it is suitable for intervention. Indeed, programmes aimed at enhancing resilience present a viable means to preventing the potential negative effects of work stress and enhancing wellbeing and performance in the workplace.

Research on resilience training in the workplace has provided evidence that resilience training can be effective in modifying resilience (e.g., Arnetz *et al.*, 2009; Grant, Curtayne & Burton, 2009; Sood *et al.*, 2011). Indeed, resilience interventions have yielded adaptive changes in wellbeing and performance. To illustrate, resilience training has been found to have a positive impact on various mental health and subjective wellbeing outcomes (e.g., lower stress, depression, negative affect) in employees (e.g., Arnetz *et al.*, 2009; Grant *et al.*, 2009; Pipe *et al.*, 2012). In addition, some resilience intervention studies have revealed performance benefits including increases in goal attainment (Grant *et al.*, 2009), productivity (Pipe *et al.*, 2012), and observed behavioural performance (Arnetz *et al.*, 2009). While the benefits of resilience training programmes are now starting to be recognised, their effectiveness as a whole has remained unclear to date since comprehensive reviews of existing primary evidence had not been undertaken. However, this limitation in the literature has recently been addressed in two reviews of resilience training (viz. Robertson et al., 2015; Vanhove et al., 2016). Specifically, the reviews located workplace resilience interventions and synthesised their effects on various wellbeing and performance outcomes with the aim of advancing the study and use of resilience training in the workplace.

With a view to bringing greater clarity on how resilience training can enhance wellbeing and performance, this chapter aims to provide a summary of the current research evidence that has determined the effectiveness of resilience training in the workplace specifically exploring the effects of resilience training on various wellbeing and performance outcomes. We also examine the characteristics of resilience training that seem to enhance effectiveness. In this way, anyone responsible for employing resilience training can determine what styles of training are effective according to current research.

Resilience training in the workplace

Robertson and colleagues (2015) conducted a review of resilience training interventions implemented in workplaces. Their review identified 14 studies that investigated the impact of resilience training on personal resilience and four broad categories of outcomes: (1) mental health and subjective wellbeing, (2) psychosocial, (3) physical/biological and (4) performance. Overall, their findings indicated that resilience training can improve personal resilience and is a useful means of developing mental health and subjective wellbeing outcomes in employees. Robertson and colleagues also found that resilience training has a number of wider benefits that include enhanced psychosocial (e.g., self-efficacy, social skills, work satisfaction) functioning and improved performance.

When examining the effectiveness of resilience training at work, typically researchers are interested in the impact training has on wellbeing and performance. Robertson and colleagues (2015) found that resilience training had beneficial outcomes for mental health and wellbeing as reported by the employees themselves. Specifically, resilience training appeared to be able to impact symptoms of depression and anxiety as well as emotional wellbeing. To illustrate, one study examining the effectiveness of resilience training in physicians showed a decrease in self-reported stress and anxiety symptoms after resilience training (Sood et al., 2011). The physicians also reported increases in their quality of life post-intervention. Similar findings have occurred for nurses, whereby reductions in stress, anxiety, and depression were observed after resilience training (Pipe et al., 2012).

These promising results are not confined to health workers. Employees working in the resource sector demonstrated significant reductions in stress post-resilience training and these effects were maintained when followed-up six months later (Millear et al., 2008). Police officers have also received benefits from resilience training experiencing reductions in negative mood (Arnetz et al., 2009), depression, and anxiety (McCraty & Atkinson, 2012) post-intervention. In fact, resilience training has demonstrated some positive effects on mental health in several other domains including: public school teachers (Jennings et al., 2013), civil servants (Liossis et al., 2009), administrative staff (Burton et al., 2010), and in executives and senior management (Grant et al., 2009). Thus, across a range of studies, it appears that appropriately designed resilience training can have positive effects on mental health outcomes across a range of employee groups.

In terms of the impact of resilience training on performance, six out of the 14 studies identified by Robertson and colleagues (2015) examined performance outcomes. For example, executives and senior managers demonstrated increases in goal attainment post-resilience training (Grant et al., 2009) and police officers have shown increases in behavioural benchmarks (e.g., tactics, communication, control) of police work performance (Arnetz et al., 2009). Interestingly, resilience training has had mixed effects on productivity. In nurses, resilience training has been shown to result in greater productivity (Pipe et al., 2012), but no impact on productivity has been shown in other studies (Abbott et al., 2009; McCraty & Atkinson, 2012).

In a further review of a greater number of studies examining resilience training, with 42 independent samples across 37 studies, Vanhove and colleagues (2016) presented a meta-analysis to determine the effectiveness of resilience-building programmes implemented within organisational settings. In general, the findings revealed that the overall effect of such programmes was small and that programme effects diminished substantially from proximal (≤ 1 month post-intervention) to distal (> 1 month post-intervention) time points. Vanhove and colleagues (2016) found that resilience-building programmes had the strongest immediate effect on improving performance, while somewhat weaker effects were observed for enhancing wellbeing and preventing psychosocial deficits. Moreover, the effects of resilience training appear to diminish over time in terms of the impact of training on examining longer-term psychosocial adjustment, wellbeing and performance. In contrast, programmes targeting individuals thought to be at greater risk of experiencing stress and lacking core protective factors showed the opposite effect over time. Programmes employing a one-on-one delivery format were most effective, followed by the classroom-based group delivery format. Whereas, programmes using train-the-trainer approaches (i.e., where leaders receive resilience training and disseminate learned knowledge and skills to their subordinates) and computer-based delivery formats were least effective. Finally, substantially stronger effects were observed among studies where the same (single) group of participants undertook resilience training, in comparison with studies where different groups of participants were utilised for one or more resilience training and control conditions.

In summary, resilience training appears to demonstrate some benefits to the wellbeing, psychosocial adjustment and performance of working adults in a variety of occupations. However, generally, the changes seem short-term and rather than improving in their ability to use the trained skills over time, the general tendency is for employees to forget or cease applying the skills resulting in a slow return to pre-training status.

What should be taught in resilience training?

One of the factors that may determine the effectiveness of resilience training is the content of training. Training content has been identified as falling into five broad categories: (1) the Penn Resilience Programme, (2) coaching-related principles, (3) mindfulness and compassion-based practices, (4) self-regulation of stress responses and (5) multimodal cognitive-behavioural techniques. The limited research available evaluating resilience training means that it is difficult to draw any firm conclusions about what the most effective content for resilience training is (Robertson *et al.*, 2015) and it would be misleading to advocate for any one approach over another at this point. However, it is possible to describe the diversity of strategies that have shown a level of effectiveness. This might be used as a guide to those considering implementing resilience training as to what might be most appropriate for your organisation.

First, it is likely that no one strategy is going to be appropriate for all organisations and a level of judgement about the 'fit' of a particular strategy is necessary considering the organisational culture, nature of the work and employee characteristics. For example, work by Britt *et al.* (2016) found that while problem solving is typically an effective strategy in most workplaces, in a low autonomy workplace (i.e., military), problem solving did not tend to be as effective. In contrast, acceptance was the most effective strategy in a low control workplace. Thus, in workplaces where there is very little decision making autonomy or flexibility regarding how work is carried out, strategies that focus on enhancing problem-solving may be less effective than those with a focus on enhancing acceptance of the stressors associated with one's employment.

Second, a couple of resilience training studies were based on coaching-related principles (e.g., Grant *et al.*, 2009; Sherlock-Storey, Moss & Timson, 2013). Sherlock-Storey *et al.* (2013) used a skills-based coaching approach and Grant *et al.* (2009) used a developmental or executive coaching approach. Skills-based coaching is typically characterised by a higher level of structure and/or more directive style of coaching, a fairly narrow skill or behavioural focus and a shorter timescale than development coaching. Development coaching is typically more complex and emergent in focus, less directive in style and more about creating the right conditions and 'psychological space' for reflective learning.

Third, a number of resilience interventions used mindfulness- and compassion-based practices (e.g., Burton *et al.*, 2010; Jennings *et al.*, 2013; Pidgeon, Ford & Klassen, 2014). To illustrate, Burton *et al.*'s (2010) intervention was based on Acceptance and Commitment Therapy (ACT), which uses acceptance and mindfulness strategies to develop psychological resilience through six core processes: acceptance, cognitive diffusion (changing one's relationship with thoughts), being present (mindfulness), self-as-context, values and committed action. Jennings *et al.*'s (2013) intervention introduced a series of mindful awareness practices, beginning with the basic practice of body and breadth awareness and extending to activities that promote a mindful approach to daily activities (e.g., standing, walking, being present in front of the classroom). To promote compassion, the intervention introduced "caring practice" and "mindful listening". Caring practice involved a guided reflection of "loving kindness" focused on generating feelings of care for self and others, and mindful listening exercises were designed to promote the ability to listen to others without judgement. Pidgeon *et al.*'s (2014) intervention was based on loving-kindness meditation described as a mind-training practice utilised to increase feelings of warmth and caring for the self and others. The programme consisted of periods of silence and training in mindfulness and other skills to increase mindfulness and self-compassion.

Fourth, a couple of resilience training studies (viz. McCraty & Atkinson, 2012; Pipe *et al.*, 2012) were primarily based on self-regulation of stress responses via technology to achieve a more coherent physiological state. Police officers from McCraty and Atkinson's (2012) study learnt a set of skills that enabled them to self-regulate their mental, emotional and physical systems. The programme utilised a set of proven techniques and technology (i.e., emWave) for achieving coherence. Pipe *et al.*'s (2012) intervention included a "Transforming Stress" workshop that focused on the impact of stress on the body-mind-spirit and several techniques for learning how to self-regulate physiological stress responses by shifting into a more coherent physiological state. Participants were also given use of an emWave heart rate variability technology, which helped them learn how the techniques were impacting on their stress responses.

Fifth, most resilience training programmes (e.g., Arnetz *et al.*, 2009; Liossis *et al.*, 2009; Millear *et al.*, 2008; Sood *et al.*, 2011; Waite & Richardson, 2003) consisted of multimodal cognitive behavioural techniques (e.g., attentional training, energy management, relaxation training, imagery and self-talk). Arnetz *et al.*'s (2009) programme consisted of relaxation and imagery training with mental skill rehearsal. More specifically, the sessions began with training and practice in both progressive and cue-controlled relaxation methods wherein police officers learned how to induce relaxation regardless of the situation. This was followed by imagery training using verbally presented scripts of various critical incident traumas to help officers create mental images of specific, police work-relevant stressors and mentally rehearse appropriate responses. The Promoting Adult Resilience (PAR) programme (viz. Liossis *et al.*, 2008; Millear *et al.*, 2008) consisted of seven main topics: (1) understanding personal strengths and resilience, (2) understanding and managing stress, (3) challenging and changing negative self-talk, (4) practicing changing negative self-talk, (5), promoting positive relationships, (6) problem solving and managing conflict, and (7) bringing it together. Sood *et al.*'s (2011) programme addressed two aspects of human experience, namely attention and interpretation. Participants were also provided with training in a brief structured relaxation intervention (viz. paced breathing meditation). Lastly, Waite and Richardson's (2003) intervention was a bio-psycho-spiritual enrichment programme designed to improve mental and spiritual health. Drawing from multidisciplinary perspectives (e.g., Chi, quanta, collective unconscious), participants learnt skills in using resilience to increase energy and focus energy in performing job functions, and develop interpersonal skills.

Mode of delivery

Although the content of resilience training is important, the way training is delivered is probably of equal importance. In their systematic review, Robertson and colleagues (2015) identified four main training delivery formats: (1) online training (Abbott *et al.*, 2009), (2) group-based sessions (Arnetz *et al.*, 2009; Burton *et al.*, 2010; Liossis *et al.*, 2009; McCraty & Atkinson, 2012; Millear *et al.*, 2008; Pidgeon *et al.*, 2014; Pipe *et al.*, 2012; Waite & Richardson, 2003), (3) one-on-one training (Sherlock-Storey *et al.*, 2013; Sood *et al.*, 2011), and (4) a combination of group-based sessions with one-to-one training (Carr *et al.*, 2013; Grant *et al.*, 2009; Jennings *et al.*, 2013). Five of the 14 studies provided opportunities for additional training in the form of group-based booster sessions (Jennings *et al.*, 2013; Liossis *et al.*, 2009; Pidegon *et al.*, 2014), a follow-up review session to provide an opportunity for participants to report back informally on how things were going (Waite & Richardson, 2003), and a follow-up session based on individual needs (Sood *et al.*, 2011).

One of the most extensive individualised programmes was that of Grant *et al.* (2009). The programme consisted of 360-degree feedback on participants' existing leadership styles, one half-day leadership evaluation and training workshop, and four individual executive coaching sessions over an 8–10 week period. This programme produced several beneficial effects and so did other programmes offering individual support (viz. Jennings *et al.*, 2013; Sood *et al.*, 2011). Since some programmes without this element also delivered beneficial results, Robertson and colleagues (2015) noted that the evidence is too limited to support a conclusion that one-on-one training is critical in overall effectiveness. They did, however, assert that the results suggest that, until conclusive evidence is available, it may be wise to include individual support in any resilience-training programme.

Vanhove and colleagues (2016) show that online resilience training programmes that have the least amount of contact with employees provide less beneficial outcomes demonstrating only small benefits to wellbeing or no benefits at all. It is worth noting, however, that the few studies available do not allow us to draw firm conclusions about the (in)effectiveness of online training programmes. Furthermore, Robertson *et al.* (2015) also observed that a resilience-building programme delivered online (viz. Abbott *et al.*, 2009) was one of the only two studies in the review to produce no positive results (see also Carr *et al.*, 2013). Having noted this, highly sophisticated computer-based resilience-building interventions implemented in non-workplace settings have been shown to be quite effective (Rose *et al.*, 2013). In this vein, Vanhove and colleagues (2016) contended that resilience training via computer-based formats may have greater potential than is reflected through the current results. Technology has made it relatively easy and cost-effective to provide and receive training on a large scale, and computer-based programmes focused on improving psychosocial health, such as cognitive bias modification, have been shown to have practical utility (e.g., Bar-Haim, Morag & Glickman, 2011; Hallion & Ruscio, 2011). If not as a primary means of programme delivery, online resources and activities may have considerable utility in supplementing face-to-face training, while providing the practical advantages of reducing face-to-face time and programme costs. However, when designing computer-based delivery systems, programme developers should draw on the abundant computer-based training literature (e.g., Hallion & Ruscio, 2011; Kraiger & Jerden, 2007) to maximise the effectiveness of these efforts.

Although previous research has shown that online interventions can be effective in changing health-related behaviour (Portnoy et al., 2008), many interventions fail to work due to the lack of take-up (Bennett & Glasgow, 2009). Indeed, Abbott et al. (2009) noted that a high proportion of their sample did not complete the training and this may go some way to explain the lack of effects for their intervention. Thus, if your organisation is considering online resilience training programmes, it is probably worth asking about the retention rates for their programmes. There is considerable diversity in the retention rates for mental health programmes. The average retention rate is approximately 70 per cent, so it is probably wise to only use an online programme that achieves at least the average or close to this amount of retention. You can also ask about strategies for increasing retention, or whether the trainers provide any direct contact with employees (e.g., weekly phone contact or coaching sessions).

Being reactive or proactive about resilience building

There are essentially two ways of approaching resilience building, one as a "response" to a defined problem such as a crisis or perceived threat, and the other as a "proactive effort" to boost resilience and enhance effectiveness in the face of continuing challenges and pressure. In this regard, Cooper, Flint-Taylor, and Pearn (2013) identified eight practical scenarios – along a continuum of reactive-proactive approaches – for resilience-building interventions in organisations. Specifically, they proposed that resilience development can be seen as a: (1) general performance enhancer, (2) remedy or response to stress or unusual circumstances, (3) accelerator of team development and/or integration, (4) enabler for the transformation of an underperforming organisation, (5) core capability in organisations that routinely face demanding and stressful conditions, (6) core culture builder in start-ups, (7) essential component of leadership development, especially in difficult and challenging times that is the norm today, and (8) supporting organisational transformation and culture change. Thus, while resilience building is generally seen as providing a buffer to stress and pressure, it can go well beyond this to act as a performance enhancement that benefits individual, team and organisational success. Indeed, in our view, the most powerful approach is not to raise resilience as an end in itself, but to use resilience to underpin, support and enhance other performance goals, especially in difficult and challenging times. More specifically, we believe that the most effective approach is for managers and organisations to develop resilience as a preventative and proactive approach to managing stress, and to incorporate resilience building within an overall change management strategy.

Matching the programme to your organisation

In our previous discussion, we alluded to the "fit" of a programme to your organisation. This is an important factor to consider when selecting a resilience training programme and trainer for your organisation. Here are some factors that may impact the efficacy of the resilience training in your organisation:

The extent of knowledge your trainer has about the industry you work in. Trainers with good knowledge about the industry and context of the work done by your organisation have a better understanding of the critical stressors faced by employees. This is important for two reasons. The first is that the strategies used in the training are likely to be more appropriate for the nature of your work demands. Indeed, resilience training should be customised to meet specific needs and requirements. Second, trainers who communicate an understanding of the industry and key challenges are likely to be perceived as more legitimate sources of information and influence.

The willingness of the trainer to tailor the language used during the training to that of your organisation. The communication of often complex and new information is a critical aspect of resilience training. It is helpful if the trainer is able to communicate this content in ways that are accessible to your employees. This may mean a careful use of language and concrete examples that are directly applicable to your employees.

The direct versus indirect nature of training. Given the categories of delivery formats present in the occupational resilience building literature, one important factor may be the *directness* with which training content is delivered. Vanhove and colleagues (2016) suggest that the more direct contact trainers have with trainees, the better trainers are able to attend to trainee comprehension, identify trainee needs and provide relevant feedback, all of which have been identified as important to effective training delivery (see Kraiger, 2003). Vanhove and colleagues (2016) demonstrated that the one-on-one delivery format show the strongest impact on employee resilience. This method provides the most direct contact with trainees and is likely to be the most tailored to the individual needs of each employee. Classroom or small group formats demonstrate moderate effectiveness, but may be more practical and cost effective for many organisations. In sum, the more direct the delivery method, the more time and resource-intensive and often impractical the approach becomes. On the other hand, indirect delivery effects such as computer-based training can potentially be highly efficient. The weak effect associated with this indirect delivery approach may suggest it is simply not conducive to building resilience.

Is there an opportunity for on-the-job application and follow-up? Transferring the training to the work context is a critical training principle. More effective resilience training is likely to establish with employees specific opportunities for the application of training techniques to their workplace. In Grant and colleagues (2009) coaching approach this is referred to as 'way forward' (p. 400), and employees are encouraged to identify specific actions they will undertake in a specified time-frame to apply the outcomes of the coaching conversation. This may be the reason that direct delivery formats are more effective at building resilience. Such formats better attend to trainees' unique needs, allow trainees to apply training content to specific experiences and situations, and hold trainees accountable.

Final thoughts

Concerns about building resilience are now centre stage in human resource management and occupational psychology not only to enhance productivity, but also to foster workplace wellbeing. We foresee an increased focus on building and sustaining resilience as a key element in transformation and change processes within organisations of all kinds, especially where time pressures and the stakes are very high. We also foresee an increased focus on resilience in organisations generally to help equip people in all roles to manage stress and pressure effectively. We have provided a summary of recent research that has determined the effectiveness of resilience training in the workplace specifically looking at the effects of resilience training on various wellbeing and performance outcomes. In addition, we have presented practical guidance to managers about how to develop psychological resilience. There is clearly no doubt that, by building and protecting the resilience in the workplace, managers not only contribute to the overall success of their organisations, but also boost the wellbeing and engagement of employees.

KEY MESSAGES FROM THIS CHAPTER

- Resilience training programmes appear to enhance the wellbeing and performance of working adults in a variety of occupations. However, the changes are generally short-term with programme effects diminishing over time.
- Training content has been identified as falling into five broad categories: (1) The Penn Resilience Program, (2) coaching-related principles, (3) mindfulness and compassion-based practices, (4) self-regulation of stress responses and (5) multimodal cognitive-behavioral techniques. For managers considering implementing resilience training in the workplace, these categories should serve as a guide (rather than a definite list) as to what might be most appropriate for your organisation.
- The way resilience training is delivered is important. It may be wise to include an element of one-to-one training and support based on individual

needs, and the implementation of online resilience training programmes requires careful consideration to ensure programme effectiveness.

- Various factors may impact the efficacy of resilience training in your organisation including: (1) the extent of knowledge your trainer has about the industry you work in, (2) the willingness of the trainer to tailor the language used during the training to that of your organisation, (3) the direct versus indirect nature of training, and (4) the opportunity for on-the-job application and follow-up.

References

Abbott, J-A., Klein, B., Hamilton, C. & Rosenthal, A. (2009). The impact of online resilience training for sales managers on wellbeing and work performance. *Electronic Journal of Applied Psychology, 5*, 89–95.

Arnetz, B. B., Nevedal, D. C., Lumley, M. A., Backman, L. & Lublin, A. (2009). Trauma resilience training for police: Psychophysiological and performance effects. *Journal of Police and Criminal Psychology, 24*, 1–9.

Bar-Haim, Y., Morag, I. & Glickman, S. (2011). Training anxious children to disengage attention from threat: A randomized controlled trial. *Journal of Child Psychology and Psychiatry, 52*, 861–869.

Bennett, G. G. & Glasgow, R. E. (2009). The delivery of public health interventions via the Internet: Actualizing their potential. *Annual Review of Public Health, 30*, 273–292.

Britt, T. W., Crane, M. F., Hodson, S. E. & Adler, A. (2016). Effective and ineffective coping strategies in a high demand, low control work environment. *Journal of Occupational Health Psychology, 21*, 154–168.

Burton, N. W., Pakenham, K. I. & Brown, W. J. (2010). Feasibility and effectiveness of psychosocial resilience training: A pilot study of the READY program. *Psychology, Health & Medicine, 15*, 266–277.

Carr, W., Bradley, D., Ogle, A. D., Eonta, S. E., Pyle, B. L. & Santiago, P. (2013). Resilience training in a population of deployed personnel. *Military Psychology, 25*, 148–155.

Cooper, C. L., Flint-Taylor, J. & Pearn, M. (2013). *Building resilience for success*. Basingstoke: Palgrave Macmillan.

Egeland, B., Carlson, E. & Sroufe, L. A. (1993). Resilience as process. *Development and Psychopathology, 5*, 517–528.

Fletcher, D. & Sarkar, M. (2012). A grounded theory of psychological resilience in Olympic champions. *Psychology of Sport and Exercise, 13*, 669–678.

Fletcher, D. & Sarkar, M. (2013). Psychological resilience: A review and critique of definitions, concepts, and theory. *European Psychologist, 18*, 12–23.

Grant, A. M., Curtayne, L. & Burton, G. (2009). Executive coaching enhances goal attainment, resilience and workplace well-being: A randomized controlled study. *Journal of Positive Psychology, 4*, 396–407.

Hallion, L. S. & Ruscio, A. M. (2011). A meta-analysis of the effect of cognitive bias modification on anxiety and depression. *Psychological Bulletin, 137*, 940–958.

Jennings, P. A., Frank, J. L., Snowberg, K. E., Coccia, M. A. & Greenberg, M. T. (2013). Improving classroom learning environments by cultivating awareness and resilience in education (CARE): Results of a randomized controlled trial. *School Psychology Quarterly*, *28*, 374–390.

Kraiger, K. (2003). Perspectives on training and development. In W. C. Borman, D. R. Ilgen & R. J. Klimoski (eds), *Handbook of psychology: Volume 12, Industrial and Organizational Psychology* (pp. 171–192). Hoboken, NJ: Wiley.

Kraiger, K. & Jerden, E. (2007). A meta-analytic investigation of learner control: Old findings and new directions. In S. M. Fiore & E. Salas (eds), *Toward a science of distributed learning* (pp. 65–90). Washington, DC: American Psychological Association.

Liossis, P. L., Shochet, I. M., Millear, P. M. & Biggs, H. (2009). The Promoting Adult Resilience (PAR) program: The effectiveness of the second, shorter pilot of a workplace prevention program. *Behaviour Change, 26*, 97–112.

McCraty, R. & Atkinson, M. (2012). Resilience training programme reduces physiological and psychological stress in police officers. *Global Advances in Health and Medicine, 1*, 44–66.

Millear, P., Liossis, P., Shochet, I. M., Biggs, H. & Donald, M. (2008). Being on PAR: Outcomes of a pilot trial to improve mental health and wellbeing in the workplace with the promoting adult resilience (PAR) programme. *Behaviour Change, 25*, 215–228.

Pidgeon, A. M., Ford, L. & Klassen, F. (2014). Evaluating the effectiveness of enhancing resilience in human service professionals using a retreat-based Mindfulness with Metta Training Programme: A randomized controlled trial. *Psychology, Health, & Medicine, 19*, 355–364.

Pipe, T. B., Buchda, V. L., Launder, S., Hudak, B., Hulvey, L., Karns, K. E. & Pendergast, D. (2012). Building personal and professional resources of resilience and agility in the healthcare workplace. *Stress and Health, 28*, 11–22.

Portnoy, D. B., Scott-Sheldon, L. A. J., Johnson, B. T. & Carey, M. P. (2008). Computer-delivered interventions for health promotion and behavioral risk reduction: A meta-analysis of 75 randomized controlled trials (1988–2007). *Preventive Medicine, 47*, 3–16.

Robertson, I., Cooper, C. L., Sarkar, M. & Curran, T. (2015). Resilience training in the workplace from 2003–2014: A systematic review. *Journal of Occupational and Organizational Psychology, 88*, 533–562.

Rose, R. D., Buckey, Jr, J. C., Zbozinek, T. D., Motivala, S. J., Glenn, D. E., Cartreine, J. A. & Craske, M. G. (2013). A randomized controlled trial of a self-guided, multimedia, stress management and resilience training program. *Behaviour Research and Therapy, 51*, 106–112.

Sherlock-Storey, M., Moss, M. & Timson, S. (2013). Brief coaching for resilience during organisational change – an exploratory study. *The Coaching Psychologist, 9*, 19–26.

Sood, A., Prasad, K., Schroeder, D. & Varkey, P. (2011). Stress management and resilience training among Department of Medicine faculty: A pilot randomized clinical trial. *Journal of General Internal Medicine, 26*, 858–861.

Vanhove, A. J., Herian, M. N., Perez, A. L. U., Harms, P. D. & Lester, P. B. (2016). Can resilience be developed at work? A meta-analytic review of resilience-building programme effectiveness. *Journal of Occupational and Organizational Psychology, 89*, 278–307.

Waite, P. J. & Richardson, G. E. (2003). Determining the efficacy of resiliency training in the work site. *Journal of Allied Health, 33*, 178–183.

15

MAKING CHANGE HAPPEN

Dr. Monique F. Crane

The purpose of this book is to assist managers to take positive steps to support the resilience of their staff and create a happier, more satisfying and healthier workplace. If you are reading this book then it is likely that you are already a fairly supportive and willing manager. While you might have the motivation to enact change and the personal resources to do so, change can still be challenging. Thus, this chapter is intended to help you answer the question: "So, what do I actually do?" by helping you identify the actions that need to be taken, the changes that need to be made, prioritise these actions/change behaviours and help you with some concrete steps to facilitate change.

In the introduction I suggested four overarching areas in which managers could support the resilience of employees, these were: (1) reducing unnecessary drains on staff resilience, (2) promoting adaptive workplace behaviours and thinking in the face of difficulties, (3) supporting the development of both personal and social resources and (4) allowing employees the opportunity to access needed resources). All these four domains are important and the more of them that you achieve the more likely your staff will experience positive benefit.

Without knowledge of your workplace or current practices it is difficult to give specific advice on how to translate these overarching themes and the lessons within each chapter into actionable behaviours. However, I can provide some guidance. Having said that, much of the thinking and hard work will need to come from you. The following five steps are expected to occur over the course of several weeks, rather than in a single sitting. Doing all five steps will increase the chance of sustainable change. The five steps are summarised in Figure 15.1 for quick reference.

I recommend that you document your progress through each of the five steps. This is important for two core reasons. First, documenting this process ensures that you are paying more thorough attention to the details of the change process and have an accurate record of events. Second, this is perfect promotional material. In the future you may consider taking on a bigger role within the organisation or

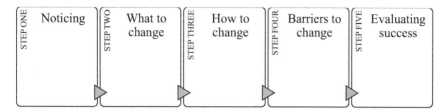

STEP ONE	STEP TWO	STEP THREE	STEP FOUR	STEP FIVE
Noticing	What to change	How to change	Barriers to change	Evaluating success

FIGURE 15.1 Steps to making change happen

another organisation. More and more emphasis is being placed on aspects of the managers' capacity to maintain the resilience of staff and manage well in times of difficulty. This is a perfect illustration of your capacity to make positive changes to achieve this and the details may be forgotten if not documented appropriately.

Step 1: noticing

The first stage involves "noticing" this is about getting some sense of the current situation in your workplace and how you currently respond to high-stakes or other stressful workplace situations. There are two central approaches that you might take to achieve this, ideally do them both: (1) self-assessment and (2) asking staff for feedback.

Self-assessment: here are some questions that you might ask yourself or find out from your employees based on the chapters in this book. Also note that some chapters provide more comprehensive checklists that you can also use (e.g., Appendix 5.1, Appendix 6.1, Table 7.2, Table 10.1, Table 10.2). Consider some or all of the following questions:

- To what degree do you pay attention to employee-organisational fit in your hiring practices? (Chapter 2)
- What post-hiring practices do you use that provide employees with stress management resources and health interventions? (Chapter 2)
- Do you model thinking and behaviours that are consistent with the four psychological resources identified in the PsyCap model: *hope, efficacy, resilience, optimism*? (Chapter 4)
- What do you do to create a positive attitude to support seeking? (Chapter 5)
- Do employees know how they can access the support they need? (Chapter 5)
- What do I do to support my employees? (Chapter 6)
- What important resources do I make available that are important to employees (i.e., skill variety, task identity, task significance, autonomy, feedback)? (Chapter 7)
- Do I employ practices that interfere with staff daily rest? (Chapter 8)
- Do you monitor the pressures placed on staff and the availability of resources to manage those pressures? (Chapter 9)

- What attempts do you make to enhance the positive emotions within the team? (Chapter 9)
- Do I see the sort of talk and behaviours in the team that reflect a strong identification with my team? (Chapter 10)
- Do we have policies that support resilient workplace practices? (Chapter 11)
- Do we monitor the wellbeing of staff? (Chapter 11)
- Do I employ management practices to enhance autonomy, competence and relatedness needs in staff? (Chapter 12)

To respond to the above questions accurately it is best to spend a few weeks taking notice, without judgement, of how you manage various situations in the workplace. In this exercise, the goal is to treat yourself as the subject of inquiry and determine whether the behaviours you display are consistent with the messages in this book, and in what ways they are not.

One effective strategy for doing this is at the end of each day take 15 minutes to think about how you and your staff have approached the challenges of that day. Imagine that you are observing yourself as an outsider or third party. Consider the way you have addressed potentially difficult or challenging situations throughout that day. Think of an interaction that you had with a staff member and imagine that you are observing the interaction. The benefit of this strategy is to get around our positive or negative biases about the way we see our behaviour in an attempt to get a more objective perspective. Try this exercise at various points over the period of several weeks gradually identifying how you typically react to others, how you manage demands, how you provide support etc.

Asking for feedback. If you are not sure about the answer to these questions than you might consider an anonymous questionnaire aimed at identifying the level to which these aspects are occurring. For this type of inquiry open-ended questions are perhaps the most appropriate. Also, you will need to limit the number of questions you ask to about 15 minutes (i.e., 5 questions) otherwise it is likely that staff will not have time to respond. Here are some suggestions, based on the above, to get you started:

- Are there aspects of the work that you feel there could be more autonomy?
- Do you feel that there are adequate opportunities for development and feedback?
- Do you know how to access the various forms of support you may need at work (e.g., advice, help with a task, emotional support)?

Step 2: deciding on what to change

Hopefully after the above exercise there are some areas that you have identified that are areas for improvement. This is a terrific start. Now, what to improve on.

Let's start with three things that you would like to improve on or change. At this step, we are just highlighting the specific (e.g., give employees more autonomy), but not necessarily going into detail about how the change would happen. If you have more than three things, pick the ones that you feel most confident and able to make changes in. Do not pick things that are too difficult first. This is for two reasons. First, achievable changes are more likely to build your confidence in tackling the more challenging goals. Second, part of this step is about getting a sense of how the change process works for you, but also in your organisation, so initially it is also about learning how change happens.

Setting your goals. Most managers have heard about SMART goal setting. This strategy is fairly effective for identifying: Specific, Measurable, Achievable, Realistic and Time-bounded actionable goals. Here are some questions to help you to fully formulate your goals. Try to answer these questions for each of your different change goals.

*   What specific changes would you like to adopt?
*   Can success be measured?
*   Are these changes achievable and realistic given your other demands?
*   What is a realistic timeframe for change?

Step 3: deciding on how to change and when

Once you have identified what your change goals are you can start thinking about how these changes will be implemented at the coalface. Perhaps the best way to achieve this is by identifying what you are going to do differently and at what specific times.

Take ONE of your goals (for now) and decide on the following:

*   What am I going to do differently?
*   What could be my first couple of steps?
*   Who can help me make these changes and how can they help?
*   When am I going to do this? (identify actual occasions – the next time a staff member approaches me with a difficulty, the next time I am performing staff professional development reviews)
*   Who can hold me accountable for making these changes? (it cannot be you, rather it should be a mentor, an enthusiastic partner or spouse)

Step 4: identifying barriers to change

There are often reasons that we do things the way we do them. Often it is because these strategies were adaptive in the past, but over time as the situation changes these strategies can become less adaptive. At times, there are barriers to change these might be internal things like feelings of frustration or tiredness that cause us to revert back to our past behaviour. Other barriers might be more about how we respond to others (e.g., "Vicky just makes me furious because she does X"). It is helpful to identify in advance where we might encounter obstacles that create a pressure to revert back to past strategies. Below are some questions that can help with identifying those things. Attempt to answer these questions with reference to the changes that you outlined as part of step three.

- What do you think might prevent change?
- When do you think these changes will be most difficult to sustain?
- Is there anything that you can do to ensure that change is sustained?

Once you have identified what you want to change, how you want to change and how to minimise the impacts of things that could get in your way, it is now time to take action. It may seem like a bit of a long road to actual action, but it is common to leap into action a little too early and it is a good idea to take the time to look before we leap and make our interventions targeted.

Step 5: evaluating success

Finally, it is probably a good idea to evaluate how successful the change has been. In doing this, it is useful to reflect on whether you were able to implement the change as you had intended, what successful outcomes might look like and how you would measure these outcomes as objectively as possible. These points are summarised in the below questions.

- Were you able to implement change as you intended? Why or why not?
- What does success look like? (perhaps consider the reasons you decided to read this book in the first place)
- How would you measure success?

Some options for evaluating success in an organisational setting include:

- Obtaining feedback from staff
- Following-up with a mentor who has been keeping track of your change process
- Performing before-change and after-change staff wellbeing surveys
- Asking targeted open-ended question to staff about key success indicators
- Self-reflection and evaluation

If you are able to do a few of the above practices for evaluating your progress this is preferable. In order to illustrate the above five steps, I have included the following illustration of this process.

Step 1: noticing

Peta is a middle manager at a small consulting firm. Peta's team specialises in helping to support organisational change. As part of their work, the team provides monthly reports about the client's and progress over the past month for all projects. The end of the month is a particularly stressful time because reporting requires contributions from all five members of Peta's team regarding their independent projects.

Peta observes that at these times staff seem more aggravated and stressed than usual and concludes that more could be done to help the staff cope better with time pressure. One option is of course having a psychologist come to talk to the staff about resilience and self-care. However, Peta also decides to review her own approaches and determine whether there is anything she can do to help support her staff more.

In a review of her management style under pressure, Peta identifies that when there is a looming reporting deadline she seems to become more irritable and short tempered with staff. Moreover, she notices her tendency to more closely monitor staff performance and be more prescriptive about the way in which tasks are done. A survey confirmed that staff feel particularly micro-managed under times of high workload and time pressure. Staff commented that this feeling of 'being micro-managed' contributes even more to their stress in addition to the experience of time pressure. As we know from previous chapters in this book, feeling micro-managed tends to reduce a sense of autonomy and competency, which are important motivational drivers.

Step 2: deciding on what to change

Peta decides that she would like to stop micro-managing staff during these times and seeks to determine whether such a change may help better support the resilience of her staff. Peta believes that this change is realistic, but is concerned that perhaps staff will not progress well enough to meet reporting targets if she fails to monitor them so closely. This makes her nervous about implementing such changes.

Step 3: deciding on how to change and when

The behaviours Peta identifies as the targets for change are: (1) resist being prescriptive about how reports should be done and (2) stop assessing every step of the reporting process and asking for daily updates. Peta decides to replace these behaviours with: (1) giving staff information about the broad aim of the report, but not micro-managing the process, (2) asking for reporting on progress only after two days and (3) giving staff more decision-making autonomy. Given her concern about relinquishing control, Peta decides to pilot this change for the next report and review how it goes.

Step 4: identifying barriers to change

Peta identifies that a major barrier to change is her concern about progress and report quality and what this might mean for her. She is concerned that without micro-management the staff will not complete the report on time at the required standard and she will look like a poor leader. She decides in order to deal with her concerns she will remind herself that the team is skilled in producing these reports and they understand the importance of meeting the deadlines. She also lets her team know that based on their feedback, she would like to take a more hands off approach that would hopefully benefit them, but regarding the expectations about the quality and timeliness of the report still remain the same. Peta also speaks to a mentor within the organisation about the change she wishes to implement and some of her concerns. In this way, her mentor is able to offer both advice and can hold her accountable for implementing the changes. Her mentor asks that she reports back about her success.

Step 5: evaluating success

Peta decides that key success indicators will be the level of reported staff stress during the next reporting period compared to the previous period, measured by a staff survey. She will also monitor whether the report is delivered on time and report quality.

Final thoughts

Hopefully, through this illustration of the change process it is clear how to use the five steps outlined above in your team or organisation. Remember that the changes you implement to support staff resilience do not need to be costly, grand or time-consuming. Many of the leadership and management practices suggested in this book are low cost, sustainable and practical; mainly requiring changes to the way you might engage staff in their work or approach organisational challenges. What is required is a bit of soul searching on the part of the manager, the courage to look at one's current approaches critically, the willingness to make change, the belief that a manager can make a difference, and an honest desire to support staff wellbeing. Armed with these ingredients and the tools outlined in this book you have everything you need to support the resilience of your staff – best of luck.

INDEX